DOWNSIZED
But Not Defeated

DOWNSIZED
But Not Defeated

The Family Guide to Living on Less

Hope Stanley Quinn

Lyn Miller-Lachmann

**Andrews McMeel
Publishing**

Kansas City

Library of Congress Cataloging-in-Publication Data

Quinn, Hope Stanley.
Downsized but not defeated : the family guide to living on less /
Hope Stanley Quinn, Lyn Miller-Lachmann.
p.   cm.
Includes bibliographical references.
ISBN 0-8362-3659-9 (pbk.)
1. Unemployed—United States—Life skills guides.   2. Finance.
Personal—United States—Planning.   I. Miller-Lachmann, Lyn, 1956–
II. Title.
HD5724.Q56   1997
640'.42—dc21
97–10331
CIP

Designed by John Reinhardt Book Design.

ATTENTION: SCHOOLS AND BUSINESSES

Andrews McMeel books are available at quantity discounts with
bulk purchase for educational, business, or sales promotional use.
For information, please write to:
Special Sales Department
Andrews McMeel Publishing
4520 Main Street
Kansas City, Missouri 64111

To Shirley Hammons Stanley—role model, teacher, mother.
—HSQ

To my mother-in-law, Lotte Lachmann,
who has faced life's tragedies with courage and wisdom
and has managed to find joy through it all.
—LML

Contents

Acknowledgments

The authors would like to acknowledge the many people who made this book possible. We would like to thank our agent, Sandra Choron, and our editor, Stephanie Bennett, for their unfailing support and essential feedback.

For their inspiration and wisdom, we would like to thank our moms, particularly those who survived the Great Depression—Shirley Stanley, Ethel Quinn Low, and Lotte Lachmann. Our husbands, Jim Quinn and Richard Lachmann, helped us make "lemonade" out of their job "lemons," and our children, Michael and Christine Quinn and Derrick and Madeleine Lachmann, offered their perspectives on what downsizing means to kids.

We would also like to thank the countless parents we met at swim meets, at PTA meetings, on soccer fields, and elsewhere, in the various places we have lived, who shared their stories. We hope this book will help many more parents in the future.

Introduction

*P*icture the lifestyle of the "typical" upscale American family: the house in the suburbs, two cars, trips to Disney World, and evenings out at movie theaters and restaurants. For the past fifty years, this "typical" family could count on more and more as the years passed: a larger house as the family grew, an assortment of pets, vacations, college for the kids, and the material goods that came with increased prosperity.

Today, all that has changed. White-collar engineers, managers, and executives, who once looked forward to reaching ever-greater heights of achievement and earnings, are now the first to be laid off as businesses "downsize." According to the *New York Times* (March 3, 1996), "nearly three-quarters of all households have had a close encounter with layoffs since 1980 . . . [and] . . . one in 10 adults—or about 19 million people—acknowledged that a lost job in their household had precipitated a major crisis in their lives."

Layoffs aren't the only problem facing middle-class families in the United States today. One in two marriages eventually end in divorce. According to recent studies, the wife and children's standard of living generally falls after a divorce while the man's standard of living rises.

Whether it's the result of a layoff, divorce, disability, death, or other tragedy, the sudden loss of the income that had provided an affluent lifestyle comes as an unprecedented shock. We wonder how we will survive, what we will tell our family, friends, and neighbors, and how we will break the news to our children.

Those were just abstract issues for me until one icy December day in 1995. That morning my husband phoned me from work and quietly announced, "What we were afraid of has just happened. I'll be home in a little while; they'll escort me offsite with my personal belongings. Cancel Christmas." He then hung up. *Cancel Christmas.* The words hit me like a pile of bricks. *Cancel Christmas!* We have

1

young children! Our relatives are coming three thousand miles to spend the holidays with us! My husband has lost his job, and we have to cancel Christmas!

The panic began to set in within a couple of seconds of hanging up the phone. How could we survive? We had just purchased an expensive house in the kind of neighborhood in which we had always dreamed of living. I had a part-time job that might cover the mortgage, but how would we eat or pay the heating bill? I immediately had visions of becoming homeless, sleeping in doorways and moving through alleys with all my earthly possessions in a shopping cart. I actually knew a girl in college to whom that had happened. As a young child she lived as neighbors with the Kennedys in Massachusetts; then her dad lost his fortune and her parents divorced. She'd told me stories of her and her mother homeless in New York City, moving from shelter to shelter, living on charity. They had recovered, somehow, and she was at school on a full scholarship. I hadn't thought of that girl in years and now I couldn't stop thinking about her.

Get a grip, I told myself.

Of course we had talked about the possibility of layoff. Everybody does where we live, in Albany, New York. It's the state capital in a time of political turnover and government downsizing. It's next door to Schenectady, the site of several large facilities of General Electric, which has cut more than half its workforce in the past twenty years. Who's the newest to join the ranks of the unemployed is all too common a topic of conversation. So we had weighed the probabilities for our own situation. But my husband wasn't employed by the state or GE. He had been brought to this area from the other end of the country "specifically for his special talents" by his company only thirteen months earlier. Surely we were immune.

However, he wasn't getting on well with his new boss, and we had been getting worried. But denial is an insidious thing. Yes, everyone knew forty people were going to be laid off. But that was out of hundreds; it couldn't happen to us. He had been given verbal guarantees of immunity. But it had happened. And now, we had to "cancel Christmas."

The first few days were agonizing as we struggled to cope with the reality of my husband's job loss. We decided we needed to do a detailed assessment of our financial situation—what money we had to work with and what we needed to live on. It was obvious that drastic cuts in our lifestyle were necessary if we had any hope of avoiding economic ruin.

As we began to make plans, I realized I had knowledge and skills that could be a significant help in our "downsizing" effort. I had been raised by a Depression-era mother who had taught me how to cook and manage a home very economically. I had used that knowledge twenty-five years ago when I was in my first apartment after graduation with a yearly salary of $8,500. I had done it then; I could do it again. My husband didn't believe me when I said I could cut the food budget to less than half of what we usually spent. But I did.

That's when I realized that others might benefit from my experience, and the idea of writing this book began to coalesce. It quickly became apparent that all the areas of the family budget needed to be trimmed, not just the food budget. I wanted to gather ideas and money-saving strategies from lots of sources and share them in a book specifically designed for those in a family situation. I wanted to find strategies that could be used either when extra time is available because an unemployed family member is at home or when time is scarce because you are working long hours at lower pay. Children, whether they are toddlers, elementary-age kids, preteens, teenagers, or college students, add a complicating dimension to the problem, but the crisis can also serve as a positive experience for them if handled well. So a sincere effort has been made to include strategies to help with children at different ages.

If a job loss or other drastic reduction in income hasn't happened yet, you are smart to read this book and think seriously about how you can plan for downsizing your lifestyle if the case should arise. Some layoffs can be predicted in advance, and a divorce often takes time to come through. Yet, crises—death, disability, or job loss—often occur suddenly. You can act now to minimize the financial difficulties and make the necessary preparations that will allow you to begin to deal with real issues quickly and successfully.

For those of you who have been thrust, as we were, into this situation without mental and physical preparation, this book is designed to offer practical advice for dealing with a sudden and drastic loss of income. Regardless of whether you have overcome the psychological effects of the crisis that has hit you, the sooner you start to implement these strategies, the sooner you will begin to gain some control over your destiny again.

—HOPE STANLEY QUINN

Chapter 1

The Upscale Dream Shattered

Adjusting to the Reality, Thinking about the Future

My husband was laid off a couple of weeks before Christmas. Being the procrastinators that we are, we hadn't purchased very many gifts yet. We returned some items. We decided the kids needed a few presents; we chose to make them more practical ones. All other relatives would be nominally served, and my husband and I would exchange only hugs and kisses, a big change from normal, when we would spend up to a thousand dollars on each other. His family generally spends the Christmas holidays with us. They came as usual.

It was a very strange holiday season. There were no parties, restaurant dinners, movies, or After-Christmas Sale shopping sprees. Instead, we put together a three-thousand-piece puzzle that had been in a box in the closet for years. Hours were spent talking and drinking coffee hunched over the puzzle. We made homemade cookies and simple meals, attended church services, and enjoyed warm fires in the fireplace. The kids received far more clothes than they wanted as Christmas gifts. The Grinch was unable to "steal" or "cancel" Christmas, but as the residents of Who-ville discovered, there isn't much left to do except hold hands and sing. Disgustingly enough, I came down with bronchitis and couldn't even sing!

—HSQ

Maintaining perspective and a sense of humor is very important for the upscale family that has to downsize following a loss of income. This income loss may result from a layoff, divorce, death, disability, or other tragedy. In any event, it means a lifestyle change is imminent. In some respects, it's like a religious conversion. One person is affected but strongly influences the other members of the household. The conversion results in a significant change in attitudes and priorities and a total change in lifestyle. Here, though, the analogy abruptly ends. Whereas the religious convert is enthusiastic about the changes and assumes it will last forever, the "outplaced" white-collar worker or the newly divorced parent with child custody is sucked into the "new life" kicking and screaming in protest the entire way. Moreover, the out-of-work professional prays fervently that the lack of a job is only a temporary situation, and the divorced mom secretly hopes a knight in shining armor will suddenly appear, sweep her into his arms, and carry her to the castle on the hill where she will never, ever, have to clean a toilet again!

True, it might be a temporary situation. On the other hand, it might be excruciatingly permanent.

Helping you to rationally accept and implement the necessary lifestyle changes is what this book is all about. It's as much about attitude adjustment as it is about specific cost-saving techniques. It is written to address two audiences—those who have experienced a loss in income and those who fear it may happen to them soon.

It explores which items—such as food, clothing, entertainment, and luxuries—can be cut quickly and extensively, and which items— such as child care, housing, and education costs—may require more planning, luck, and creativity to reduce. Strategies for cutting each category of items, both in the short term and in the long term, are provided in individual chapters. Timing for changes is also explored throughout the book. Some things you can implement immediately, like trimming the food budget or finding less expensive sources for clothing. Other changes with long-lasting implications, such as moving to a less expensive part of the country, can be explored theoretically, but should be not be rushed into. You will be able to assess your true needs and remaining income in order to plan effectively.

There are three special topics in three separate chapters. Chapter 14 offers advice on how to prepare in advance for a potential loss of income. Much of this book is applicable, but this chapter explores ideas you can implement ahead of time (when you have money) to minimize the financial impact later (when you don't). The second special topic is about poor decisions that can end up costing a family far more than they save, and thus Chapter 15 is suitably entitled "Pennywise, Pound-foolish." Finally, Chapter 16 describes the types of public services and benefits that are available. For affluent Americans who have never had to seek low-cost counseling, unemployment compensation, or food stamps, there is a discussion of how to apply for the assistance and benefits to which you are entitled and how to find help through other community organizations.

The book assumes that you have children. Both authors are mothers of "typical" middle-class children of various ages. The approach throughout the book is to deal with the downsizing of the family as a group. Continually, the children are considered, their help enlisted, their emotional well-being cherished.

Most important, throughout the book, you will find lots of stories. Each author's personal stories, experiences, and reflections are indented and followed by her initials; the experiences of others are indented and presented in italics without initials. Names and details have been changed to protect the privacy of friends and acquaintances who have shared with us; in some cases, the stories combine the experiences of more than one person. The purpose of the stories is to illustrate vividly otherwise abstract concepts, to provide solace and support, and to help shape your attitude toward the changes you are undergoing. These changes start the moment the loss occurs.

Grief—The Unexpected Companion

Whatever loss has precipitated your current situation, it's extremely important to recognize that the loss most likely produces grief. This may come as quite a surprise.

Fourteen years ago, our firstborn child died when she was three weeks old. It was the most traumatic event of our lives. Thus, I was dumbfounded when my husband equated his job loss to the death of our daughter! Deciding to accept his statement at face value, I attended a nationally televised teleconference on grief at our local hospital. Sure enough, someone phoned in during the question and answer section and asked the distinguished panel of psychologists, grief counselors, ministers, and professors if the loss of a job could be analogous to the death of a loved one. They all heartily agreed that it was!

—HSQ

We all know that the death of a loved one produces grief. It may seem strange, but, likewise, the death of a relationship can produce grief when it is one that significantly defines who you are and how you feel about yourself, and is the basis for your entire lifestyle. Therefore, if "the job" or "the marriage" has defined you, the layoff or the divorce can affect you as strongly as the death of a loved one.

Our neighbor down the street had worked for GE for twenty-eight years. He received the largest bonus ever for outstanding work one month and a layoff notice the next. Another neighbor believed her marriage was great. Then, one evening, her husband walked in and announced he wanted a divorce; he had fallen in love with someone else.

The suddenness of a significant loss complicates the grief process. People who have lost a loved one unexpectedly due to accident, suicide, homicide, or disease are characterized as being particularly traumatized because they have no context in which to define or place the event. They feel powerless and angry and, most important, unsafe. Even if they successfully grieve the individual and move on to reconstruct their life, the feeling that the world is unsafe and cannot be trusted never goes away. They carry that burden their entire life.

The lost job or the divorce produces similar feelings. When the tragedy strikes, the assumptions and opinions you've always had are shattered. The more suddenly the event occurs, the more acute and lasting will be the effects. Even if the person gets another job, he or she will feel afraid it could end at any time. The divorcée has much to deal with before someone new can be trusted.

Tragically, job layoffs have a high coincidence with subsequent divorce. This may be the result of misdirected or unacknowledged grief.

Imagine the wife whose primary role in life is to support her corporate husband as he climbs the ladder of success. She entertains company executives and attends social functions with her husband that are designed to "move him along." If he suddenly loses his job, so does she. Although her loss is less obvious, it has to be acknowledged if she, as well as her spouse, is to heal. If their grief is similar and simultaneous, the marriage should be stable. However, if her expression of grief involves continued anger and guilt directed at her husband, as it often does, then it's easy to see that the marriage can be threatened.

The life of a college professor or corporate executive often involves cross-country moves and life in remote or unfamiliar places. That was the case for Karen and Martin when he got his first teaching job in Iowa. Karen had an interesting job as a children's book editor in New York City, with which she supported Martin in his years in graduate school. When they moved to Iowa, Karen could not find a position that was remotely comparable. She worked at a series of low-level, dead-end research assistantships and eventually quit altogether to take care of their new baby and to entertain his colleagues as the dutiful faculty wife. Six years after moving, Martin was de-

nied tenure. Karen blamed him for making her leave a job and a city she loved, for moving them to the middle of nowhere, and then for not publishing enough to keep his position. Fearing they would continually have to move from college town to college town with no job security to show for it, Karen left Martin and returned to New York.

On the other hand, imagine a wife whose defining role has very little to do with her husband's job. When the layoff comes, if she doesn't recognize the grief process in her husband, the marriage relationship is likewise shaken. "Instead of moping around, why don't you get off your duff and go find another job (or even take care of the kids)!" may be a typical response, but it doesn't show any empathy for the situation and the husband's grief.

During the years I spent as a professional in the business world, I noticed a general trend distinguishing the men and women I worked with. The men identified themselves with their job far more than the women who had children. Women without children were more like the men in their attitude toward the overall importance of their work. Mothers who were also professional, however, tended to see "the job" and "motherhood" as more balanced, equal roles. This isn't to say that the men with children were lousy fathers. They weren't, but their defining role was influenced primarily by their avocation, not their fatherhood.

—HSQ

Although this may be contrary to the politically correct concept of men's and women's roles, there still seems to be lot of truth to it. Obviously then, a layoff affecting a man may have deeper repercussions than the working wife may anticipate. If she belittles the grief based on her own bias, she threatens the stability of the marriage. Who would belittle the death of a loved one? No one. Yet, this can easily happen in a job loss situation when understanding is lacking.

Think for a moment about how our society deals with a death in a family. Friends and family members gather, tears and sorrow are shared. More distant colleagues send cards acknowledging the grief. Funeral rituals and memorial services help to move along the grief process. Family members are encouraged to talk about it, and the talk is important to the healing.

The only type of death where many of these social functions break down is death by suicide. A stigma surrounds a suicidal death. No one feels comfortable relating to the surviving family members. No one encourages the family to talk about it. Neighbors and friends don't know how to react, so often they don't. Fewer people attend the funeral. The surviving family members struggle with a horrible loss that has limited avenues for release.

Job loss and divorce are more similar to the suicidal death. They carry a stigma. "What's wrong with you that this happened?" people think. It's very awkward for family members (close or distant) to discuss it openly. Many may completely miss the fact that grief is an important factor now. No wonder this is a difficult situation! There are no rituals, like funerals, to help the grieving process along.

The Grieving Process

If you have recently experienced an unexpected drop in income due to a lost job, divorce, death, or disability, then you are already in the midst of the grieving process. Hopefully, as you read this short passage, you will recognize your reactions as normal and natural responses to a loss. If you are reading this book as "preventive medicine," then just consider this as "forewarned is forearmed" information. It may very well be new to you as our American culture rarely educates us about grief.

Grief must be acknowledged, permitted, and worked through. It is a process. Its duration and intensity are unpredictable, but six to

twelve months is typical. It is also intensely personal and individual-
istic. A variety of responses occur—there is no "proper" or "one" way
to express grief. It's also important to remember that all members of
the immediate family will be affected. Each one needs the latitude to
deal with loss their own way.

Dr. Elisabeth Kübler-Ross has written extensively on the five stages
of grief. The first one is denial. This is a common initial reaction to
a job loss or divorce as well. Many people who suffer a job loss continue to leave the house at the same time every morning dressed for
work and return at the same time every evening. Some do not even
tell their family they are out of work. They may believe they will be
called back soon, even though all signs point to the layoff as permanent. Families going through a divorce experience the same process of
denial when they believe the spouse or parent will soon return. Children, especially, may try to reunite their parents.

If you are in denial, you will find it particularly difficult to make
the hard choices necessary for living on less income. You may believe,
for instance, that you or your spouse will return to the same job soon
and therefore it's OK for you to run up a lot of credit card debt to pay
your bills and maintain your normal lifestyle. You may find yourself
believing that if you continue to live as you did before, then the
layoff, divorce, or other tragedy never happened. This attempt to maintain a sense of "normalcy" is certainly understandable—and normal—
but it's a dangerous pitfall.

Eventually, reality sets in. If you are reading this book, you have
probably gotten past the denial stage and are looking for ways to
cope with your situation. After denial, people going through the grief
process experience anger or rage. This is most often directed at the
employer in a job loss situation.

I was fired from my first job as a teacher in a private
school. Since all the teachers in my department except
me were male and since my department head had made
several sexist remarks, I wanted to sue the school for dis-
crimination. I contacted a lawyer, who said I had a case,

but she wanted $1,000 up front. The fact that I would have to dip into my meager savings, which had to tide me over until I found a new job, made me think. I realized I didn't want my job back; I mainly wanted revenge. I dropped the case.

—LML

Anger after a job loss may also be directed at a spouse, especially if the unemployed person perceives the spouse as unhelpful or unsympathetic. Anger in a divorce is usually directed at the ex-spouse, but may be deflected onto the children.

A third stage in the grief process is bargaining. In some ways this stage is similar to denial in that you think you will get your job or spouse back or be able to maintain your lifestyle if you change in some way. You have begun to think that change is necessary—which is important—but you have not yet accepted the new reality. Remember how a person in denial will seek to maintain his or her upscale lifestyle via credit cards? Someone who has advanced to bargaining will think, "If I cut up my Visa and MasterCard, I will be able to keep all my department store cards."

A fourth stage is sadness or depression. This occurs when you begin to realize the full impact of all that has been lost. To continue the analogy: You have now canceled not only your Visa and Master-Card but all your credit card accounts. But shopping was your favorite activity—you enjoyed buying new things for yourself and your family, and perhaps it was an activity that brought you and your preteen daughter together every Saturday. Now your favorite pastime is gone, along with a cherished ritual you shared with your daughter.

Depression is a tough stage to get through, but in experiencing it, you will come to the final stage—acceptance. In accepting the changes, you begin to develop new rituals and activities that you enjoy. You may, for instance, spend Saturdays riding bikes or baking cookies with your daughter instead of shopping, and actually find yourself enjoying the new activities more. Even if you continue to miss your old pastimes, you have accepted the new realities, changed your life in accordance with them, and, most important, gotten on with your new life.

While most people go though all the stages of grief (though perhaps in a different order and at various rates), they will express their grief in different ways. These "manifestations of grief" are listed below. Some ways are more typical of the anger stage or the depression stage. Not all people will experience all these feelings. It's possible for people to go back and forth or experience several of these feelings at the same time.

- Shock
- Sobbing
- Rationalizing
- Anxiety, panic, or fear
- Withdrawal from human contact
- Irrational thought
- Physical symptoms: tightness in the throat, shortness of breath, need to sigh, empty feeling in the abdomen, lack of muscular power, aching limbs, trembling, diarrhea, change in sleep habits (increase in sleep or insomnia), change in appetite (increase or decrease), fatigue
- Relief (of being spared some aspects of what was lost)
- Guilt
- Regret
- Anger, hostility, or irritability toward others

How do you know when the process is coming to an end? Your confidence starts to rise. Recognizing that there is something to be learned from the struggle indicates that healing is occurring. Also, starting to take good physical care of yourself is a positive sign.

How do you know if your grief has turned into serious depression that requires professional intervention? Danger signs include social isolation, mounting use of alcohol or other drugs, destructive behavior, hostility or rage directed at specific persons, and a preoccupation with suicidal thoughts. Extreme manifestations of the normal grief stages or feelings may also point to problems. Many grief-stricken people consider suicide, but *suicide with a plan* is the significant difference. If you, or someone in your family, are exhibiting these behaviors, then skip ahead to Chapter 16 and read about the low-cost counseling options that are available.

The following sections offer advice for the first few hours, the first few days, and the first few weeks. Because so little has been written on this subject, the focus is on people who have experienced a job loss. Many of the suggestions, however, can be used by those going through a divorce or other family tragedy that results in a drop in income.

The First Few Hours: Telling the Immediate Family

Since "the ax" hasn't fallen yet for some of you reading this, it makes sense to start at the beginning. The bad news has just been received. How should you tell the immediate family?

Emergency room caregivers who have to deliver bad news to a family try to do so face-to-face, in a private area. They are encouraged to touch the person's arm or hand, look them straight in the eye, and speak honestly and directly.

That's probably the best way to deliver any bad news. Doing it by phone should be avoided, if possible. However, phoning is a natural reaction when any tragedy strikes. What do you do when the car breaks down on the highway, when a storm brings a tree crashing into the house, when your child breaks her arm at school? You phone your spouse. You need immediate assurance of security, and the spouse's role at those moments is to provide it, at least verbally. However, the most important tragedies are going to produce the greatest amount of shock. It's best to wait until you can discuss it in person.

Whether you are giving or receiving the news, it's crucial that you realize that confusion and disbelief are the natural consequences of shocking news. This is nature's way of "cushioning" you. It helps alleviate the physical responses produced by adrenaline rushing into your system.

This is a time to keep expectations low for each other. The way you each react to the news will very likely be quite different. Try not to be disappointed if the other person doesn't say what you expect or react in the manner you want. Keep reminding yourself that this is a grief situation and everyone needs permission to react individually. Shock is most acute during the first few hours. Slowly, rational thinking will resume.

My husband came home from work late in the morning the day he was laid off. His face was expressionless, his eyes blank. When he walked, it was like a zombie. Most of the time he just sat and stared off into the distance for long periods of time. I didn't know what to say, so I said almost nothing. My husband has a volatile temper, and I was scared to death I might say something that would trigger an explosive outburst. I assumed he wanted "space" and quiet.

For that reason, I went outside to meet the children as they arrived home from school. My eight-year-old daughter came home first. As she got off the bus, she noticed my husband's car in the driveway. "Why is Daddy home?" came her innocent question. "Your dad lost his job today," I explained as we walked up the driveway together. "He's very upset. He needs lots of love." Similarly, I met my junior high son when he came home. I waited for him on the steps so I could tell him privately before going inside. I used basically the same words that I had with his sister. At the time, it never occurred to me to be concerned about how the kids would react to the news. In fact, I didn't think about that at all for many weeks.

Then, I asked them what they thought about the way I broke the news to them. "It was like being hit by a train," said my son. "Couldn't you have written me a letter and told me?" asked my daughter. In retrospect, I realized that I hadn't done a very good job. My husband and I had never shared with them the possibility of such a thing happening, even though we knew he might be laid off. If we had, it would have made the situation a little easier for them to grasp.

—HSQ

Parents generally try to shield their children from bad news or tragic events. We want to keep their lives simple and innocent. In the long run, it isn't helpful. Being honest with children old enough to understand (school age) about the family situation is healthier for them. You don't need to paint doomsday scenarios for them, but if a loss of income looms as a possibility, it's best to let them know. As a family, discuss the challenges—both emotional and financial—that such an event would present. Enlist their suggestions on how one might save money if it happened. By discussing it openly, it lessens the impact for them if, and when, it becomes a reality.

When the kids were very young, we lived in northern California, an earthquake-prone area. I made a game of discussing earthquake preparedness. At any time (in the supermarket, on a street, in the bedroom) I'd say to them, "If an earthquake happened right now, what would you do?" We would discuss the safest places around, what to avoid, and how they should act to protect themselves. They treated it like a game too, and we had great fun with it. However, it was important mental practice for an event they knew could happen without notice. When the Loma Prieta earthquake hit—while I was out of town on a business trip—they knew exactly what to do.

—HSQ

Another thing to realize about children is that they are inherently self-centered. They want to know how it's going to affect them. Chances are, they are not going to have the maturity to express the kind of empathy you might desire or expect. While you may be fretting over the mortgage payment, the kids are concerned about their allowances, the planned vacation, the anticipated computer upgrade.

During the first few hours, when the kids bring up such questions, you will probably react in horror and anger at such trivial nonsense. However, it isn't trivial to them. If you can't answer these questions (because of your own confusion and grief), it's best to be as honest with them as possible. "Yes, I realize you're concerned about such and such, but we haven't made any decisions yet. We'll talk it over as a family in a day or two."

Children who may be away from home (at college or "grown and gone") don't need to be notified right away. You can wait until tomorrow and deal with the situation at hand with fewer distractions.

Extremely small children also do not need great explanations at this point. Time, work, and money are fairly abstract concepts for preschool-age children. If the unemployed parent is still out of the house, say at the outplacement center, or the children remain in the same day care, chances are they won't even realize there has been a change in parental schedules as a result of a layoff. A divorce, death, or parental illness, in which one or both parents are unavailable, is an entirely different story. So is a situation in which the unemployed parent is home all the time and/or day care arrangements must be changed. Obviously, the new circumstances will have to be explained to children in simple terms. Avoid piling on too much information at one time. If parents are upset (fighting or crying), even extremely young children will be aware of the unusual circumstances. They are quick to recognize the stress, internalize it themselves, and react by suddenly exhibiting deplorable behavior. What they need at this point is reassurance that they are safe, loved, and not responsible for what has happened. Hugs and simple statements expressing love will do much to calm their fears.

The First Few Days: Begin Financial Assessments

The good news is that you can expect the initial shock and confusion to dissipate. The bad news is that it'll probably be replaced with fear. You don't know how bad your financial situation is, and your imagination can conjure up all kinds of nightmares. You feel a distinct lack of control, another source of deep-rooted fear.

It's time to do something concrete about the finances. First, put a moratorium on all spending except for essentials. Then, begin the work described in the next chapter, "Assessing Your Financial Situation." This involves going back and itemizing all your expenditures in the previous six months. Identify the luxuries along with the bills that must be paid. This exercise will take some time and require concentration. Directions are provided in the next chapter. What's important to recognize here is that this is a constructive activity. Organized lists, neatly written, provide a feeling of accomplishment and a measure of control. At this point, the psychological help you receive by this little bit of control is just as important as the information you glean about your financial situation. The subsequent budgeting activities will help you assess your income, and the reality of your monetary status will start to crystallize. Abstract fears may be replaced by substantiated fears, but at least you know what you're actually facing without imaginative embellishments.

Now is a logical time to evaluate current financial commitments. Do you have an upcoming vacation for which you've made reservations? Have you recently made any significant purchases that could be returned? Are there special restaurant dinners on your calendar in the upcoming weeks? No matter how much you may feel you've "earned" these luxuries, you probably ought to cancel them and save the money. This is not an appropriate time to keep up appearances. It's a time to be ultraconservative. Even if you went on your vacation, you'd probably not have a very good time. Knowing that you're spending money you don't have doesn't make for peaceful sleep at night!

The First Few Days: Telling Close "Others"

The first few days are also the time to tell absent children, grown children, and your closest confidants. It's completely appropriate to contact your minister, priest, or rabbi. Helping you when you hurt is part of their job description.

Young adults away at college pose a different problem. Remember, they are immersed in a completely different world and schedule than yours. The news that their college future may be jeopardized shouldn't be thrust upon a young person cramming for finals or writing end-of-term papers. Give some thought to your timing of the message. On the other hand, it's important to start setting the correct expectations and enlisting their help. The on-campus student has the opportunity to visit the Financial Aid Office. Since your income has dropped, the student may now qualify for aid that was previously denied because of income levels. It's important to start the search process quickly. Are there financial aid deadlines that have to be met? (This topic is explored in more detail in Chapter 9.)

Adult children (out on their own), extended family relations, and dear friends can help share the burden by sharing your hurt. However, don't be surprised if they don't really know what to say. Remember, this situation is analogous to a suicidal death; it's a real conversation stopper. Once the individual has expressed concern, it's difficult for him or her to offer anything else. There may be no tangible way to help you. Odds are, they aren't going to loan you money, and the possibility you'd ask for it may even create barriers in the relationship. So where can you find the support you desperately need?

The First Few Days: Finding Support

You should seriously consider finding a support group. Support groups can be formal—like People Without Partners, a nationwide network of singles—or informal—get-togethers or phone conversations. The objective is to locate people who understand what you're going through. The best support groups are made up of people who have experienced exactly what you have. Having been there, their empathy is strong and their advice worthwhile.

Look at library bulletin boards, read the small announcements in community newspapers, and check with churches and community centers. If nothing else, use word of mouth to find someone to talk to.

There were thirty-nine other people from my husband's company who were laid off along with him. The layoffs had been from many different departments and levels. For the most part, these men hadn't known each other at work at all. Yet, within a week of the layoff, they had begun to find each other by phone. They began to meet once a week at a local coffee shop. The meetings have been extremely helpful. There, the men can vent, share stories, exchange information, and generally commiserate in a group where everyone feels accepted and understood. Usually, my husband returns from these meetings more relaxed, with a clearer perspective on his own situation.

—HSQ

Sometimes, the tragic circumstances that bring people together in support groups unite those who otherwise would have little, if anything, in common.

The best example I can give you of this was the time the hospital social worker asked my husband and I if we would meet with another couple who had a dying baby that could not be saved. A few months earlier, we had experienced the same thing.

The couple were migrant field workers from Mexico. They spoke no English. The woman believed her baby was dying because she had been pregnant and outside during a partial eclipse. My husband and I, members of Corporate America with graduate degrees, believed our child had died as a result of genetic defects. We spoke no Spanish. Differences between us couldn't have been greater.

We met with an interpreter in a small room at the hospital. As I recall, very little actual conversation took place. For the most part, we hugged each other and cried. We were all parents who were sorrowing and devastated. Surprisingly enough, nothing else mattered. Afterward, both the social worker and the interpreter told us how deeply grateful the Mexican-American couple was for the meeting. They wanted us to know that it had been a truly healing experience for them.

—HSQ

When you stand back and think about it, we are all just human beings, pretty much alike as we walk this earth. The tragedies that affect us, affect us fundamentally much the same way. When we share with others, it helps.

The First Few Weeks: Adjusting to New Roles

Chances are, it's the magnitude of the many changes during the first weeks and the difficulties adjusting to them that have prompted you to pick up this book. There are lots of books available with advice for the newly divorced individual and suggestions for helping the kids adjust to that situation. School counselors are well versed in this area and deal with it daily. Emotional adjustments to white-collar layoffs is not a well-documented subject because the phenomenon is too new. So again, much of this section is focused on the family in which the major breadwinner has lost his or her job.

Children's Changing Roles

Children are resilient and can adjust to new situations. However, they will accept new responsibilities better if they are involved, from the beginning, in defining them. This is the time for lots of family discussions.

Years ago, I was working at a manufacturing division that was on the verge of collapse. Our future depended on successfully launching three new products in the course of a couple of months. Product designs had to be finalized, software finished and tested, manuals written, and all marketing literature produced. Since it looked like the company was "going under," employees were leaving to take other jobs all the time. It meant more work and stress for fewer and fewer people. The General Manager announced that everyone in Marketing and Research & Development would meet together at 4:30 every afternoon to assess our daily progress and try to deal with difficulties that had arisen that day. At first, we thought it was a horrible waste of time. In the long run, however, we realized how important it was to air problems openly, deal with them before they became crises, and monitor the daily progress of bringing these products to market. It knit the group together in an unbelievable fashion. And it worked. We introduced the products on time and the division survived.

—HSQ

Likewise, frequent family discussions are a necessity. This is a learning process for everyone. Ideas may be tried and discarded. New insights will occur. Seriously consider suggestions children make. Be sure to explain adequately your concerns and what you need them to do. There are probably new responsibilities for school-age children.

We sat down and negotiated with our kids about their allowances. I wanted to take them away altogether; my husband wanted to cut them in half. The kids quickly picked up on the difference in our opinion and sided with their dad. They were unhappy to hear that new chores were being added to their "to do" list even though the money was being cut in half. If I were working full time again, I would need significantly more help with the housecleaning and maintenance. Working more for less money was a staggering concept for them, as it is for all of us!

—HSQ

If you and your spouse are working longer hours at lower-paying jobs, or if you are now a single parent, it may be necessary for your children to become "latchkey" kids. This means they arrive home from school to an empty house and are on their own for a period of time without adult supervision. This situation demands lots of instruction prior to implementation and careful observation and listening to their concerns as they begin this new independence. There will be more on this topic in Chapter 7.

Older teenagers often have jobs outside the home. They may need to give up these money-earning opportunities to care for younger siblings. If this isn't a problem, your teenagers may consider increasing their work hours to earn more money to help the family out. How will this affect their schoolwork? Tradeoffs and experimentation may be necessary. Again, frequent family discussions are crucial to finding workable solutions with which you all feel comfortable.

As parents, we must remember that the children will go through their own grief process. They will learn a lot about handling feelings during this time by watching you and how you handle yours. There are certain things you can do to help them. Regardless of their age, answer their questions briefly, honestly, and tenderly. Hug or hold them more frequently. Keep to normal routines and bedtime schedules. Never let the children feel responsible for bringing on any aspect of the job or marriage loss. For younger children, acknowledge their feelings of loss, but don't pester preteens with questions to make them vocalize their feelings. Recognize that children of all ages tend to act out their troublesome feelings behaviorally. A normally active child may become withdrawn and sedentary. A quiet child may suddenly turn hyperactive. Other behaviors that signal unhappiness are a resump-

THE UPSCALE DREAM SHATTERED

tion of bed-wetting, thumbsucking, nail-biting, nightmares, and temper tantrums.

Older children are more apt to exhibit a combination of these behaviors and those the adults experience. Anxiety can lead to lack of attention, and school grades may suffer. Their self-image can be damaged if you don't have the money to allow them to keep up with their peers.

All these situations can be dealt with in family discussions. Keep blame and lecturing to a minimum. Keep unconditional love and communication at a maximum.

Adult Adjustment to New Roles

> When my husband lost his job, his dignity was destroyed, his self-image shattered. He set up an "office" in the basement for the organization of his job search efforts. He literally buried himself there. He refused to go outside—he didn't want anyone to see him. The only time he would leave the house was to go to the outplacement agency or to visit his coffee shop support group. He would have spent the entire winter in the basement if it hadn't been for two events. I got desperately ill with pneumonia in February, and we had record amounts of snowfall. If he wanted to eat, he had to shovel the driveway and go to the grocery store.
>
> —HSQ

In a layoff situation, the first few weeks may challenge you with something you have never faced before: How are you going to spend your time? The day may seem amazingly long without a commute, a boss and clients to please, projects to finish, and endless meetings.

How you choose to spend your time will begin to define your new role or roles. The role may be "job searcher," "cook," "baby-sitter," or all of the above. It's no longer "engineer," "production supervisor," or "accountant," but it *is* a role. You have to start somewhere. Decide to play this role well, properly, expertly even! Find some reason to feel good about yourself.

Establish a daily routine. Most people feel most comfortable with structure and activity. Build both into your schedule. Set goals and deadlines for yourself. ("I'm going to read four chapters of this book and write two letters today.") Keep the goals realistic, and revel in their accomplishment.

Exercise is a fantastic activity to include in your new schedule. There's nothing like firming up and slimming down to make you feel better about yourself. Chances are, you will be competing against younger people in the job hunt. Exercise can improve your overall health and appearance. This will help boost your confidence during interviews. Also, hard exercise is one of the best stress relievers known.

Heaven knows you need to reduce stress! These new roles and activities will frequently seem like pathetic attempts to rebuild your shattered ego. Pessimism and frustration will seem insurmountable at times. Acknowledge that you're moving through grief. Continue to talk with your support group. Find solace where you can—your friends, religion, family, and pets.

Complicating a man's layoff situation is when he has to take care of the kids too, now that the income has plummeted. This is usually less of a problem for laid-off women, who are at least perceived by society as performing a traditional and accepted role. It's bad enough to move through the community feeling like a fish out of water, but to be pushing a stroller while doing it may make him feel like a landed fish toting a flashing neon sign.

Imagine trying to use the outplacement agency's services while you have an eight-month-old baby in tow. Your former employer has set up this service for you so you can get job counseling, get help with résumé writing, do computer searches, and have a place to fax and make phone calls, but you are now the baby-sitter while your wife works. This would be difficult for a woman who has been laid off and can no longer afford child care, but it's often much worse for a man.

Walking into a place like this with a baby is a situation that has to be faced with the same bravado you used when you were fifteen and decided to ask a girl to dance for the first time. Remember how that went? You casually saunter across the gymnasium floor from the "boys' side" to the "girls' side" with a carefully composed visage to show how "cool" you are. With mustered confidence you quietly ask her to dance, then mask your surprise when she says yes. "Oh boy, it's great she didn't destroy me by saying no, but now I have to dance for the first time—in front of everybody!" you think to yourself. You gulp down the fear, share a nervous laugh with her, and start to try to move to the music. It's awkward, and you're terrified, but you can't let anyone know! The interminable song finally ends and you sheepishly smile at her and thank her for the dance. You walk back to your buddies, working hard to maintain your balance and keep looking "cool." From the corner of your eye you see the girl disappear into the Ladies' Room with a pack of giggling friends. You lived through it. The next time should be easier. You hope.

Whether it's at the outplacement agency, the public or university library, or simply the grocery store, when you have to appear in public with the baby stroller, assume the same attitude that got you through your first dance. If you could do it at fifteen, surely you can do it now. Anyway, assuming a look of confidence and coolness is excellent practice—isn't this exactly what you do at job interviews?

Don't misunderstand. A baby is not appropriate everywhere. You will not be able to utilize the outplacement agency as much as the person who isn't also a baby-sitter. It is an office environment, and children do not fit into this environment. However, this place exists because of extenuating circumstances, so not all the regular rules apply. Be smart, though. Don't take a tired or hungry baby. Do pack lots of quiet toys. Everyone enjoys an unobtrusive, smiling cherub. No one likes a screaming tyrant. There will be people trying to get serious work accomplished around you. Use your brains and common courtesy. Then, when the child fusses, leave.

The First Few Weeks: Who Else Has to Know?

You need to maintain your dignity. This is partially accomplished by maintaining your privacy. Don't feel obligated or compelled to tell everyone about the loss in income. It's only their business if you choose for it to be their business. Discuss with your children what is appropriate and not appropriate to say to their friends and teachers. Lower elementary children tell their teachers everything; assume those teachers know. If you are seeing behaviors in children of any age that indicate they are experiencing difficulties that could affect their schoolwork, it's best to let the teacher know what is going on. A simple, handwritten note will suffice. The teacher can contact you if a consultation is needed.

Odd circumstances will occur when you have to tell people that you'd otherwise prefer not to.

Lyn, my coauthor, is a neighbor down the street. One day, shortly after Christmas, she came over and asked if my husband could hand-carry some materials she had to a coworker at his office. No, I tentatively explained, he couldn't. My husband had been laid off a few weeks earlier. She was, of course, speechless with surprise.

—HSQ

When Hope told me about her husband's layoff, I was surprised mainly because the company had brought him East only a year ago. I could certainly empathize with her situation because my husband had been denied tenure six years earlier. The thing that most upset me when he lost his job was our isolation. People who were once our friends avoided us as if we had a catching disease. I felt we had no one to turn to for help or support.

—LML

Unfortunately (or maybe fortunately) you really learn who your friends are in a situation like this. Yes, some of your neighbors and fair-weather friends will start to avoid you. But others may reveal their own stories and reach out to help. Often you can't predict who's going to come through and who isn't, so if you don't want to know, don't tell. If you're looking for support, your best sources are generally people in similar circumstances, or who have experienced similar circumstances in the past. Support groups offer the best chance of meeting these people, but you may have some friends and acquaintances who have gone through hard times in the past and whom you can approach. Hopefully, you haven't been a fair-weather friend to them!

While you are trying to maintain your privacy and dignity, you also must guard yourself from falling into the trap of "keeping up appearances." Carrying on, spending money like you used to, is a form of denial that is extremely destructive. The American Dream, for you, has been shattered. This is reality. It's imperative that you face this reality with utter honesty.

Chapter 2

Assessing Your Financial Situation
How Deep Is the Hole You're In?

$\mathcal{S}$omewhere, I understand, there are people who actually plan how their paycheck will be spent. Their money is carefully allocated to bills, savings, and other expenditures, and all records are meticulously maintained in ledgers or in a computer program. At the other extreme, there are people whose idea of money management consists of piling all incoming bills in the same place on the kitchen countertop with the hope that someone will remember to pay them before they're due. Most of us fall somewhere between these two extremes. We have a general feel for how much discretionary money we have each month, live within our means, and plan to start seriously saving soon, maybe next year. Most of us don't follow a strict budget plan, and the vast majority of Americans are notoriously poor savers. However, those relaxed days are now behind you. If you have never budgeted before, now you must. This simply means that every penny has to be accounted for and spending it must be a calculated undertaking. *Every* penny.

Start by Looking at the Past

The best way to begin to get a handle on your spending is to review what you generally spend. Start with the last six months. (You may want to increase this and review the last twelve months—you're less apt to miss items by remembering the entire year. It's just more work!) Go through your checkbook register, credit card bills, and receipts, and organize and account for all of your expenditures as best you can. You have several objectives in doing this. First, it will help you see where "fat" can most easily be cut. Once the easy stuff has been cut out (at least in your mind), then the "squeezing" begins to help you save every cent possible.

Second, categorizing your expenditures will help you spot where your priorities have been, regardless of whether you recognize them as priorities. ("For where your treasure is, there will your heart be also." Matt. 6:21) What's important now has probably changed. You are "back to the basics" of food and shelter, but it's wise to recognize where your weaknesses for spending lie. Forewarned is forearmed!

The third objective you have in this endeavor is to let it help you construct a monthly target budget that covers the essentials. You have to determine how much money is necessary, per month, to continue to live where you do. Can you stay in your current home—pay the rent or mortgage—by downsizing in other areas? It may be clear to you that the answer to that question is no. OK, that may be true. The exercise is still valid because you need a clear idea of all the expenses you must meet (somehow!) until the house sells.

Categorizing your expenditures will be most helpful if you keep your categories fairly specific. Instead of Food, break your expenditures down into Groceries, Restaurant Meals, Fast Food, Lunches, etc. Don't forget the kids' cafeteria meals at school. If you buy nonfood items (paper, detergent, lightbulbs, etc.) at the grocery store, estimate what percentage of each grocery bill is food and what is nonfood, and put these amounts in separate lists. For a category like Entertainment, break it down, if possible, to the different types of entertainment your family enjoys: Movies, Concerts, Theater, Rented Videos, Athletic Games, etc.

Every family will be different, but here is a list to get you started. The first is the general category (present on most family budgets) and some possible subcategories are in parentheses. Modify this as you see fit.

FOOD groceries, restaurant meals, fast food, lunches away from home

ENTERTAINMENT movies, concerts, theater, parties, videos, cassettes/CDs, games requiring tickets, computer games, cable TV, books, newspaper/magazine subscriptions

RECREATION sports, music, arts, club fees, equipment, lessons, other fees

CLOTHING per person in the family, dry-cleaning costs, special sports clothing

TOYS/GIFTS birthdays, major holidays, miscellaneous

CHARITIES per charity

UTILITIES gas, electric, water, phone, sewage, garbage

HOUSE MAINTENANCE supplies for inside, supplies for outside, yard service, cleaning service, home repairs, appliances

HOUSE—MAJOR PURCHASES remodeling, landscaping, furniture, home computer, audio/video equipment

TRANSPORTATION per person costs or per vehicle costs such as lease payment, gasoline, repairs, maintenance, licenses, parking costs, etc.

PERSONAL INDULGENCES alcohol, cigarettes, gambling

PERSONAL CARE cosmetics, haircuts, tanning salons

PETS per pet

CHILD/ELDER CARE per person

CHILD SUPPORT

ALIMONY PAYMENT

EDUCATION per person: tuition, books, supplies, transportation to and from school

MEDICAL/DENTAL deductibles, co-payments, prescriptions

CREDIT CARD INTEREST/FEES per card

BANKING/FINANCIAL SERVICES

NONMEDICAL PROFESSIONAL SERVICES accountant, lawyer, etc.

MORTGAGE/LEASE/RENT separate out costs of insurance and taxes if an escrow account is part of the monthly payment covering these items

INSURANCE car, life, medical, dental, homeowners, disability, long-term care

LOANS auto, installment, personal

TAXES local, state, federal

Obviously, if you do this on separate sheets of paper, you are going to have a *lot* of sheets. That's OK. Staple the different subcategories together and the pile will seem more manageable. It's important to get this level of detail. Trust me, the effort will pay off in the end with the amount of information you discover in this process.

Some folks will prefer to do this exercise on a computer utilizing commercially available budgetary or spreadsheet programs. Don't go buy software for this—it's not worth the expense now. Paper lists have sufficed for several hundred years!

Once you have most of the expenses in the last few months allocated to the different lists, it's time to do some serious thinking about the differences between *wants* (luxuries) and *needs* (necessities).

Luxuries and Necessities

Most of us have never visited a convent, but we've all seen movies that portray the simple life of a nun. Her bedroom has few furnishings; her clothing changes are minimal. Basic foods are prepared and eaten communally. The starkness of this lifestyle shocks us. It would take a direct call from God to induce one to embrace a life like that!

But thinking about it helps you realize how really very little around you comprises the basic necessities. There's your home, your clothing, your food, your family. Your home provides shelter—its purpose is the same regardless of whether it's an apartment, a mobile home, a $150,000 house, or a million-dollar mansion. Your clothing is meant to protect you from the elements. When it's cold, you need a jacket. When it's hot, you need a hat. Your food is meant to sustain you. Your health is maintained regardless of whether your main source of protein is steak, hamburger, or lentils and rice.

Exaggeration is done here with purpose. Of course, your home and clothing serve many other functions beyond simple shelter and protection from the elements. They define your position in our complex society. The trappings with which you surround yourselves furnish you with a role to play. The marketeers in our consumption-based free enterprise system make sure your identity continues to be rede-

fined with more and more complex and expensive material possessions.

A Luxury is a "want"—a desirable thing to have to increase comfort and make life more interesting and fun. You'll find plenty of these
on your lists. Go through your lists and mark each item with an "L"
or an "N" depicting Luxury or Necessity. A Necessity is a "need"—
fundamental to existence and survival. You'll find some of these in the
lists you have compiled. Your home, food, insurance, and medicines
are all necessities.

There was an exercise like this in the Sunday School
curriculum last year. My class of third-, fourth-, and fifth-
graders had been given a list containing about twenty
items such as TV, phone, tape player, jacket, lunch, and
house. There were to circle the items they needed for
survival. Out of the eight kids, none was willing to live
without a TV. No matter how I tried to explain what the
word "survival" meant (stranded on a desert island, on a
rocket ship bound for the moon), they absolutely, res-
olutely refused to consider that life could be sustainable
without their beloved televisions. I was really shocked! I
drew a time line and showed them how many generations had lived before the invention of TV, and how children had managed to be busy and happy then. I finally
gave up. Perhaps, with time, they will mature enough to
realize that TV is a luxury, not a necessity. At least, I
hope they do!

—HSQ

As you go through your lists and mark items and categories with
Ls and Ns, you may find some real surprises. Although we always assume we know where our money is being spent, you may very well
find yourself saying, "Wow! I didn't realize we spent that much money
at such-and-such a store last year!"

A friend from California did an exercise like this and discovered she was spending more than $1,000 a year on cappuccino at coffee shops. Obviously, the cappuccino in Northern California is very good, but if she's that addicted, she should seriously consider buying a cappuccino maker for her kitchen and learn how to foam her own milk!

Also, as you do this exercise, you are going to come across items that you normally would want to buy, but you know could be purchased more economically or that perhaps have much cheaper reasonable substitutes. If we aren't forced to buy the most economical variety, we often don't, but instead opt for other features that drive up the cost. When you come across these items, give them a special notation, like an asterisk (*). Much of this book is devoted to helping you with this process—finding less expensive substitutes. That's the whole point of downsizing. There's no reason not to begin the thinking process now, the first time you review these lists of prior expenditures.

Don't confuse "necessary bill to pay" with "necessity." A loan on a boat is a necessary bill you have to deal with, but the boat itself is a luxury item. Mark it with an L. If your child is involved in an expensive sport (like ice hockey or karate) and you're in the middle of the season or have a contractual agreement, these represent expenditures that must be made unless you withdraw your child from the sport. Although it seems like a necessary bill to pay, the fact remains it is a luxury activity.

The world isn't entirely black and white. You're bound to find things on the lists that are extremely difficult to mark either as a Necessity or a Luxury. No problem—mark it with an NL and move on. You can come back to it later.

The careful analysis of each expenditure as a Necessity, Luxury, an NL, and/or an asterisk will be most beneficial for the nonbudget type person. This exercise should clearly show you where your discretionary money has been spent. If you use this N vs. L exercise as the basis for a family discussion, it will probably launch some hot debates. Each person in the family will have his or her own "sacred cows" that couldn't possibly be cut out! However, that is precisely the reason behind the exercise—to get you to analyze seriously your spending habits and begin to prioritize your luxuries.

An interesting, but optional, step to take after the lists are completed is to sum up all the luxury items. Calculating what percentage of your prior income was spent on luxuries can also be enlightening. However, that's all in the past now. It's more important to move on to dealing with your present circumstances.

Creating a Typical and a Target Monthly Budget

Having reviewed all your accounts to assemble the categorized lists of expenditures, it should be a fairly straightforward exercise to construct a "typical" month's expenses. This is where you list the "necessary to pay" bills regardless of whether they are a necessity or a luxury.

Use the same categories and subcategories that were listed at the beginning of the chapter. Where there is a preset, constant cost, include it (like the rent or mortgage, which doesn't change). For the utilities, you can average your costs (best done over a twelve-month period to account for weather changes) and calculate the typical bill. For the items that are highly variable (food perhaps), an average cost is a good starting point for the figure to put on the budget. If you have purchased anything on credit and haven't yet paid it off, create a special category called "Necessary to Pay" Bills and place the payment there. This category will include auto loans, loans from retail stores, and credit card payments. Note that this is a different category in your budget from, say, Transportation, House—Major Purchases, or Entertainment. These are debts left over from past purchases, not purchases you will be making now.

Concentrate on the necessities and "necessary to pay" bills. Now would be a good time to put a special notation (like a star) next to items that normally are monthly bills but are complete luxuries (for example, newspaper and on-line subscriptions or cable TV channels). If you can continue to pay for these on your downsized income, then fine, they can stay on the budget plan. If you can't, then you'd better start getting used to the idea that they are going to be cut from your life, at least temporarily.

We all have expenditures that happen only once or a few times during the year. Property taxes and different types of insurance payments are typical bills of this sort. If your mortgage includes an escrow account to cover some of these expenses, then they won't be as much of a concern as it will be for those who don't have these accounts. The IRS can be a problem, however, if someone in your family is self-employed and/or you have investment income and file quarterly payments.

When my husband was laid off in early December, we were facing upcoming Christmas expenses, and property taxes and a quarterly payment to the IRS for my home-based business were due in January. These were frightening expenses to be looming over our heads.

—HSQ

As a professional writer, I am accustomed to wide swings in income from one year to the next. Although our family's expenditures are based on my "worst year" earnings (plus my husband's salary and income from savings) and anything beyond that is put into savings, my biggest problem is that quarterly IRS payment. Quarterly payments are based on one's income from the year before, and several times I have had good years followed by bad years, so that I owed huge payments at a time when I was least able to pay. The worst was the year I took a maternity leave from my writing and ended up having to take a part-time job to pay the IRS.

—LML

As you construct your typical monthly budget, include these "occasional" costs. If something is due once a year, put one-twelfth of that cost in the monthly plan; if it's due quarterly, put one-third of the quarterly payment in the monthly plan. In other words, average the cost over the number of months between payments.

It's generally quite helpful to construct a time line of the year, January through December. For each month, write down the normal amount of bills you need to pay, but mark clearly where the "occasional" bills crop up. Note what big payments are pending in the next couple of months. You need a plan that can deal with them.

Up to this point, you've been dealing primarily with expenses that are similar to your past ones (using your historic data). As you put your "typical" monthly budget together, you may run across expenses you had in the past but don't have now. For instance, if you're out of a job, transportation costs may be significantly less. Note these. There are also expenses you may now have that you didn't before—child care, perhaps, if now you're working outside the home and you didn't previously. There may be job search costs (phone, postage, education) that need to be factored in.

Your "typical" budget needs to start its transformation into your "target" budget. Begin this by adjusting the costs and categories to represent more accurately your best guess for expenses ahead. As you read this book, you should discover new ways to help you save money in all the categories in a normal family budget. Unless your income has fallen only a little bit, you'll see the need to downsize most expenses in the budget significantly. The budget you just put together can have several columns: Past, Present, and Target for each category. (See the sample budget worksheet on pp. 49–51.) Continue to update this budget document as you read, discover, and implement downsizing strategies.

Figuring Your Income

It's fine to figure out how much your bills amount to; the trickier problem is getting to match it with your present income. Your plans may include getting a new or different job that will pay you more. However, whatever you have for income *now* is where you need to start.

If you are downsizing because of a layoff, then you likely have severance pay, unemployment compensation, and perhaps back vacation pay. If your situation is a result of divorce, then hopefully, you have some employment income to supplement your divorce settlement, spousal support (alimony), and child support payments (assuming the divorce is finalized). If the death of a spouse has led you to downsize, you have probably received a lump sum payment through a pension or insurance. This lump sum should be invested carefully, in safe, income-producing investments. Your children are also entitled to Social Security Survivor's Benefits until they turn eighteen.

There may be other income streams possible if you have certain kinds of investments. If you have investments that pay dividends that are normally automatically reinvested into the investment fund, you may be able to get the dividends paid out to you directly in cash. It may not be much, but every little bit helps. Some life insurance policies have a cash savings program that accompanies them. You may be able to access this money now, as a direct payout or as a loan. If you have investments like stocks that are in long-term growth accounts, ask your broker about switching the funds to short-term cash generators like bonds. Don't forget or ignore rent from property, gifts, or royalty payments. Most of us who have experienced layoffs, however, have to rely primarily on the other spouse's salary and unemployment compensation.

Once you add up all your possible income, then compare it to your monthly bill obligations. If your financial commitments are significantly greater than your income, you've got to figure out other ways to raise revenue in the short term.

Contingency Thinking

The ideas in this section are meant to be just that—ideas. At this point, they should just be things to consider rather than to act on. You shouldn't be in any hurry to make critical, life-changing decisions until everything is reviewed. However, you should examine different ideas, brainstorm new ones, do some research, and carefully evaluate their financial implications. You may or may not need to implement some of them to make ends meet.

Look carefully at your savings, investments, and retirement funds. You may need to liquidate some of these, but most types have penalties for early withdrawal. Some have severe penalties.

Cash savings in passbook accounts shouldn't have any penalties associated with them. CDs (certificates of deposit) are investments in which the money is tied up for short periods of time, like 90 days, 120 days, or 1–3 years. You *can* get your money before the time of maturity is up, but the bank will charge you a penalty for doing this. Check with the bank to see how much you stand to lose if you withdraw the cash from a CD.

Stocks and bonds can both be sold. You'll be taxed on any profits you've made, and there will probably be a cost of sale. Mutual funds can be sold like stocks and bonds, but they might be better used to generate a cash stream by redirecting growth-oriented funds into income-generating funds.

Annuities, 401Ks, and IRAs are designed to be long-term, tax-deferred investments that are to be used for funding your retirement. Liquidating these will be very expensive because you'll generally pay a 10 percent early withdrawal penalty (if you're less than fifty-nine and one-half years old) plus income tax on the withdrawal. Annuities sometimes have the penalty dropped if you hold on to them for more than five years. It is something worth checking on if you've had one for a long time. A 401K account usually has your own investment money plus matching money from an employer. You should check with the plan manager to see whether or not you own the company contribution before you think seriously about withdrawing it. An IRA has only your contributions in it, no company matching money. However, both 401Ks and IRAs should be "last resort" investments to liquidate. Borrowing against the funds in them, though, may be a possibility to investigate.

If you decide you need to liquidate an investment, think about your tax consequences and where you are in the calendar year. Does this year or next year look to be the year with the lower income? If you can, withdraw the money in the year in which your income is lower, in order to keep your income tax to a minimum. Don't forget that you will owe income tax on your unemployment compensation as well. It may seem like adding insult to injury, but it's the law.

If you have contributed from your paycheck to a pension plan and now you're no longer an employee, you may be able to get the pension plan money, plus interest, in a lump sum payout. Plans differ, and you will probably have to pay a penalty and taxes on the withdrawal. If the pension plan was paid for by your employer but not by you (noncontributory pension plan), then you won't be able to access the funds at all until you retire.

As mentioned earlier, many people buy life insurance that has some kind of savings plan built into it. (This is the opposite of "term" insurance.) If you have this, check with your agent to see if you can withdraw the savings accrued or if it's possible to qualify for a loan based on that savings.

Some people have money invested in real estate that was designed for long-term appreciation and/or a tax shelter. This kind of investment can be a terrible burden to hold on to now that you've had a significant drop in income. Look into what it will take to sell and how long it might take to get rid of the property.

The same thing applies to your house, if you own it. It doesn't cost anything to meet with a couple of local real estate agents to discuss the present value of your home, its marketability, how long you can expect to wait before it sells, and to get some realistic suggestions on what improvements are necessary before you place it on the market. Meeting with two or three agents should help you get a fairly accurate representation of the current market situation. If you end up deciding to sell, you'll probably use a real estate agent, so this exercise can be used to "interview" agents as well.

In the past, when home values were rising steadily, those who had lost a job or had to sell due to a divorce could count on making some money from the sale of the house. The situation today is far more complicated. In areas with high unemployment, real estate values have actually fallen, and many people have discovered, to their dismay, that they would continue to owe money on the mortgage even after the house is sold. If you think the balance of your mortgage is greater than what you could get from the sale of the house (a situation known in real estate jargon as an "upside-down house"), you need to investigate the other options discussed in Chapter 12.

We were shocked to discover that the house we had owned for a mere thirteen months had lost about $50,000 in a market that was falling rapidly and it would take six to twelve months to sell. If my husband found a job in another state, it would probably mean living apart from each other for a very long time, at least until housing prices came back or until we had saved enough from his new job to pay off the mortgage. This was something we'd never wanted and never thought could happen.

—HSQ

My brother in Houston, Texas, found himself in a similar situation. First, oil prices crashed and the bottom fell out of Houston's economy. Then, the economy recovered, but his neighborhood fell out of fashion. When he married and moved to a different neighborhood with his new family, he chose to rent out his old house rather than bring a very big check to the closing. Renting it offered enough tax advantages for him to break even until prices rebounded.

—LML

Besides your house, do you have other assets that might be liquidated to provide additional income? Many affluent families have money invested in artwork, jewelry, furs, silver, antiques, cars, and collectibles. Even though they may carry great sentimental value, are they potential "nest eggs"?

My husband owns an antique Porsche. He bought it years before we met, and he affectionately refers to it as his Mistress. On a sunny day, one of his greatest joys is to remove its top, start up the engine that sounds like a rocket taking off, and zoom around the country roads. Most of the time, however, it sits in the garage and appreciates in value. A couple of years ago, my mother gave my husband a hand-painted sweatshirt with the picture of his sports car. Under the car it read "MY FOURTH LOVE." I always hoped the kids and I came first! We clearly do, because shortly after he was laid off, he rechecked the current value of the car. It would be a gut-wrenching experience for him to sell it, but if our backs were to the wall, he would. He constantly reminds us, though, that the car is worth more on the open market than the three of us are!

—HSQ

To sell your valuables, it helps considerably to have the original receipts or an up-to-date appraisal. If you've had a special rider on your homeowners insurance policy for these items, you may have needed to determine their value when you took out the policy, so you may have gone through this already.

To get an appraisal now, you'll probably have to find an appropriate appraiser and pay a fee. Phone calls should tell you what that may cost. You'll have to decide if it's worth the cost to get the appraisal; you might be able to sell it for close to your asking price without the cost of the formality.

To sell artwork, start by contacting the gallery it came from. Most galleries will not take artwork back and resell it, but occasionally you'll find one that will. If it does, expect to have it sold "on consignment" (you are paid only when the painting sells) and to be paid only a fraction of what the gallery receives for the work, say $8,000 for a painting the gallery sells for $20,000. (The gallery expects to make a healthy profit on it too!) Chances are, though, you'll need to sell it on your own. If you're successful in finding a buyer, you'll make the most money on the transaction by doing it yourself. The trick is finding your target market. Your best bet is to advertise in major newspapers in areas of the country that cater to art or tend to be highly affluent. (New York City and Beverly Hills come to mind.) Advertising in regional editions of *The Wall Street Journal* is an excellent way to target certain areas of the country. Unfortunately it's quite expensive; expect to pay several hundred dollars daily for a very small ad. Selling artwork through an auction house should be a last resort; you won't receive very much.

Auction houses are a better bet, however, for valuable antiques. The major auction houses, such as Sotheby's and Christie's, take a 15 percent commission on each item sold, but most won't accept an item for sale unless it is quite valuable. You may have to wait a while too, because the big houses sometimes hold pieces for theme auctions or special events. Local and regional auction houses have a lower minimum value than the major houses, but don't expect to realize as much from the sale either. You can also try advertising your pieces in trade publications such as *The Antique Trader,* which focus on your target audience. Other options include selling through a dealer on consignment and selling through the newspaper.

Jewelry and furs are best sold through advertising in newspapers. Because of the abundance of pre-owned jewelry and furs and because stores want to sell their new wares at high prices, jewelry stores and furriers will not buy back these items. There are establishments advertised in the Yellow Pages that claim to buy them, but you'll get only a tiny fraction of what you paid for them initially. Check with a few if you want; it never hurts to ask. The one exception to this bleak situation is antique or estate jewelry and silver from a time period that is currently in fashion. At the time of this writing, for example, many collectors were seeking certain styles of jewelry from the 1930s and 1940s. If you have pieces of unusual distinction and/or provenance, an auction house may be interested in them. You may also be able to sell your estate or antique jewelry on consignment through specialized dealers. If you do choose the consignment route, be sure to ask the dealer about its policies on compensation if your piece is damaged or stolen while on its property.

When you sell items yourself, through advertising in the newspaper, you will have to weigh in your mind the costs involved to sell them versus the amount of money you expect, realistically, to receive.

Exotic cars and collections tend to have cult followings and frequently have magazines and clubs catering to a very select audience. Advertising in the magazines' classified ads is the logical way to proceed. Some clubs or organizations have free or low-cost appraisal services too, which will also help you determine the value of your merchandise.

Most of the topics in this section on "Contingency Thinking" need research of some sort on your part to determine feasibility. Use the phone, library, and knowledgeable friends and contacts so you make sure you can fairly evaluate the benefits, disadvantages, and pitfalls.

Accurate information is valuable, even if it's not what you want to hear. It sets realistic expectations. It provides a framework for evaluating plans and making decisions.

Challenge the assumptions you've always held. Your world has been turned upside down. The things you've always taken for granted may no longer be valid. Work hard to keep an open mind.

In addition, you should think things through carefully so you won't later regret decisions that were made with too much haste. This also applies to selling cherished heirlooms and other valuables; it's much easier to replace stocks and bonds than your mother's jewelry. You should wait and make sure you have to sell these heirlooms and try to sell more easily replaceable things first. Grief counselors usually advise surviving spouses not to make a major decision—such a selling the house, moving out of town, or making a large investment—for six months after the death. While outside factors—an offer in a distant city or dire financial need—might force an earlier decision in the case of a job loss, this advice still holds. Your job loss is like a death. It has changed every aspect of your life and the way you view the world. You need time to recover and get your bearings first.

Credit Cards

Most Americans view credit cards as a child sees Santa Claus. The child enjoys the presents without realizing their hidden cost, and today's adults use the credit cards to provide instant gratification, deliberately ignoring the fact that the purchase isn't affordable and will take a while to pay back "on time." The multibillion-dollar credit card industry thrives on people's willingness to pay 18–21 percent interest on their short-term debt.

Now that your income has plummeted, your precious credit cards provide tantalizing temptations. Credit card companies don't give you a shovel to dig your financial hole; they'll provide a backhoe so you can dig deeper and faster than ever before!

You can take cash advances on your credit cards. Pull out the cash, pay your bills, run the card up to its limit, then start on the next card. Pay the minimum due each month. There are no forms to fill out, no loan approval committee to pass, no definite schedule for repayment.

However, do this for a few months and you'll end up so far in debt you may never get out. The road to bankruptcy is paved with credit cards. It's a lot like a playground slide, effortless to go down. Have you ever watched a toddler take his first solo trip down the slide? The shrieks of delight turn to cries of pain when he flies off the bottom and smacks his rear on the playground surface. Use your credit cards in this manner and your fate at the bottom is the same as his. It's unbelievably painful.

A friend's husband lost his job in the 1990–91 recession, only months after they had purchased their dream house. It took him almost a year to find work. They survived, she said, by taking cash advances on one credit card, then going on to the next one when that one was "maxed out." In fact, one of the major advice books on surviving a recession recommended just such a strategy!

Unfortunately, two weeks before her husband was to

*begin his new job, our friend fell desperately ill and
ended up in the hospital. Without medical insurance,
they had no means of paying the $3,000 bill. By that
time, all their cards were "maxed out."*

*Today, the two of them are working four jobs between
them to pay all their debts, including the credit card debt
at 18 percent interest. Their cards have been canceled,
and their credit rating is ruined. "We managed to hang on
to our house, but there's no money for the 'extras,' ever,"
she observes sadly. "We'll be paying off our credit cards
and the medical bill for the rest of our lives."*

Save credit cards for emergencies only. Emergencies are like your
child needing to be hospitalized before your new medical insurance
policy begins or when you have an unexpected car repair that is absolutely necessary. If you use your credit cards indiscriminately, they
may not be there when you most need them—they'll already be at
their maximum charge limit.

There are two other reasons why you shouldn't take cash advances
using your credit cards. One is the interest. No other legitimate lender
of money is allowed to charge the rates charged by credit card companies. These companies then go further by adding exorbitant late fees onto
their outrageous rates if you are even one day late paying your minimum
balance. In addition, interest on cash advances applies the moment you
take the advance—there's no thirty-day grace period here—and it is
tacked on immediately to everything you have charged that month.
You'd have to go to a pawnshop or a loan shark to find a worse deal.

The second reason you should avoid taking cash advances on your
credit cards is in the event you have to declare bankruptcy. (For more
information on declaring bankruptcy, see Chapter 13.) Most states ex-
empt from bankruptcy protection any credit card debts incurred in
the six months before your bankruptcy filing. You may even be
charged with bankruptcy fraud, especially if you've run up big debts
and purchased items considered to be luxuries.

Credit card usage is too easy. It's much too tempting to use them to maintain your old lifestyle, keep up appearances, or purchase the expensive goodies you miss so much. These things can "slip in" while you are convincing yourself that you are only paying for the necessities.

Dig deep into yourself, locate the common sense, maturity, and self-discipline you know you have. Put the credit cards aside and really work at solving your financial difficulties without using them. You may very well need a loan, but any loan at conventional rates is better than the interest rate on credit cards!

Conclusion

This is only the second chapter of the book. This topic isn't ended—it's only begun. If you have done the suggested exercises, you should now have a very accurate picture of what you used to spend and how much was spent on luxury items. You should have a typical monthly budget for your present circumstances that is turning into a target monthly budget. You should have started researching ways to tap into more revenue.

Now the "squeeze" begins. The subsequent chapters are designed to help you cut, trim, and substitute your expenditures to help save every cent possible. Use the monthly budget form presented in this chapter (make photocopies!) to keep track of your expenses from month to month. Then the overall financial picture is examined again in Chapter 13 in an attempt to pull it all together.

You can start right now, though! Begin by locking up the credit cards, carrying less cash, and writing down everything you spend. Continue to read and keep an open mind.

	Past Budget	Present (Typical) Budget	Target Budget
Categories (with suggested subcategories; yours may differ)			
Food (groceries, restaurant meals, fast food, lunches away from home)			
Entertainment (movies concerts, theater, parties, videos, cassettes/CDs, games requiring tickets, computer games, cable TV, books, newspapers/ magazine subscriptions)			
Recreation (sports, music, arts, club fees, equipment, lessons, other fees)			
Clothing (per person in the family, dry-cleaning costs, special sports clothing)			
Toys/Gifts (birthdays, major holidays, miscellaneous)			
Charities (per charity)			
Utilities (gas, electric, water, phone, sewage, garbage)			
House Maintenance (supplies for inside, supplies for outside, yard service, home repairs, cleaning service, home repairs, appliances			
House—Major Purchases (remodeling, landscaping, furniture, home computer, audio/video equipment)			

	Past Budget	Present (Typical) Budget	Target Budget
Transportation (per person costs or per vehicle costs such as lease payment, gasoline, repairs, maintenance, licenses, parking costs, etc.)			
Personal Indulgences (alcohol, cigarettes, gambling)			
Personal Care (cosmetics, haircuts, tanning salons)			
Pets (per pet)			
Child/Elder Care (per person)			
Child Support			
Alimony Payment			
Education (per person: tuition, books, supplies, transportation to and from school)			
Medical/Dental (deductibles, co-payments, prescriptions)			
Credit Card Interest/Fees (per card)			
Banking/Financial Services			
Nonmedical Professional Services (accountant, lawyer, etc.)			
Mortgage/Lease/Rent (separate out costs of insurance and taxes if an escrow account is part of the monthly payment covering these items)			

	Past Budget	Present (Typical) Budget	Target Budget
Insurance (car, life, medical, dental, homeowners, disability, long-term care)			
Loans (auto, installment, personal)			
Taxes (local, state, federal)			
"Necessary to Pay" Bills (credit purchases; add to **Present** and **Target** budget)			
TOTALS			

Chapter 3

Not by Bread Alone

Cutting Back on
Discretionary Spending

$\mathcal{E}$veryone needs "treats" sometimes. Without them, you can become overwhelmed with depression, or at least, find it difficult to preserve the positive attitude necessary to continue to face the challenges ahead, whatever they may be. However, most Americans move subtly beyond this concept of occasional diversion and feel that besides our "daily bread," we actually *deserve* to have fun, entertainment, and rewards. Hence we say that "man cannot live by bread alone." Sorry to disappoint you, but the full quotation (from the Book of Deuteronomy) is, "Man cannot live by bread alone, but by every word that proceeds from the mouth of God." It doesn't indicate that we are due any luxuries!

Whether or not we are "due" them, whether or not we can afford them, we still want to have some treats. But if you are facing a financial crisis, giving up your expensive luxuries is a quick and important step in gaining control over your situation. What you lose in fun activities you will make up in fewer sleepless nights. (For busy parents, a good night's sleep may very well occupy position number one on the treat list!) Since downsizing may become a permanent condition, this chapter will help you find lower cost, but still reasonable, substitutes that you can adjust to and enjoy over the long run.

In Chapter 2, you were encouraged to itemize all your expenditures for at least the last six months before your sudden need to curtail spending. It was suggested that you list the amount of money you had spent in separate categories and then mark which ones were luxuries.

If you did that, then you have a clear picture of how much you used to spend for different items. Pull those out again and look them over carefully.

Do you still want to spend money on the same kinds of things, or have your priorities changed? If your downsizing is the result of divorce, disability, or a death, then your preferences for recreational activities may be quite different now.

When Chris and Laura got divorced, they included their health club membership in the settlement. Laura realized that, like more than half of the members, she almost never used the upscale club. Her two kids went there only occasionally, and usually with their father. Laura saved a lot of money by giving up her membership, and Chris reduced his to an individual membership.

While newly single spouses frequently change their spending priorities, you may find that after a job loss, your needs and priorities in this area may have changed significantly as well. This is especially true if you take a new job in a different field or even with a different employer.

A bank vice president, Chad was laid off when his bank merged with another. After searching for almost a year, he took a position with a government agency that paid about half his previous salary. In his new job, however, Chad didn't have to keep up appearances or engage in the expensive pursuits that were mandatory in his old line of work. He resigned his family membership in the exclusive country club and instead joined the local Y, where his daughters competed on the swim team. No longer did he have to attend the costly black-tie political functions so important to his boss. When he had to sell his BMW and drive a second-hand Toyota instead, he came to re-

> *alize that no one cared what kind of car he drove into the*
> *parking lot.*

Put a list together of the activities you and the family actually want to continue. Prioritize the list from the things that are the most important to the things that are the least important. Be sure to let everyone in the family contribute their thoughts. Open discussion should be encouraged. It's important for all members of the family to listen to each other and respect divergent opinions.

Continuity is something to think about as you weigh the possibilities. Children, delighted with the prospect of giving up forced practice sessions, may eagerly agree that their music lessons can be sacrificed. However, the parent who has endured hours of listening to the basics being mastered and now delights in listening to real music being played may be extremely reluctant to see the investment cast aside. Club and association memberships often have an initiation fee. Canceling them can save money now, but another fee may be charged to resume the membership at a later date.

Besides continuity, another important thing to consider is self-esteem. A loving parent is going to be quite reluctant to withdraw a child from a sport or activity (no matter how expensive) that has been the child's source of acclaim and newly discovered pride. A child needs the confidence boost that is tied to his or her ability to excel in certain activities. On the other hand, the expensive "toys" that adults like to operate (sports cars, boats, etc.), although they may pamper an injured ego, should not be considered with the same seriousness.

> Every family's priorities will be different for which luxuries stay the same, which ones get downsized with cheaper substitutes, and which are eliminated altogether. In our house, coffee is practically sacred. We buy dark roast beans at an exclusive coffee house, grind our own, and brew a substance with deep, full-bodied flavor. (We

love it; my mother thinks it's strong enough to ream out clogged pipes and shouldn't be used for anything else!) My husband and I mutually agreed that the coffee was not to be altered in any way. Wine, on the other hand, was open to discussion. Having spent years living in the midst of the California wine country, we had grown quite fond of many varieties and certain wineries. When we moved to upstate New York, we were shocked at how expensive wine could become after being shipped three thousand miles. We had already started cutting back. After some thought, we decided to reduce our consumption even further and to shift to much cheaper brands, but not give up a daily glass with dinner. Some luxuries, though, had to go completely. We canceled the newspaper, the YMCA family membership, and most cable TV channels. I now go to the library to read the paper, we exercise at home, and my husband is going through withdrawal symptoms having to live without his cable sports channels.

—HSQ

For each category of luxury, you have three options: to keep it as is, to find a cheaper alternative, or to eliminate it altogether. You may be surprised at the options available if you do choose to substitute. More and more communities, for instance, have second-run movie theaters, which offer feature films at less than half price for those who are willing to wait a few weeks. There's no law requiring you to buy the overpriced popcorn and watered-down soda either. To help you make choices regarding common luxuries, the next part of the chapter discusses many of them individually.

Restaurant Meals

Most people consider sit-down restaurants and fast-food establishments in separate categories. Certainly, fast-food restaurants cost less, but they are not as economical as eating at home or packing a lunch for work or school. Still, if your family's idea of an occasional treat is eating somewhere else and not having to do dishes, you might want to consider substituting a fast-food dinner for one at a sit-down "family" restaurant.

If eating out is one of your family's top priorities, here are some other options:

- buy dessert and coffee instead of a whole meal
- go for early-bird specials
- eat lunch rather than dinner out
- use 2-for-1 coupons
- order appetizers instead of entrees
- go to all-you-can-eat buffets

When we lived in California, we went out to eat with the kids at least once a week. Not only did we enjoy eating at restaurants, but we also felt our kids would learn proper restaurant decorum by eating out on a regular basis. However, these excursions cost us a minimum of $25, for fast food or breakfast at a sit-down restaurant, and often up to $125 for the entire family at our favorite steak houses. After we moved to the Albany area and I quit my full-time job, that was one of the first indulgences we cut back. We stopped eating out altogether when my husband was laid off.

We still enjoy eating out at restaurants and consider it an important priority. However, it is very expensive, and, frankly, we don't enjoy the meal if we know we're spending money we don't have.

—HSQ

Movie Theaters

Many big cities are notorious for high movie ticket prices. Movies in smaller cities can also be expensive if there is little competition among theater companies.

Movies also tend to be a high priority among older children and teens. Having seen the latest hot film often confers social status, and kids don't want to be left out. Younger children, too, may badger you to see the latest Disney release, not just once but multiple times.

The key here is getting kids to wait until the film arrives at second-run theaters or comes out on video. Younger children, who tend to like seeing the same film over and over again, will probably be appeased if you take them to see an old favorite at a second-run theater, a museum, or the library. Then, when the new film's first run is over, you can take advantage of seeing it at a less expensive venue as well.

If you or your older child are fairly indiscriminate moviegoers—seeing just about anything that is "hot," a genre that you like (be it action/adventure, comedy, romance, or foreign films), or with an actor or actress that you like—you must become more selective. If you're watching each penny, you don't want to waste it on a movie you won't enjoy. Wait for the reviews to come out, or wait for someone you trust to give his or her opinion first.

What should you do if a friend invites your child to the movies? Although the price of a children's or student ticket at even a first-run theater is less than $5, this may be more than you can afford. It is really difficult for children to lose social opportunities because of financial hardship, so, if possible, you should budget for these kinds of spontaneous invitations. Perhaps your child can earn the money through yard work or baby-sitting in the neighborhood, or he or she can do additional chores around the house. (Since you will probably have to give up your yard or cleaning service, any help is certainly welcome!) Pack a snack so he or she won't be tempted to buy from the concession stand.

If watching movies is one of your family's top priorities, here are some other options:

- wait until the movie comes out on video
- go to matinees rather than evening showings
- go to the area's cheap theater
- watch for film festivals or regular series at local colleges, museums, and libraries
- wait for it to come to cable TV

We've been appalled for years at the price of taking the family to the movie theater. Even before downsizing, we negotiated with our kids and said that we could go together as a family, but nothing would be purchased at the snack bar. That, in itself, cut the cost of the venture almost in half. Then, utilizing the lower matinee prices, it's almost an affordable activity again.

—HSQ

A friend of mine is the director of a public library in our area. For years she has run an award-winning film festival that consistently draws full houses. If you're willing to wait for six months, you can see top-rated films for free, meet other fans of the same genre (mostly art and foreign films, but often interesting and critically acclaimed commercial films as well), and sometimes even meet the filmmakers.

—LML

Video Rentals

Renting videos is a good "downsized" option for your family if you are accustomed to going to the movie theater but can no longer afford it. Even with renting videos, you can save money. If you've been using one video store for years, it's worth your while to shop around. Stores vary widely in their selection, rental plans, and prices. The largest stores with the greatest selection will charge the steepest rates. Try the smaller places.

If renting videos is one of your family's top priorities, here are some other options:

- borrow them from the library instead
- go to a cheap video store
- rent them Monday–Thursday (off-peak) for less

We love to rent videos and watch them together as a family. It was decided that no more would be rented; we would only borrow them from the local library. Since our library carries primarily the "classics" (generally adapted from the original literature), our kids have been introduced to a very different kind of film. Old films are slower-paced and have little gore and violence compared to modern day films. As parents, we have been startled by the contrast as the kids consider many of the movies we treasure to be quite boring.

—HSQ

My daughter is one of those kids who likes watching the same Disney movies over and over. If our library didn't carry the video, we found it cheaper to buy it rather than to rent it several times. We discovered that once a video is no longer a top ten rental, the video store puts in on sale at half-price, and that's when we snap it up. That's how our son obtained some of his video games as well, until kids in the neighborhood abandoned their old systems for the "latest and greatest" and simply gave him their old games.

—LML

Sports Events

Big-ticket sporting events, featuring highly paid athletes, seem to get all the publicity these days, but in small towns and cities across the country many sports events are free or very inexpensive. Minor-league baseball games, for instance, often cost less than a movie ticket, and the antics of your fellow spectators (and perhaps you!) may be much more entertaining to watch. If your children are older, they will probably want to see their high school team play, and perhaps you too will want to see their friends compete.

Another issue arises if you have season tickets to a major sports event. These tickets are quite expensive, and once you give up your seats, you may never get them back again. (It is said that New York Giants season tickets are passed down from generation to generation.) Do you have a friend or relative who can buy your tickets from you until your financial situation improves? Perhaps you can split the season passes with someone else, especially if you need to cut back for the long term. You might also be able to sell some of the tickets individually, thereby recouping part of the cost, and still see some of the games yourself.

If watching sports events is one of your family's top priorities, here are some other options:

- watch on TV or listen to radio coverage
- buy cable TV subscriptions to events
- watch the games with other fans at a sports bar or restaurant
- buy only cheap seats
- take advantage of special promotions
- go to a few events rather than buying season tickets

Several years ago, when the Houston Rockets first won the NBA Championship and ticket prices rocketed into outer space, my father introduced me to the sports bar/restaurant, where we could watch the games in the company of other rowdy fans (which is pretty much the whole point of going to the live event anyway). While you usually have to buy a meal (or drinks), the prices are cheaper than at the arena or stadium and you don't have the price of admission. If you don't want to drink or don't want to take the kids to a bar, most cities that have major sports teams also have "family" sports restaurants.

—LML

Concerts/Theater

If your tastes run to music and theater, you probably know that there is a wide range of shows and places to see them. You can spend $100 per person for orchestra seats at a "hot" Broadway musical or pay $6 or less apiece for a community theater production.

The same holds for music. The efforts of some alternative bands notwithstanding, rock concert tickets, like major sporting events, have skyrocketed in price. At the same time, many communities offer free classical or folk music concerts, especially during the summer.

Just as you can rent videos as a "downsized" option to seeing a first-run movie, you can downsize your preferences for concerts or theater by buying a CD of your favorite musical group or borrowing from the library a video of a classic theater production.

If seeing concerts or plays is one of your family's top priorities, here are some other options:

- go to free showings in the park
- buy tickets at a half-price booth for same day showings
- buy standing room tickets or cheap seats
- buy the CD or borrow it from the library
- rent or borrow from the library a video of the concert or theater production

We did not judge theater and concerts to be a high priority. While we had gone go to a couple of local shows, this was something we dropped after my husband's lay-off. Fortunately, our kids haven't asked us to get them tickets to rock concerts, but if they did want to go, they'd have to spend their own money.

—HSQ

CDs and Cassettes

Despite falling costs in the production of compact discs, their prices seem to be going higher and higher. Recording companies have taken the attitude of charging "what the market will bear." However, if you can grab a new release just as it comes out, the prices are generally five to seven dollars lower. You may also find lower prices for many classical recordings and popular recordings that may have been "cut out" or discontinued.

If buying CDs or cassettes is one of your family's top priorities, here are some other options:

- buy them secondhand
- borrow them from the library
- trade with friends

There are a lot of things I'd give up before I stopped buying music. Fortunately, I have a large network of friends and relatives who share my musical tastes, and we've been trading CDs, cassettes, and even those old-time vinyl LPs for years.

—LML

Cable TV

It's time to reconsider your motives for the cable channels you are purchasing each month. Under your present circumstances, are they necessary? If you have to cut back on other forms of entertainment, television is a relatively inexpensive substitute. However, you can rent a number of videos for the price of a premium movie channel.

If cable TV is one of your family's top priorities, here are some other options:

- trim down your package of channels
- eliminate cable from all but one of your TVs
- see if there are other cable companies in your area that have lower rates

---

My husband was heartbroken when we decided to trim our cable service to the basic package. Although it cut our monthly bill in half, the basic package did not include the car races he so loved to watch. But in the overall scheme of things, we decided the car races were a lower priority than our children's activities.

—HSQ

Books, Magazines, Newspapers

Explore the resources at your local libraries—not just the one nearest to you, but further afield. Small communities often complement each other rather than simply duplicate. If you have access to a college or university library, you'll find a different range of publications and services there as well. Most local libraries also have the resources of other public and academic libraries available through interlibrary loan, so you may not even need to travel. Show your children the vast resources available, generally free of charge.

You may need to cancel subscriptions to get the refund, or not renew the publication when it runs out. Look for your favorite newspapers and magazines at libraries, friends' houses, and your office. Many libraries also have out-of-town newspapers, which you can use for a job search or researching other communities.

If books, magazines, and newspapers are among your family's top priorities, here are some other options:

- use the library
- wait for best-sellers to come out in paperback
- swap magazines with friends
- take advantage of free trial offers and then cancel the publication

---

We cancelled our daily newspaper and let our magazine subscriptions run out. As a family, we started going to the library more. I caught up on my local paper and magazines, and the kids checked out books. Now we're in the habit of using the library regularly, which has become a permanent benefit. Too many people are unaware of the range of things that are available at the library, from the latest best-sellers to older books, newspapers, magazines, videos, films, lectures, and children's programs. Our library even has computer classes and software for the public to use.

—HSQ

Computers

Many families have computers at home, which serve a variety of purposes. Kids and other family members use them to play games. They can help with homework, and adults can use them for hobbies and keeping financial records. Computers also serve as a mainstay of the home office.

For those who have decided to set up a home office and use a computer for work, strategies for purchasing the computer and setting up the office will be discussed in Chapter 6, "Household Necessities for Less." The suggestions detailed below are geared to families who use computers primarily for educational and recreational purposes:

- cancel on-line services
- shop for the cheapest on-line service
- take advantage of on-line services' free trial offers
- buy computers and add-ons secondhand
- play shareware games
- trade games with friends to provide variety

We bought our computer in July 1995, five months before the layoff. I used it for my part-time job, but the
main fan of the computer was our teenage son. He had
been eagerly anticipating an upgrade, so he did not welcome the prospect of our downsizing, which forced him
to cut back his game purchases and put his upgrade plans
on hold. The truth was, our 486 computer was perfectly
adequate for his school assignments, my work, and my
husband's job letters (the old 286 in the basement could
even handle the schoolwork and the job letters). Nobody
else considered the upgrade a top priority.

We suggested that if he wanted the upgrade badly
enough, he could look for yard work in the neighborhood
to pay for it. After one hard afternoon of weeding, he decided to make do with what he had. On the other hand,
he discovered a wealth of shareware games, and they in-
spired him to write his own games.

—HSQ

Club Memberships

For many affluent families, membership in a club—either a country
club or an upscale health club—is an important part of life. The club
provides not only recreational activities but a social circle as well.
Frequently, children participate in classes and on teams, and many of
their friends are drawn from the children of fellow club members. De-

pending on how exclusive a club is, having to cancel a membership because of financial difficulties may make it difficult to rejoin, and you may have to pay a steep initiation fee if you do rejoin. However, no exclusive club in this country has been untouched by recession and corporate downsizing, and most will accommodate members who have temporarily encountered hard times. If possible, you should take advantage of the provisions your club offers, because your fellow members may serve as an important source of contacts in your job search. Keeping fit is also important, both for your job search and your mental health.

Keep in mind, however, that club memberships are among the priorities that you might want to change if your long-term circumstances have changed. If your ex-spouse played golf but you hate it, there's not much point in paying for the golf club membership now that you're divorced. Also, if you no longer work for the company or in the industry that dominated your country club you probably wouldn't feel comfortable as a member there now.

If club memberships are among your family's top priorities, here are some options:

- explore less expensive membership options
- investigate whether your club will let you take a temporary leave of absence
- if you do have to resign, find out if you can reinstate your membership at a later time without a new initiation fee
- go to a YMCA instead of a fancy health club
- explore the public recreational facilities, such as pools, tennis courts, and golf courses, in your area

---

For us, membership at our local Y (a brand-new, magnificent facility) seemed a luxury we should sacrifice. Our dilemma arose with our daughter, a member of the Y's swim team. It was mid-season and she had already qualified to go to the state championship meet. We decided

to continue her on a very limited, inexpensive membership. Later, we found out that scholarship money exists to
help those children who are "financially strapped." We
could have taken advantage of that, but by the time we
learned about it, swim season was almost over.

—HSQ

Vacations

Due to the stress of your situation, time "away" may be a good idea.
However, adapting to very cheap vacations may take some real planning, discipline, and effort. Your cheapest vacations are where you still
prepare your own food—camping or staying in a house/cabin with a
kitchen facility. This kind of vacation offers primarily a change in routine and scenery because there is still a lot of work. You have to get used
to the idea that you still need to buy groceries, cook, and clean up. Aim
this kind of trip toward a beach or lake (don't stay on the waterfront)
or stay near state or national parks. Get outside and enjoy the sights.

A driving vacation can also be low cost. Stay at the nationally
known, but very cheap motel chains. Carry your own coffeepot and
ice chest. Eat breakfast in the motel room (simple things like cereal
and bananas) and lunch at a picnic area with homemade sandwiches.
Eat out only for dinner and then aim for diners and coffee shops to
keep the costs down.

Many people are reluctant to take a driving vacation with young
children. It's true that they provide a real challenge. As a parent, you
have to realize that most children can't entertain themselves very effectively and their little bodies need movement. This means you either
drive at night when they are sleeping or you drive during the day with
many stops for play. Every town has a playground. It pays to get off the
main highway and ask directions at the first gas station for the nearest
park. A half hour of fast-paced play is actually good for everyone.

If vacations are among your family's top priorities, here are some
other options:

- visit relatives where your meals and lodging are provided
- drive, don't fly
- go camping (rent a tent, pop-up trailer, or RV)
- stay in nationally known budget motels
- visit national and state parks and historic sites; avoid big cities and expensive attractions
- stay close to home and visit places you've always "planned to" but haven't yet
- look for hotels that cater to business travelers for good week-end rates in major cities
- look for hotels and motels with children's specials (such as children staying and/or eating for free)
- if you have to be in a major city and have access to transportation, stay in a less expensive suburban motel rather than downtown
- plan trips around zoos, parks, and museums
- avoid trips where shopping and gambling are the primary activity

---

Having been raised in the West where one always has to drive long distances between places, my husband and I both spent many hours in the car when we were children. Once we grew up and had our own, we had to learn what worked best given the temperament and disposition of our own kids. We learned always to give my daughter medicine, or she'd get carsick. We also discovered that one parent in the backseat between the kids, in charge of entertainment and fight mitigation, seems to be the most effective way to maintain order and keep everyone sane. Even as old as they are now, the kids still beg for Mom to drive so Dad can tell them stories. He's got a gift of story–telling that keeps us all enchanted, mile after mile.

There were, however, many trips to my mother's when the kids were young and my husband couldn't come. This six-hour drive worked best if I started at 3:00 in the morning, driving in the dark with the kids asleep in their car seats. By the time they woke up, most of the driving was done. We would stop for breakfast, a welcome break for us all, then I would make the last hour and a half dash to my mom's doing my best to sing songs, play games, and lead the entertainment from the front seat. It was fairly manageable that way.

Nowadays, vacations are a very low priority. If we do anything, we go camping.

—HSQ

Ironically, our biggest trip occurred at our leanest time financially. My husband had been denied tenure and had a year to find another job or face unemployment. I had closed down my small publishing company and gone back to school so I could get a decent-paying job if he were unable to find one. In the midst of all this, a writer's organization called to tell me I had won a grant to research a book in Chile. I had applied for the grant nine months earlier, but in the chaos had forgotten all about it. So we took a break for a few weeks and traveled six thousand miles to Chile!

—LML

Toys and Gifts

It's not just children who love toys. Many affluent American adults have toys and hobbies that can carry a stiff price to operate or maintain. If your toys are expensive, then you ought to consider selling or storing them for the time being. Are they consistent with your new lifestyle?

If toys and gifts are among your family's top priorities, here are some other options:

- for relatives: photos of the kids
- for relatives: handmade gifts from the kids
- for kids: shop at garage sales
- for kids: buy the old-fashioned "basics" like yo-yos, Frisbees, rubber balls, decks of cards which are inexpensive and long-lasting
- for the family: get inexpensive things you enjoy doing together, such as craft kits and jigsaw puzzles

---

As a family we enjoy doing jigsaw puzzles and playing board games together. Our financial crisis forced us to give up the expensive toys (such as stuff for my husband's antique car and computer games and upgrades) that we'd do alone, and we focused instead on those inexpensive things we liked to do together. We found ourselves spending more time with each other as a family than with our pricey "things."

—HSQ

Children's Lessons/Activities

As we said earlier, lessons and activities that offer your children skills, enjoyment, and self-esteem should occupy a high priority. Your children will fare better in this crisis and maintain a more positive attitude if their favorite sports activities and lessons are not disrupted. If your son or daughter has successfully tried out for a competitive soccer team, for instance, you have an obligation to keep him or her on the team even if something else you enjoy has to be sacrificed first. Even if your child is not an accomplished athlete or musician, if the activity gives him or her pleasure and a feeling of competence, then it should be continued, even though you might want to look at less expensive options.

If children's lessons and activities are among your family's top priorities, here are some other options:

- take lessons less frequently
- enroll in group lessons rather than private ones
- investigate scholarship money possibilities
- propose work-for-lessons exchanges
- have the child pay part of the cost of the lessons with money earned through baby-sitting, yard work, etc.
- look for low-cost substitute lessons in city programs or YMCAs

---

Our children are both involved in Tae-Kwon-Do, a form of karate. They have been training for several years and currently are brown belts. Having invested a great deal for years (over a hundred dollars a month and all their effort!), the entire family was devastated at the prospect of dropping the sport. The kids were heartsick the day we had to explain our financial dilemma to the head teacher of the school. To our surprise, he suggested that the kids work at the school in exchange for the cost of their lessons. The kids eagerly agreed. Each has been given several hours a week of lower-level classes they are expected to assist. They've discovered that it's time-consuming and fairly uninteresting work, but neither has complained. Instead, they are extremely grateful and now appreciate the training more than ever.

—HSQ

Household Services

It seems unfair to lay off the cleaning lady and the landscaping service, but that is exactly what's necessary. (If possible, give individual service providers advance notice so they can find other work.) It's time to clean your own floors and bathrooms, cut your own grass, and weed your own gardens. While you're at it, you now need to maintain whatever you can without hiring someone else to do it. For repair jobs, get a book from the library and learn how to do it yourself. Painting, wallpapering, plastering, deck, and driveway maintenance are all jobs that you may need to do if you are preparing your house for sale. They can all be learned by reading and asking for advice from knowledgeable folk. Even if you have to invest in some new tools, you'll save a lot of money.

Of course, it's time-consuming; mastering new skills goes slowly at first. Don't assume that just because you haven't done it before, the job will turn out looking terrible. In many cases, you'll discover that the job you do is perfectly adequate, better perhaps than one done by the person hired who really could not care less what you think of their work the moment after you pay them.

When something around the house has to be done, you need to consider seriously how you will tackle the job with your own resources. After some investigation, it may be that you decide you really can't do it and you have to hire someone, but this should definitely be a last resort decision. In the end, you have to use your wisdom about what you can and cannot realistically accomplish.

A month after my husband was laid off, we had a series of major snow and ice storms that dumped several feet of snow on our roof. Because of the design of homes in our area, most people were hiring professionals to remove it from the roofs. Here we were, "greenhorns" from California never having experienced upstate New York winters. Coupled with the fact that we have a very high roof and we're both afraid of heights, we decided we absolutely had to spend the money to hire knowledgeable individuals to remove the snow and open up the ice dams for proper melting. It was excruciating to fork over several hundred dollars for this, but neighbors assured us that if we didn't clear the roof, we were apt to experience major structural damage. After we heard their own horror stories from the past, we were persuaded.

On the other hand, we do minor repairs ourselves. We

stopped using a cleaning and yard service, and now we divide up the chores. The kids do their part. Although we have had to reduce their allowance, our kids are now doing a lot more to earn their money. What they earn, they certainly appreciate.

—HSQ

Personal Indulgences

These are how we adults "pamper" ourselves. It might be the expensive haircut at a fancy salon, the routine pedicure, a weekly rendezvous with friends at a restaurant or bar, or the well-stocked liquor cabinet for the drink at day's end. If you weren't particularly aware of them before creating lists in Chapter 2, then certainly you should be able to put an accurate dollar figure next to them now.

To downsize these, like everything else, you have to either "cut out" or "cut back." Reduce the frequency, establish strict limits on what you spend, or find reasonable substitutes.

I have worn acrylic nails for eight years. I've always taken pride in my flawless manicure. When people ask me, "Are those your own nails?" I always answer, "You bet! I pay for them every two weeks!" That kind of extravagance had to go. Now I have short, paperthin nails—the "au naturel" look.

—HSQ

Many people spend a great deal of money on cigarettes and liquor. Enormous savings can be realized by curtailing these. It's difficult at a stressful time such as this, but you need to both save money and get some control over your life. If cutting back in this area proves to be impossible, or you discover you are actually increasing expenditures, then it's time to seek professional help. (See Chapter 16.)

Gambling of any kind is not a wise investment, especially now. Save the dollars you might have thrown away on the lottery and apply them instead to groceries.

Charitable Contributions

Chances are, you don't want to contribute money to charities now. (In fact, you're probably trying to stay out of the soup kitchens yourself!) However, that doesn't mean you can't give something if you are feeling guilty about "letting down" some organization. You can volunteer your time and energy to work for it. It's a rare organization that couldn't use a helping hand with paperwork, packing, running errands, phone calling, or assistance in some other manner. If you have only provided monetary support in the past, you will now experience a different dimension to charitable work. It may even end up meaning more to you as you get to see, firsthand, what your contributions are doing for others.

If you have tithed your income (given a certain percentage) to a particular church or organization, you may feel compelled to continue this practice. Your income is down substantially, so your financial contributions will be too. However, where you may have been giving "from plenty" in the past, now you are giving "from need"; your gift is coming from the housing or grocery money. Sacrificial giving will provide new insights—look for them.

Free or Low-Cost Entertainment Ideas

Before the days of electronic baby-sitters, families did things together to have fun. These "old-fashioned" ideas are applicable again. If you've never done many of these activities, the kids may be suspicious and reluctant to participate at first. Older children may worry about looking ridiculous. Gently insist on their participation, set the example with your own, throw back your head, laugh, and have fun!

Outdoor Activities:

- games: ball, soccer, Frisbee, croquet, handball, badminton, volleyball, etc.
- picnics and cookouts
- hiking
- biking
- cross-country skiing
- sledding
- ice-skating/roller-skating
- concerts/plays in the park
- the zoo
- visiting the airport/train station with little kids
- camping out in the backyard
- utilizing parks (city, county, state, and national)
- street fairs
- ethnic festivals
- parades

Indoor Activities:

- games: board, card, charades
- jigsaw puzzles
- making a home video movie (write script, make costumes, plan the actions, etc.)
- writing a play (same as above)
- museums
- crafts
- reading to each other
- cooking/baking together
- drawing/painting
- lectures/slide shows at libraries, civic organizations, and colleges

These are by no means exhaustive lists of activities. Look in the community newspaper and watch bulletin boards (at libraries and around stores) for more ideas. Many organizations have fairs, pancake breakfasts, and get-togethers of all kinds that are generally cheap, interesting, and fun.

These pastimes may be quite different from how you have entertained yourself and your family in the past. However, don't assume they are poor substitutes. You might discover that they offer more opportunities for conversation with each other, more chances to develop skills long forgotten (when was the last time you rode a bike down a park trail?), and more ways to know your own community and neighbors better. These are valuable trade-offs.

It's important for you to realize that you can cut back and still have lots of fun. You simply have to establish priorities that are agreeable to you as a family and be willing to experiment with novel activities that work within the budget.

One of our favorite ideas for inexpensive family fun comes from friends who downsized when the father left a well-paying job to attend divinity school and, ultimately, to become an assistant pastor at a local church. The family owned a video camera from the old days. Whenever one of the three kids had an appropriate school assignment, the entire family would join in, writing the script, making costumes, and acting the various parts. For example, the youngest child learned about the rainforest in third grade, and the family produced The Attack of the Killer Lionfish. *The story, which was set in the Amazonian rainforest, featured him and his sister as reporters, his older brother as the victim, his father as the fisherman who rescued the victim, and their big dog as the lionfish. (Mom was the cameraperson and his sister provided an ominous musical score on her clarinet.) When he entered the film in the school's creativity festival, it attracted large and enthusiastic crowds. The festival did not include awards, but if it had,* The Attack of the Killer Lionfish *most certainly would have won first prize.*

Chapter 4

Downsizing the Food Budget, Part I

Thinking Differently about Meal Preparation

After luxuries, the food budget may very well be the area in which you can make the greatest change in the shortest amount of time. Depending on how you generally shop and cook, you could potentially reduce your food budget to a third or a quarter of what you spent in the past. This can mean a savings of hundreds of dollars each month.

The typical American cook takes advantage of the many timesaving conveniences built into products throughout the grocery store. Anything that saves you time in the kitchen adds a cost to the product; the greater the time savings, the higher the additional cost. The produce section has precut salad ingredients and vegetables. The dairy/deli sections are full of pre-grated cheeses, presliced meats, packaged desserts, and tubes of biscuit, roll, and cookie dough. The aisles are full of bottled sauces, packaged noodle and rice dishes, and dehydrated soups and cake mixes. The frozen food aisle has everything from simple vegetables to complete meals ready for the microwave and almost instant ingestion.

Food manufacturers are well aware of the fact that our lifestyles are so busy that food preparation is simply not a high priority. Most of us are more than willing to spend enormous amounts of money to purchase these convenient, timesaving products. At least we were before we had to watch every penny spent. In fact, if this is how you have always cooked—if you have considered the four food groups to be freeze-dried, microwavable, take-out, and delivery—then you may have never considered the alternatives, or at least considered them seriously.

Of course, I'm getting to the idea of making many or most of your foods "from scratch." Now, before you throw the book down in frustration, please read on a bit further.

After my husband's layoff, I went from working part-time to working full-time at my marketing job. Thus, with even less time on my hands, I faced the challenge of cooking without timesaving conveniences. I found that putting the labor back into the food preparation doesn't necessarily mean sweating over the stove for hours like I remember my mother and grandmother doing. Those memories, I realized, were memories from holidays—not everyday life. In the "olden days" homemakers had many more time-consuming chores to do daily than we have today. They couldn't spend all their time in the kitchen. But their approach to meal preparation was different than the modern way and their "secrets" are rediscoverable. Besides, we still have our microwave ovens, food processors, and bread machines to ease our tasks.

—HSQ

So, yes, you can prepare dishes "from scratch" and save an enormous amount of money. You will also be feeding your children food with no extra salt, food that is completely free of preservatives, nitrates, and other additives. Your meals will be full of vitamins, minerals, and fiber. Your children will be eating the freshest, healthiest food you could possibly give them. It's not really such a bad trade-off for a little more time and effort. You will all find the food tastier, healthier, and definitely cheaper.

Meal Objectives

You need to save money by reducing the food budget, but you still have certain important objectives that must be met. Meals should be nutritious and filling, offer interesting variety, be acceptable to the family, and hopefully be quick to prepare and clean up.

ORANGE JUICE	Premixed	$.04 per ounce
	Made from concentrate	$.02 per ounce
MOZZARELLA CHEESE	8 oz. pre-grated	$2.59
	8 oz. block	$1.34
CAKE	Grocery store's bakery	$9.99
	Cake mix and homemade icing	$3.50
POPCORN	Popped and bagged	$.07 per cup
	Microwave	$.05 per cup
	From kernels	$.016 per cup
SALAD MIX	2-lb. bag of iceberg lettuce, red cabbage, and carrots	$2.59
	Equivalent ingredients for 2 lbs.	$1.46
CHICKEN NOODLE SOUP	Canned	$.22 per cup
	Dehydrated	$.18 per cup
	Homemade	$.10 per cup
BLUEBERRY MUFFINS	Grocery store's bakery	$2.36 for 4
	Muffin mix	$1.26 for 4
WHITE BREAD	22 oz. store brand	$1.40
	22 oz. homemade	$.86
PANCAKES	Frozen (4-inch)	$.17 each
	From mix	$.05 each
CHICKEN BREASTS	Skinless and boneless	$3.79 per lb.
	With skin and bones	$1.85 per lb.
RICE KRISPIE TREATS	Prepackaged, boxed	$.32 each
	Homemade	$.09 each

CHOCOLATE CHIP COOKIES	Grocery store's bakery	$.22 each
	Made from tube dough	$.09 each
	Homemade	$.028 each
MACARONI & CHEESE	Frozen dinner	$.90 per cup
	Box mix	$.30 per cup
JELL-O	Little container for kid's lunch	$.31 each
	Prepared from box mix	$.18 each
PUDDING	Little container for kid's lunch	$.27 each
	Prepared from box mix	$.22 each
APPLESAUCE	Little container for kid's lunch	$.32 each
	From large bottle of applesauce	$.10 each

Notes: Prices are based on the average of as many brands as could be found, but at least the average of the store brand and one commercial brand whenever possible. Princes are meant to be a "snapshot" view. They are from one store in a suburban, middle-class neighborhood, in the summer of 1996. When a "mix" is mentioned, the additional ingredients (like margarine, eggs, or milk) are also included in the calculated price.

Nutritious and Filling

Remember your class in Health back in the seventh grade? In the days before the microwave oven, you learned about the Basic Food Groups: meat and poultry, dairy, breads, and fruits and vegetables. You were taught to put a meal together with items from each group and you'd eat a healthy meal. More recently, the Food Pyramid has gained popularity. It's much the same idea, but helpful in showing the relative proportions of the different foods we should consume.

The Food Pyramid is particularly helpful in showing us that fats (present in many different foods) should comprise the smallest part of our in-

Food Guide Pyramid
A Guide to Daily Food Choices

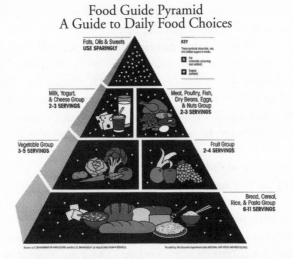

take of daily calories while the foods in the bread group (actually, the grains and legumes group, which include bread, rice, beans, peas, and nuts) should comprise the most. We really don't need to consume very much meat, but the healthy consumption of fruits (2–4 servings daily) and vegetables (3–5 servings) may seem enormous to the average American family. It's important to keep these facts in mind as you plan your meals.

Fortunately for the budget-conscious, the foods at the bottom of the Food Pyramid are generally the least expensive ones. Examples in the typical American diet include rice, beans, peanut butter, and bread. These foods, and their variants—lentils, couscous, tortillas—form the staple diets of most cultures throughout the world. With far fewer material resources than we have in the United States, many people in Asia and Latin America actually lead healthier lives because of their diet.

What does it mean, scientifically, to have a "healthy" meal? It means that when the foods are eaten and digested together, the body can make, from the components, all the essential compounds needed to keep you alive and well. The body is capable of producing all the vitamins, proteins, and enzymes it needs when the raw ingredients are present in the meats, fresh produce, grains, and legumes you eat. The bread group foods become sugar when they are digested and are "burned" in the cells to provide the energy for all the body processes and to keep you warm. Bread and other grains provide a number of vitamins as well, most notably, those of the B complex, which aid in digestion, cell formation, and the operation of the nervous system. Fats are stored for energy burning so you can still maintain life processes when the sugar levels drop. An excessive amount of fat, however, can lead to obesity and heart disease and increase the risk of some forms of cancer. And just as grains and legumes are generally the least expensive foods, high-fat foods—such as chips, chocolate bars, and premium ice cream—are among the most expensive. At the same time, peanut butter, if consumed in moderation, is a relatively healthy and inexpensive high-fat food.

The reason you are supposed to eat a balanced diet is that then all the raw components your body needs will be present at the same time. This allows the body to operate at maximum efficiency. For instance, suppose you need a particular vitamin to help you fight off an invading bacterial disease and you haven't eaten the foods to provide the components for the vitamin's immediate manufacture. The body may or may not be able to conjure up the needed chemicals from storage reserves to make the needed vitamin. Your ability to fight the infection can be seriously impaired.

In your efforts to cut back on the food budget, you still must make it a top priority to make nutritionally balanced meals for your family. When you do, these meals will be "filling." Imagine a meal with a tossed green salad, turkey and gravy over potatoes, broccoli, and a sliced apple. After consuming that, you will probably feel "satisfied" because you have eaten everything your body is craving.

One of the key ingredients your body needs is protein. In the typical American diet, the principal source of protein is meat—generally red meat, but also pork, chicken, and fish. Most scientists acknowledge, however, that we do not need as much protein as we consume, and red meat is also a principal source of fat and cholesterol. It is also expensive, relative to other sources of protein.

Throughout the world, people with limited financial resources have combined grains and legumes to provide protein. The key is to eat both grains and legumes at the same meal; one without the other is a source of carbohydrates and vitamins, but only when eaten together do they provide "complete proteins" necessary for proper nutrition without meat. A children's favorite that combines grains and legumes is a peanut butter and jelly sandwich. The sandwich gives the body complete proteins, and if real fruit preserves are used, adds some vitamin C as well. Some other grain-legume combinations, eaten for thousands of years throughout the world, are as follows:

red beans and rice	Cajun food from Louisiana (of West African origin)
black beans and rice	China, Latin America
white beans and rice	Western Europe
peas and rice	Africa
lentils and rice	India
lentils and couscous	the Middle East, North Africa
chickpeas and couscous	the Middle East

In a city where we used to live, my husband and I would frequent a popular Cajun restaurant. Two of the restaurant's signature dishes were a bowl of spicy red beans and rice with a few chunks of sausage and a plate of blackened redfish with fresh steamed or sauteed vegetables. Before it became fashionable with the boom in Cajun cuisine, redfish was a "garbage" fish. It was practically given away when it got tangled in the net along with the day's more desirable catch. Once Cajun became "haute cuisine" the restaurant could charge almost twenty dollars for each of these tasty, healthy, and filling dishes, which could be made at home for less than three dollars each. Well, what about the atmosphere, you may ask. The restaurant didn't even play Cajun music.

—LML

That leads us to the next topic . . .

Variety Is the Spice of Life

No one wants to eat turkey (or anything else!) six meals in a row. It's boring, and it's also not healthy.

As we've explained, balanced meals are important, and changing the different members of the food groups is also very important. Providing lots of variety increases the chances you will eat the great number of nutrients your body requires, including the trace elements, such as iron, zinc, potassium, and iodine.

This is true for all the food groups. It means interspersing fish and poultry with meals based on beef and pork. It also includes cooking without meat, which will cut your food budget the most.

I have been a vegetarian for fifteen years. I started in college, when I lived in a vegetarian co-op that spent fifty dollars a month per person for food. (Since then, food prices have risen little, and it is still possible to enjoy a varied vegetarian diet on fifty dollars per person per month; the price of the college education, however, is an entirely different story!) Not only did I save money, but a weight problem that plagued me throughout my life disappeared entirely, and I am generally healthier than most of my friends. It is said that if you eat a vegetarian diet for ninety years, you will live to be very old!

—LML

Eating vegetarian—for several meals a week or on a permanent basis—does not mean doing without variety. To be most economical, though, you need to buy the fresh fruits and vegetables that are in season. In the depths of winter, you may not find as many vegetables as you'd like in the produce section. You can supplement the fresh with frozen (using the store-brand to keep costs down). Most stores provide an ample supply of fruits all year long, but out-of-season and/or fragile ones will carry a steep price if imported. So shop sensibly.

Combining grains and legumes is particularly important for those on a vegetarian diet. In addition, you should not forget about the potato, a vitamin-rich vegetable (eat the skin!) that is always in season. The supermarket features big Idaho potatoes, small round red potatoes, and sweet potatoes, among others. Potatoes can form the basis of a casserole or soup. You can bake and "stuff" a potato with all kinds of goodies like cheese and broccoli (a standard of the fast-food circuit, but at a third the price), turkey à la king, or ratatouille. Potatoes can be baked, roasted, fried, and steamed.

For many years I have volunteered at a local community service agency. One day the coordinator of the information and referral hotline told me about a couple in their late fifties who were facing a crisis. He had lost his job, and to save money, the coordinator explained, the couple was "forced to eat potatoes."

At that time, I was "forcing" my family to eat potatoes as their principal dish at least twice a week. I explained to her that potatoes were very healthy, that they had sustained my ancestors in Russia for generations (and almost all of the ones I knew about had lived into their eighties!), and that after I had cooked the potatoes in a half-dozen different ways, my family hardly felt deprived.

—LML

Be creative, persistent, and set a good example for your kids. Then, be content with what you can get them to eat. Even if it's a small group of fruits and vegetables that will be eaten, mix them up and provide as much variety as possible on a weekly basis. Different herbs and spices (many of which you can grow at home, in your garden or even in your kitchen) can add a variety of flavors to the fruits and vegetables that you use.

Getting Them to Like It

Besides being nutritionally sound and providing an interesting variety to your meals, another important objective in economical meal preparation is finding foods that are acceptable to your family. It is not economical to have food go to waste because the children won't eat it, and you probably don't have the time to make individual meals to accommodate everyone's taste.

As you experiment with new, low-cost meals, try to keep close to the kinds of food you've traditionally eaten. Your family members have already experienced a shocking and upsetting event, and they will have to deal with major changes in other areas as you cut back. The entire family will feel more comfortable if you change your menus gradually, introducing, for instance, one new vegetarian entrée per week if you're used to eating meat every night, and reducing or phasing out meat over a period of weeks or months. If your family is more adventurous, you might try nightly or weekly "themes" focusing on the cuisine of a particular ethnic group. (If you can tie this in with whatever your children are learning in school, you can save money, enhance your children's education, and distract them from the real reason you're serving, say, beans and rice.) Some of the new theme meals may become weekly staples, as your family slowly becomes more willing to accept the change in meals over the long run. Downsizing your lifestyle may be a permanent condition; you have to find meals that you enjoy preparing and eating.

Children pose the biggest challenge to changes in meal content and preparation. Most of us have kids who view anything unusual on the plate with a great deal of skepticism and, if made to taste it, taste it with the enthusiasm of someone who knows they are being poisoned. And even the most adventurous children go through picky periods or have one or two things they absolutely will not eat. How can you minimize this?

There are a number of strategies depending upon your general style of parenting. Some parents insist their children eat the day's entrée or else go to bed hungry; eventually, the children will become so hungry they'll eat anything. A variant of that strategy is to let the children make peanut butter sandwiches and/or munch on carrots, celery, or other inexpensive fruits and vegetables as a substitute. As long as no junk food's kept in the house, the kids will find something else to eat, and they'll eat a healthy, well-balanced diet if that's all you have.

A second strategy—best for finicky kids with more adventurous parents—is to alternate dishes and leftovers. For instance, on Monday night, you can make macaroni and cheese and a salad, which the kids like. Make enough so that you can serve them the leftovers on Tuesday while you and your spouse feast on spicy vegetables with chickpeas and couscous. What you don't eat on Tuesday becomes Wednesday's leftovers, which you can enjoy while the kids have grilled cheese sandwiches and roast potatoes. If you're lucky, your kids will see you trying something new and become more adventurous themselves.

If you don't like the idea of the kids and grown-ups eating separate dishes, you can plan your weekly meals to include old favorites (now made by hand) with some of the new recipes that are "dirt cheap" meals.

For example, my children had never eaten bean-based dishes until we had to downsize, and they have not been popular. Now I plan a bean dish between two dinners that I know they like. That way, if they don't eat much of the bean meal, they're still assured enough nutrition over the course of several days.

—HSQ

Often, there are some fruits and vegetables that are a struggle to get children to eat—sometimes it's an outright fight. Please do not give up. Children's tastes often change over time, and what was unacceptable a year ago may not be a problem anymore. If possible, try alternative methods of preparation. Try cutting up fruit in different shapes. You can remove the skin. You can mix two or more fruits together. Offer the chance to dip the fruit pieces into something like honey, yogurt, or homemade cheese sauce. For vegetables, try breading and frying things like zucchini or eggplant. Would green beans be more acceptable in a white sauce? Will the child eat mashed peas or shredded brussels sprouts instead of the "whole" variety? As with fruits, sometimes dipping the vegetables into salad dressings or sauces is much more appealing. If your children have always eaten canned or frozen vegetables and now you're cooking fresh ones since that is generally cheaper, the texture may seem very strange to them. Although adults may prefer the "crunch" of lightly steamed vegetables, perhaps cooking them longer to make them softer may make them more palatable to young mouths.

One of our kids is a notorious waster of food. She'll insist upon trying everything—pleased with her openness to new experiences, we give her what she asks for—but then she'll take a bite and spit it out right in the middle of the plate. We've learned to serve very small portions and to limit her to the food at hand; otherwise, we'd have a refrigerator full of cucumbers with one bite taken out of each of them.

—LML

In addition to serving smaller portions to kids (and making seconds available), serve yourselves smaller portions so that you can finish whatever the kids have left and don't end up wasting food.

One other general principle to planning acceptable meals is to get the entire family involved. As soon as they can talk, children can express their preferences and be taken into account in menu planning. You can also enlist children in appropriate meal preparation. If children have a stake in preparing the meal, they will be more willing to eat it, and as their skills develop, they can relieve you of many tasks. Some age-appropriate tasks are listed below:

If the child is:	
a preschooler	washing fruits and vegetables
ages 5–8	setting the table, using a measuring cup, making sandwiches

ages 9–12	cutting vegetables, making salad dressings, cooking simple meals, using a microwave to cook and to reheat leftovers
a teenager	making all but the most complex meals and cleaning up the mess

At the age of eleven, my brother-in-law became the principal cook for his family—which included an older brother, a younger sister, and his mother—after their father died and their mother had to work three jobs to survive. My husband (his older brother) recounts that the initial meals were virtually inedible as the young cook experimented with all the spices in the spice rack, but within two years, he became quite accomplished at making elaborate, nutritious, and tasty dinners. At first, he used his mother's recipes primarily but then developed his own, mostly vegetarian, dishes. Ultimately, he worked his way through college as a chef for various restaurants.

—LML

Training a child or teenager to cook from scratch will require some effort and supervision, if only for reasons of health and safety. Not only are children exposed to sharp knives, hot flames, electrical appliances, and water; they also need to know how to cook meat to kill possible bacteria and how to prevent bacteria from spreading to other foods before the meat is cooked. (This is yet another argument in favor of vegetarian cooking!) Once they have learned these food preparation basics, there are a number of cookbooks—including a wide selection of ethnic and international cookbooks—that are geared to teenage chefs. Most libraries have a wide selection of cookbooks that teenagers can use.

Quick Preparation

My husband is a wonderful gourmet cook. He does holiday and company meals. His specialty is French cuisine, and he's willing to spend days preparing masterpieces for the table. He is also slow, methodical, and manages to dirty every pan in the kitchen.

On the other hand, I specialize in meals for Monday through Friday that can be prepared in thirty minutes or less. I spent years working full time outside the home. At the end of a long workday, I'd pick up the kids at day care and be greeted with "Hi-Mom-what's-for-dinner?" Dinner had to get to the table quickly, or I had a riot on my hands.

During those years, I learned to utilize the weekend to minimize cooking during the workweek. Since we love to barbecue, we would generally grill two or three meats at a time. We'd eat one that night and freeze the others for later in the week. Hot dogs, hamburgers, chicken, and even fish spring back to life after a couple of minutes in the microwave. That's not unlike the meals you can purchase in the freezer section of your local grocery store; however, I paid considerably less since they weren't prepackaged.

—HSQ

In the winter, meat-eaters can rely primarily on cooking roasts on the weekends. Cooking a big turkey, ham, beef roast, or roasting chicken each week provides an enormous amount of meat in the most economic way possible. (It also keeps the kitchen nice and warm on those weekends when everyone is home, thus saving on heating bills.) When the meal is over, you simply take 15–30 minutes to cut the meat off the bones, divide it into meal-size portions, wrap these individually, and put them in the freezer. You may want to leave a small amount of meat in the refrigerator to slice for lunch sandwiches.

By alternating the types of roasts you cook, you will end up with a wide variety of meats and poultry in your freezer, ready to be used for last-minute meal preparation. Thaw in the refrigerator or microwave, and you have the pork to add to a Chinese stir-fry, strips of beef for the tacos or fajitas, or chicken to add to a sauce and pour over pasta. Preparation time is actually quite reasonable.

Of course, many dishes don't lend themselves to quick fixings. The cheapest pieces of beef often need marinating overnight or long, slow cooking to be tender enough to enjoy. Planning ahead for marinades is necessary. A Crock-Pot or slow cooker can be used for the less tender meats, bean dishes, and stews. Even though the time for cooking is long, you can arrive home after work with the main part of the meal done.

What may seem very time-consuming to you initially is cutting up fresh vegetables. Speed comes with practice and finding a knife with which you feel comfortable. You might love to be able to wield a huge knife like the chefs on TV cooking shows, but be careful. Using a small knife you can control may take more time but save you from cut fingers. Be sure your knives are sharp. It is easier to cut yourself on a dull knife because you are leaning on it and lose control of it.

"Practice produces speed" when cooking from scratch was illustrated most clearly to me by a cooking duel that occurred one holiday when the extended family was visiting at my mother's home. We were casually chatting over coffee when my mom boasted that she "could make a cake from scratch as quickly as one could put a cake mix together." The challenge was quickly taken up by my sister. Mom was allowed to bring her butter to room temperature while someone went to purchase a cake mix.

Then the stopwatch was started. My sister went first and six minutes later was putting her cake pan in the oven. Then my mother began to fly around the kitchen producing her magic. She lost the duel, of course—but only by two or three minutes! I never could have imagined that someone could put together a cake that quickly, but she had made them all her life and didn't even have to refer to a recipe. I learned an important lesson that day

about food preparation. Cooking "from scratch" doesn't
have to be so time intensive as to make it impractical.

—HSQ

Bread—The Staff of Life

My mother was the eldest of six children, raised by out-
of-work parents during the Depression in a coal town in
Pennsylvania. Her most vivid memory of foods they ate
then is that of the homemade bread her mom made daily.

My husband's mother was the eldest of eight children
growing up in a small town in northern Utah during those
same Depression years. Ask her about that time, and the
first thing she'll tell you is remembering her father walking two miles uphill, from the mill downtown to their
home, carrying a hundred-pound bag of flour on his
shoulder. This was because her mother baked eight
loaves of bread every other day.

—HSQ

Homemade bread is still considered by most people in the world
to be an almost perfect food. Biting into a piece of still-warm bread
is one of life's greatest pleasures. It's also incredibly cheap. There's a
reason the children of the Depression remember homemade bread—
it was the primary food they consumed.

If you make your own bread, you'll save at least $1.00 per loaf over
the store-bought variety. It also tastes infinitely better and has no
preservatives.

Please don't dismiss this concept as totally ludicrous. Yes, it takes
time, and kneading involves real labor. But is there a way, realistically, to
include homemade bread in your downsizing effort? There just might be!

Do you have a laid-off person at home? That individual can't spend
the entire day job-hunting. Could he or she be enticed to make bread?
Do you have any teenagers who can help out? Usually the reward of
enjoying the finished product is enough to encourage the person to

continue baking. Many men who rarely cook anything else pride themselves on their bread-making skills.

Does your electric mixer have dough hooks for kneading? Many do, but you may have forgotten about the dough hooks and let them drift to the back of the cupboard. Removing the hurdle of kneading by hand can make the entire idea more palatable.

Of course, if you happen to have one of the newly popular bread machines, then you're in great shape. Nothing is simpler than combining the few ingredients in the pan, setting the timer, and coming back a few hours later to a freshly baked loaf of bread.

If you plan to do a lot of bread-making, buy your yeast in bulk, if possible, certainly by the jar. The little three-packs are not economical. The refrigerated jars are often in the cheese section of the supermarket rather than the bakery aisle.

We were fortunate to have received a bread maker for Christmas last year, right after my husband's layoff. It seems like it goes nonstop at our house now. My teenage son, with his insatiable appetite, snacks incessantly on the fresh bread. It has replaced the junk food snacks we used to buy, and it is far healthier. The entire family agrees that it is the nicest addition to the home routine in years.

—HSQ

We encourage you to give this idea serious consideration. Bread is wonderful to eat, it's healthy, and there is no air freshener available that can come close to the delicious aroma of baking bread permeating the house!

Conclusion

In this chapter we have tried to convince you that buying the basic ingredients and really cooking can save you a lot of money and will provide healthier and tastier meals. Hopefully, we've also shown you that it doesn't have to be so time-intensive as to make it impractical.

Chapter 5

Downsizing the Food Budget, Part II

Strategies for Cutting Back

$\mathcal{A}$rmed with a general purpose cookbook, an open mind, and a determined attitude, you can save a lot of money on your grocery bills. This chapter will explore some general ideas for grocery shopping styles, then move through the topics of dinner, lunch, breakfast, snacks, and baby food. It will also offer suggestions for growing your own food and forming or joining a cooking co-op.

Shopping Styles

People have different grocery shopping styles. Some do a major shopping expedition once a month with small trips to the store for perishables like fresh vegetables and milk. There are others who plan their menus weekly and shop once a week for only the needed ingredients. Then, there are the ones who shop daily for what is needed for just that day. All three types believe that their shopping style is the best way to save money.

Frequency of shopping probably isn't as important as planning in the overall scheme. Discipline is also critical if you're in stores frequently. You have to have the discipline to stick to the plan and not buy additional items that strike your fancy. That is called impulse shopping. Don't shop when you're hungry. Avoid, if possible, taking any family members—adults as well as children—who are susceptible to the ploys of the marketing experts. Stick to your list and pre-determined budget for the day's/week's meals.

As you read this chapter, you'll find that the advice is to buy larger quantities of things like meat and stretch these quantities to cover several meals. This type of cooking lends itself to purchases of fewer pieces of meat less frequently and therefore fits a scheme of shopping once a month for major items. But if you like to shop daily, you can still cook in the recommended manner; you just wouldn't need to buy your meat on a daily basis.

When I lived in New York City, I got into the habit of shopping daily. I didn't have a car, and the greengrocer and fish market were just around the corner. As a vegetarian, I still like to shop every other day, to take advantage of specials and to get the freshest produce. My strategy is to budget for each meal, keeping in mind the other items I need besides produce—milk, juice, yogurt, cheese, etc. I take just that amount of cash to the store and decide what to make that night (and the next) based upon what's cheap and looks fresh. Nothing ever goes bad, and I generally stick to a budget of about $6 per day. At the same time, I've learned to be adaptable. If the artichokes my kids have clamored for are too expensive, we settle for stuffed zucchini, corn chowder, or baked potatoes with broccoli.

I generally shop for staples—canned goods, paper goods, and the like—in bulk once a month. Again, I've learned to make do and substitute. Sometimes we use folded paper towels rather than paper napkins. If there's no tomato sauce for the pasta, I can always substitute a cream or butter sauce with vegetables or a basil and cheese pesto.

—LML

If you're lucky enough to meet the membership qualifications at a discount warehouse store, you can save a great deal of money on all types of grocery items that can be purchased in bulk. For instance, rice, flour, and sugar can be purchased in 25–50-pound bags. Keep in mind that you must be able to store these staples properly and use them up in a timely manner so nothing goes bad. An alternative strategy is to team up with friends and divide up the bulk packages among yourselves.

Neighborhood grocery stores won't carry all items in bulk quantities like the warehouse stores, but it's still generally true that buying the largest size saves money.

As you choose items to purchase, stick to the ones that can be used in a variety of dishes. You are buying basic items now, but you want ones that are versatile. For example, a can of mushroom soup is useful in several different recipes but New England clam chowder has fewer general uses.

Allow extra time for your grocery shopping trips. You need to do comparison shopping for every item, and that's time-consuming. Act as if you are buying every item for the first time. Look at its price, ingredients, and the alternatives on the shelf. Bring your calculator to the store if you need to and figure out which brand and size costs less. This is a great learning experience for elementary school kids if you want to enlist their help—and if they can resist temptation! Look all around the shelves, particularly way up high and way down low. This is where the cheapest brands often hide because their producers can't afford to buy the prime shelf space like the market leaders can. Open your mind to trying cheaper alternatives, such as store brands and generics, even though you may feel as though you're abandoning a trusted friend. Most of the time the kids won't know you've substituted a cheaper alternative for their favorite brand, and some of your new choices may even taste better.

We normally utilize generics and store brands, but we greatly increased the number of these when we had to downsize. I can't tell the difference between generic and name brand rice, sugar, honey, salt, and pasta. The cheaper flour makes slightly smaller loaves of bread than the name brand "bread machine flour," but I don't think the difference is worth the extra expense. I won't buy the generic equivalent of my favorite breakfast cereal, though. I tried it only once and hated the aftertaste it left in my mouth. I'd rather do without my cereal than eat that poor substitute. On the other hand, the generic peanut butter was greeted by whoops of delight by all. We think it has a much better flavor than the name brand I had always used, and it's considerably cheaper. It made my day to save money and to get something we like even more at the same time!

—HSQ

If you like using coupons, by all means continue to use them. However, cooking more "from scratch" will mean that very few coupons apply to your new cooking style. Coupons are generally designed to entice you to try new products, almost always prepared foods and convenience foods. Use coupons if they are for food you would normally purchase anyway in your downsized condition.

Rather than counting on coupons, channel your time and energy to take advantage of sales. All stores run great sales periodically to attract new customers. Storage is often the limiting factor. So, reorganize your cupboards, clean out the refrigerator and freezer, and make room to pack in good deals when you find them.

In some areas of the country food co-ops exist. These offer savings on food and other items in exchange for the members' working several hours a month. Most offer a trial membership. They are definitely worth checking out.

One last "rule of thumb" for saving money based on shopping styles is to buy only food at the grocery store. Find another store to purchase nonfood items. It's convenient to be able to pick up laundry detergent, paper goods, cleaning tools, and shampoo at the grocery store. However, you pay extra for the convenience. A store that caters to bulk purchases of nonfood items will save you lots on those, so unless you can do both grocery and nongrocery shopping at one warehouse discount store, separate shopping trips will save the most money over time. Don't get carried away, however. It's not worth the time, effort, and gasoline to run all over town to catch everything on sale. Limit where you go, but maximize savings at each place.

Strategies for Dinners

The most expensive part of the dinner meal is usually the meat. You can save money by adding vegetarian meals into your normal routine, but most people aren't willing to give up their meat completely—and there is no reason to. You can eat meat and still save money simply by altering the way you purchase and prepare the meat.

After my husband lost his job, I went to the store and bought a ham, a turkey, and a roast chicken. That was $38 worth of meat. With that, I got the meat for the following meals for four people:

	dinners for 4	soup for 4
$10 ham	5	2
$20 turkey	9	3
$8 chicken	4	1
$38	18	6

The $38 divided by eighteen dinners meant I averaged $2.10 a dinner for the meal's meat. But I also used the bones to make hearty soups, which I used primarily for lunches (but were adequate for dinners). There were six more meals based on soup. In total, then, the $38, averaged out over twenty-four meals, brought the cost for the meat per meal down to $1.58. How else could one spend this little and feed a family that includes a growing teenage boy, a.k.a., "the bottomless pit"?

—HSQ

If you purchase large meat roasts and whole chickens and turkeys, you'll want to use the entire piece you have purchased. The meat can be used in a variety of meals. These are examples of uses of ham, poultry, and beef for multiple dinners and soups:

Ham Roast
- sliced ham
- small pieces on a lettuce salad
- ham and cheese scalloped potatoes
- ground ham made into meatloaf
- ground ham plus mayonnaise for sandwiches

Ham Bones
- pea soup
- bean soup

Poultry Roast
- sliced turkey or chicken
- small pieces in gravy served over potatoes, toast, biscuits, rice, couscous, puff pastry shells, etc.
- small pieces used in Chinese stir-fry
- small pieces on a lettuce salad
- pot pie
- tetrazzini
- dark meat in enchiladas, tostados, fajitas, and tacos
- ground poultry plus mayonnaise for sandwiches

Poultry Bones
- stock for vegetable soup, noodle or rice soup, leek and potato soup, etc.

Beef Roast
  • sliced beef
  • beef "au jus" on rolls
  • small pieces in burritos, fajitas, and tacos
  • small pieces in Chinese dishes like broccoli and beef
  • small pieces on lettuce salads
  • stroganoff
  • ground or diced in hash
  • chili

Beef Bones
  • stock for vegetable soup, noodle or rice, or barley soup, etc.

There are so many meals that can be quickly and easily prepared after you have put the time into the initial roasting of the meat. You need to think big. Buy larger portions than you probably ever have except at holidays or when you've had a house full of company. The extreme of this concept is to buy a whole or half cow (dead and cut up, of course!) or a whole pig from a butcher. If you do, you'll pay the least per pound of anyone. However, you have to have someplace to store that much meat (a large separate freezer), and, more important, your family will need to eat all the different cuts of meat presented to you. If no one in your family likes the dark meat of a turkey, then it is ridiculous to purchase a full bird. In this case, try to buy large bags of frozen poultry cuts at discount warehouses that also sell groceries. It's hard to beat the price per pound of the boneless chicken breasts you can buy in bulk at these places.

Red Meat

The meat department in the grocery store has learned to cater to what people want, as have all the other departments. People want things that are easy to prepare and quick to cook.

A common and frustrating situation is this: I decide to buy a roast of beef, agonize over the decision at the meat counter because there are so many confusing names to choose from, pick one, bring it home, and then can't locate the cut in any of my cookbooks. I call the store to ask how to cook it and am given directions (by whoever answers the phone in the meat department) that are hesitant and uncertain. Often, I cook it incorrectly out of ignorance and end up with tough, dry meat.

—HSQ

According to the meat manager in my local store, any cookbook more than ten years old will often not have the names of cuts of meat commonly found now. That's because meat processing has changed significantly in the past ten years. The days of receiving whole cows hung on hooks at the back door are gone. The local chain store receives meat already cut up and, most likely, even packaged. Only the most marketable meat cuts are sent to the store. Older cookbooks have names of pieces that were cut to "use up" the cow. In other words, portions were cut deliberately with both desirable and undesirable parts just so everything could be sold. Since this is no longer true, the names have subtly changed.

Along with the changed names have gone the many meat cuts that were dirt cheap. In a spacious, brightly lit store in an affluent suburb, you'll have to hunt for things like smoked ham hocks, beef marrow bones, and sometimes even stewing beef. These basic, cheap items are the foundations for some of your best hearty soups, stews, and chilis. The briskets and least expensive pot roasts are also no longer in abundance. Don't despair and don't give up. Ring the bell and ask for them. The store almost always has some "in the back." If more people request these meats, they'll find their way back to the front again.

The price of all meat varies greatly with swings in the market. Reading ads and utilizing sales can save you a lot of money. Since meat is such a significant portion of the cost of groceries, planning is critical to maximize your savings.

Beef is the most abundant red meat in American grocery stores. It's generally less per pound than comparable cuts of veal, lamb, and pork.

Veal is pricier than beef because veal is young cow that has been slaughtered to take advantage of the tender meat of youth. Because a grown cow would be much heavier when killed, veal is priced higher to compensate for the fewer pounds in the overall animal.

Lamb is more expensive than beef because the market for it is smaller in this country. (If you were to go to Greece or the Middle East, the situation would be quite different!) Lamb chops can also be cooked quickly, so their price is higher for the convenience, as it is with high quality beef steaks.

Pork is second to beef in popularity in this country, so you'll generally find an abundant supply of it. Pork is either "fresh" (uncooked) or "cured" (smoked and cooked—these are your hams). Fresh pork usually runs less per pound than the hams. All pork needs to be fully cooked before eating to avoid transmission of any possible disease-producing organisms.

The cuts of meat you'll find most prominently displayed in the meat department will be those that are easy to work with and cook quickly. These will be the ones that can be grilled, broiled, or pan-fried. They are also the most expensive.

Expensive Steaks

Beef:	porterhouse, New York, sirloin, minute, club, eye round, and T-bone steaks
Pork:	center ham slice, bacon, Canadian style bacon
Lamb:	loin chop, rib chop, sirloin chop, leg steak, arm chop, shoulder chop

If you're trying to save money, these are to be avoided. Turn your attention to the cuts of meat that take longer to cook and are generally cooked with some liquid, often covered. These cuts can be used with marinades to help tenderize them. Many of these are also called "steaks," but don't be misled by the term. A steak is a type of meat cut, not a definition of cooking style.

More Affordable Steaks

Beef:	chuck, blade, flank, Swiss, top round, round, and rump steaks

Pork: blade steak, shoulder steak, pork cutlet spareribs

Large chunks of meat are called "roasts," regardless of how they are cooked. The highest quality, most expensive roasts are cooked in a shallow open pan in the oven without additional liquid. Although pricey, they do provide a great deal of meat with very little fat and gristle waste. Buy these if you get the opportunity to save significantly with a sale.

Expensive Roasts

Beef:	tenderloin, rib, rib eye, sirloin tip roasts
Pork:	rib crown roast, loin center roast, loin roast, sirloin roast, country style hams (whole or half)
Lamb:	leg of lamb, sirloin roast, crown roast

More Affordable Roasts

Beef:	round tip, round rump, rolled rump, eye round roasts
Pork:	ham shank, shoulder or picnic roast, canned hams
Lamb:	shoulder roast, lamb shank

The most expensive cuts of meat generally come from the back (rib), rear end, and back legs. The front and belly of the animal generally produce the less expensive cuts. The extremities (neck and thinner parts of the legs) are also more affordable. Terms to look for in the name that indicate these areas are: chuck, shoulder, shank, neck, flank, and brisket. (Corned beef is cured brisket. Brisket can be purchased both raw and cured.) These cuts of meat are generally cooked in a covered pot with liquid. Terms for this cooking method are "braising" or "pot-roasting." The cheaper the meat, the longer it takes to cook, and the less amenable it will be to easy carving because it often has a large bone.

Affordable Roasts for Pot-Roasting

Beef:	chuck roast, bottom round roast, round rump roast, round tip roast, brisket, corned beef, chuck short ribs, shank cross-cuts
Pork:	ham butt, shank, picnic (shoulder) ham

The extremity pieces also include little miscellaneous chips of meat. These are packaged and sold as "stewing" beef, lamb, or veal. Stewing is simply long cooking in a larger volume of liquid (usually water). All cookbooks include recipes for stews because they are an old-fashioned (cheap!) way to use up odd meat pieces.

As mentioned, these low-cost cuts of meat frequently have an embedded bone. Yes, this adds to the overall weight and may seem like a waste of money, but if you use the bone, it's not a waste. Cut the meat away from the bone to use for a meal. Then, boil the bones to extract the deep flavors. This is how soup "stock" is made—directions are in a basic cookbook. You can also purchase marrow bones to make soup stock.

Hamburger used to be named for the section of beef from which it was ground (ground round, ground chuck, etc.). But now, it's labeled by fat content. The leaner the meat, the more expensive it is. The most expensive is 93 percent or 90 percent lean.

My store carries a ground meat called "meatloaf mix" that is a combination of beef, pork, and veal. It isn't rated for fat content. I assume it's quite high since it runs almost a dollar per pound less than the leanest hamburger. I don't buy it often because of the fat, but my kids love the grilled "hamburgers" I make with it.

—HSQ

These different suggestions for cuts of meat and how to cook them are really only guidelines. Different grades or qualities of meat exist. They are defined and designated by the Department of Agriculture. An "expensive" cut of meat (listed earlier) of low quality may be equal in tenderness to a high quality "affordable" cut of meat that was listed. It's not clear-cut. Find a newer cookbook, don't hesitate to ask the butcher for advice, and learn over time as you experiment with what your local store offers.

Poultry

Chicken has been popular in this country for a long time. More recently, turkey has crashed onto the scene as a meat to eat at other times of the year besides Thanksgiving. Its popularity has been driven primarily by the "low fat" craze. Turkey has very little fat and is generally low in calories, so the marketeers have done a wonderful job of creating a new market for this bird. This is to your benefit. It's a delicious, versatile, low-priced source of meat protein.

Chicken and turkey will always be cheapest per pound if you buy the whole bird, as opposed to the parts already cut up. Chickens of either sex are usually sold unfrozen and are named by their size: broilers are about two and a half pounds, fryers are two and a half to three and a half pounds, and roasters are over three and a half pounds. Turkeys are sold fresh (more expensive) and frozen (less expensive). The hens are usually more per pound than the tom (male) turkeys.

You can purchase either chicken or turkey already cut up into individual parts. (For turkey, you'll usually find the legs and breast portions being sold.) The most expensive parts will be those that are already deboned. Stores will generally carry certain parts in bulk and buying these large bags of parts will save you money. When you get home with a big bag of parts, you can store them more easily by washing and drying them, laying them out on a cookie sheet, and freezing them. Once frozen, you can rebag them, but now it will be easy to pull out only the couple of parts that you may want to cook at any one time.

Ground turkey meat is growing in popularity as well. It's quite reasonably priced and can be substituted for hamburger in almost any recipe for a cheaper and leaner meal. It's usually sold as light (mostly breast meat) and dark (mostly dark meat) varieties. The dark has more fat, but many people prefer it because the flavor is stronger and the extra fat content makes it easier to work with; it doesn't burn as easily when you fry it.

Any general purpose cookbook will provide instructions on how to cut up poultry and also provide explanations on how to debone it. Since you save the most money by doing this chore yourself, it's worth the effort.

I've improved over the years in my ability to cut up a chicken, but I have to admit that a butcher would probably get a good laugh out of the pieces I end up with when I'm making fried chicken. On the other hand, what difference does it make if my cut-up chicken doesn't look "store perfect"? The kids certainly don't care, as long as the drumsticks are fairly intact. I have never mastered deboning either, but I don't let that bother me. I'm not cooking at a restaurant, I'm simply feeding the family!

—HSQ

You'll get the most "mileage" out of a roast chicken or a full turkey. Don't feel obligated to make Thanksgiving dinner every time you cook a big bird. Don't even feel that you have to stuff it. Wash it, inside and out, boil the giblets in a small pan of water for an hour, and roast the bird in an oven or an enclosed barbecue grill. The meat is fantastic, plentiful, and can be used in many ways. Use the giblet water to make gravy, and after cutting all the meat off the bones, boil the carcass for soup stock. You can read the particulars in a cookbook, but it really is that simple. Minimize your effort the first few times you tackle this if you've never done it before. Once you get comfortable with the basics, you can begin to explore different stuffings if you desire.

Also, don't let the carving of the bird intimidate you. Again, cookbooks will provide instruction. It's really not that difficult. If you mangle it, so what? It's not going to bite you! Imagine how the practice will make you the "expert" carver next Thanksgiving when you can impress all the relatives!

One thing that is extremely important with regard to handling raw poultry is to make sure you do so safely to minimize the risk of contracting the bacteria that causes food poisoning. Nowadays, commercial poultry comes from farms where literally millions of birds are raised together. Growers work valiantly to keep bacteria to a minimum but under these conditions cannot eradicate it entirely. Recent estimates indicate that one in ten raw chickens and one in three raw turkeys are contaminated with salmonella.

When you work with raw poultry, you need to devote a cutting board surface to *just* poultry. Never cut anything else on that surface. Wash your hands, knives, and cutting board thoroughly with hot soap and water when you are finished. Then, use an old spray bottle filled with lightly chlorinated water (2 teaspoons bleach per pint of water) and spray the board, tools, and your hands. Clean up with paper towels so you don't contaminate dishrags and sponges. Make sure your meat is cooked completely before you eat it. Right after the meal, cut off the meat, divide and freeze or refrigerate, and always remove any stuffing from the cavity of the bird before storing it. These simple precautions should ensure that you and your family stay healthy.

Seafood

As a rule, seafood is more expensive than red meat on a per pound basis. It is usually sold in a couple of places in a typical grocery store—in the meat department, in boxes in the frozen food aisle, and in cans.

In the meat department area, you'll generally find fresh fish (more expensive), previously frozen fish (less expensive), and frozen fish (least expensive). You pay the most for fresh because people feel it tastes better and costs are high for the fishermen who have to move the fish quickly to market. However, frozen and previously frozen are often indistinguishable from fresh now that freezing techniques aboard ships have become extremely sophisticated. The fish are "flash" frozen in a couple of minutes, the ships can stay out at sea a long time, and the savings on overhead are passed along to the consumer. So consider these to be very reasonable, cost-saving substitutes.

It's difficult to generalize on types of fish by name that are the most expensive, moderate, and cheapest because this varies dramatically from region to region. Many fish that are extremely costly in the East like sole and red snapper (because these are "fished out" along the Eastern seaboard) are plentiful and inexpensive for those in the states bordering the Pacific. Different areas of the country "specialize" in certain fish (like salmon in the Northwest), so they are more reasonable in price locally but may run much higher in remote places. Of course, fish costs are higher further inland than along the coasts.

You'll find savings if you purchase a whole fish; salmon is one that transports well and is therefore available cross-country. If you buy a whole, very big fish, you can either request the market people to cut it up for you in smaller sections for your storage, or you can roast or barbecue the whole fish and divide and freeze the already-cooked meat just like you would do with a turkey. Unfortunately, most ocean fish are not available in the "whole" variety, so this option doesn't often apply.

The two most common freshwater fish, trout and catfish, are usually sold in two ways—either as fillets (trimmed and deboned) or as whole fish with or without the heads. It's always cheaper to purchase the whole fish and prepare it yourself.

Your best bet for savings in this area is to keep track of your favorite varieties and monitor their price. Catch them on sale and buy them only then. Ask the fish counter folk what time of the year your favorites are most plentiful in your area and therefore have the best chance of being lowest in price.

Fish sold in boxes in the frozen food aisle don't really save you much money. Here, you'll find your breaded and fried fish fillets and fish sticks. Even though these are made from fish chips and leftovers, because they are pressed, shaped, battered, and packaged for ease of use, the cost per pound is usually quite high. You'll save the most if you can purchase in very large quantities. An alternative is to look for bags of frozen orange roughy fillets, which you can bread and fry yourself.

The different varieties of shellfish are also quite expensive. The only way to save much money on something like shrimp is to be willing to clean, devein, and cook them yourself. Even so, they will still run $6–$13 per pound. If you really love these kinds of seafood, shop the sales and save them for special occasions. In your downsized lifestyle, they will be a rarity.

Everyone is familiar with tuna sold in cans. You'll also find canned salmon and various shellfish. The taste is quite different from their fresh or frozen counterparts, but many find them perfectly satisfactory. The amounts are convenient and cookbooks abound with recipes for them because canned seafood was the only kind available inland before modern transportation and distribution systems. The sizes are small, but most people use these in recipe "stretchers" like casseroles or pasta sauces, so a small amount is adequate for a family. If you calculate a per pound cost for the tuna to compare it with fresh fish, even the most expensive type (solid white tuna packed in water) costs under $3.50 a pound, which is quite reasonable for seafood.

Other Dinner Strategies

One of the most common and effective ways to reduce the costs of dinners is to reduce the amount of meat in the meal. This is traditionally accomplished with casseroles utilizing noodles and rice with a smaller amount of meat. Dishes like spaghetti, tuna fish and noodles, and lasagna are old standbys. To make it easier for you, make large quantities, divide, and freeze.

Meatless Meals: How to Save Time

I was a vegetarian long before the kids came into existence, and as a result, they've grown up eating lots of meals without meat, though they're not vegetarians themselves. Has eating meatless meals hurt them? I doubt it. Although my kids are smaller than average, they're a lot healthier. My son hasn't missed a school day due to illness in three years. They suffer slightly fewer colds and a lot fewer stomach viruses than their peers.

—LML

The methods for purchasing and cooking meat described above make its price comparable to varied and well-balanced vegetarian meals. (This, of course, includes the many meals that use only a little meat and a lot of nonmeat "fillers.") However, you may not be able to invest the time to cook cheaper pieces of meat, and you may have been scared off by the prospect of *E.coli*, salmonella, and other bacteria in the raw meat and poultry you are preparing yourself. (Some medical experts have argued that many outbreaks of intestinal viruses are actually undiagnosed cases of food poisoning!) Since you don't want to risk getting sick without health insurance, the meatless option may be your safest bet.

At the same time, you may have the misconception that vegetarian meals take a long time to cook. Certainly some do. A good vegetarian chili is an all-day affair, but you can also ladle the leftovers into smaller containers and freeze them. Pestos, tomato-based pasta sauces, chowders, stews, and quiches are good candidates for freezing. Freezing nonmeat meals also allows you to buy produce when it is in season and enjoy it in the cold, barren winter months.

Our family joined a farm cooperative this year. We pay a flat rate and receive whatever that farm produces from the end of April to the end of November. The first three weeks, all we got were spinach and garlic greens. We had no problem finishing off the spinach—everyone in the family loves spinach. The garlic greens were another story; they're the kind of thing we'd enjoy eating about once every two weeks. We made pesto with the greens, and now there are six meals' worth sitting in our freezer. By June, the farm had harvested all their garlic greens, but

instead of waiting until next April for more, we'll enjoy
them—in small quantities—this coming winter.

—LML

Other meatless meals rival fast food in their speed of preparation.
You can buy a falafel mix and tahini dressing, chop lettuce and tomatoes, and make your own falafels in ten or fifteen minutes. Tacos, burritos, enchiladas, and quesadillas take only minutes to prepare. All
you need are a can of refried beans, a block of cheddar or Monterey
Jack cheese to grate, a few vegetables to chop, and the appropriate tortillas. If you already have the crust, even pizza is a snap. Just ladle on
the tomato sauce, grate the cheese, sprinkle on some canned or sautéed
vegetables, and pop it into the oven. If you aren't bothered by the idea
of eating "breakfast" foods for dinner, a hearty omelette or egg-based
variant (such as huevos rancheros) is a quick, tasty, and nutritious option. Those who enjoy Chinese food know how easy and quick it is to
sauté vegetables together in a wok or saucepan. Change the vegetables
and the spices, and your sauté becomes a French-style ratatouille.

Things like baked stuffed potatoes may take a half hour to an
hour to cook, but the actual preparation time is short. Once you put
the potatoes in the oven, all you have to do is grate some cheese and
sauté the vegetables (asparagus in season or broccoli are big favorites,
but you can use other veggies as well—just don't use anything with a
high water content). The rest of the time you can spend with the kids.

Pastas with a tomato-based sauce or pesto also don't require a lot
of preparation time. In the summer, salads are especially good choices
for quick meals because they're easy to make, they're well-balanced,
and they don't heat up the house. If you're not a strict vegetarian, you
can toss a can of tuna or some leftover meat on top of the salad. Vegetarians can add protein to a salad cheaply through cheese, peanuts
(be sure to include some bread with the meal), or hard-boiled eggs.

Tofu (soybean curd) is an inexpensive source of protein and a staple of Chinese, Japanese, and Korean cuisine. Simply throw it into the
wok to sauté along with the vegetables or cut up into squares and add
to a soup. You can also add tofu to non-Asian recipes; it goes especially

well with vegetarian chili. Many people say they don't like the texture or flavor of tofu, but others (especially those who encounter it in Chinese or Japanese food) love it. It's also one of those ingredients that takes on the flavors of whatever's around it. Many stores sell a variety of textures of tofu. You never know until you try.

If you are cooking on the run, you will want to focus on a few dishes that you know well and that you can vary based on what's available cheaply. You won't have time to pore over recipes. Stick to a few basic ingredients that are versatile; expert cooks recommend no more than three ingredients if you want to make a successful quick dinner.

Strategies for Lunches

Pack lunches, don't buy them. Invest in a couple of small thermoses and plastic-topped containers to pack things like soup and pudding. Even though buying these things costs more initially, it won't take long before you've recovered the expense and from then on, you'll save a great deal.

Lunches are a great way to use up leftovers from dinners. Sandwiches can be made from slices of roasts, or leftover small pieces can be ground up and mixed with mayonnaise for a spread. Meats and mayonnaise are safe as long as refrigeration is available for your lunch. If there is no refrigerator, you may want to invest in a reusable cold pack. Cheese spreads on crackers or bread can provide variety. Cheese slices or chunks are also good. Hard-boiled eggs pack well or you can grind up the egg, mix with mayonnaise, and make egg salad. Homemade soups make a great central portion of a lunch. Add crackers or a small sandwich to round it out. Don't forget to pack a piece of fresh fruit.

Salads can be packed as well. Again, it's best if refrigeration is available. Pack toppings and salad dressings separately and combine just before eating. If you don't want a full chef salad, consider packing sliced carrots and celery, cherry tomatoes, and radishes. These crunchy vegetables are healthy and filling.

Kids particularly enjoy a variety of desserts with their lunch. Try Jell-O jigglers (Jell-O made with less water and extra gelatin to make durable chunks of Jell-O that pack well). Pudding, homemade cookies, and bars are usually hits too.

Quite popular with kids are little boxed juices that you can buy in the grocery store. The cheapest varieties are not much more expensive than making juice from frozen concentrate yourself and putting it in a thermos. Some of these juices, though, get quite expensive, so shop with care. Buying boxed juices by the case is definitely a money saver. A healthy substitute would be a thermos of milk; it may not be as "cool" to drink, but we all know the kids can use the vitamins and calcium that milk contains. If your kids balk at using a thermos for juice or milk, try a "sports cup."

Providing the kids with a permanent lunch box or bag helps ensure the return home of knives, forks, and spoons. (It's too easy to throw these out accidentally along with a brown paper bag.) You can save on utensils by purchasing heavy plastic forks and spoons, washing, and reusing them.

Many kids, as they get into secondary school, don't want to be carting along a lunch box. If peer pressure demands they purchase their lunch, then you can reduce the amount you give them slightly, teach them how to shop the cafeteria line to get the most for their money, and/or consider having them put some of their own money into lunch—perhaps buy their own dessert. Every little bit of savings helps.

Before sending a lunch to school or giving kids money to buy it, investigate whether you qualify for free or reduced price school lunch (and breakfast). The application is entirely confidential, and students receive the same lunch tickets their classmates use—only their families have paid nothing or a reduced amount for those tickets. Eligibility rules vary by state, but you'd be surprised at the number of families that qualify. In the "typical" affluent suburb, from five to ten percent of the children receive free or reduced price school lunches; still others with incomes below the cutoff may not know they're eligible. To find out more, check with your school or district office.

Strategies for Breakfast

Breakfast is an important meal. Don't skip it thinking you'll save money that way. You're far more likely to get hungry before lunch if you do and make an impulse purchase. Breakfast isn't generally an expensive meal. By all means, feed the kids. Study after study shows breakfast improves children's performance at school. (This was the main reason the school lunch program was extended to include breakfast.)

In most homes, breakfast must be quick and simple to accommodate frantic schedules. However, your days of buying convenient, prepackaged, expensive(!) foods are over. You'll need to find acceptable substitutes for frozen pancakes, waffles, French toast, strudels, and other delicacies.

Cold cereal is a very popular breakfast food. To save money, buy the largest sizes you can and/or buy generic equivalents. Avoid the highly advertised children's cereals. Homemade granola is delicious, and assembling it is a wonderful activity to do with small kids. Be careful with ingredients, though. People can make scrumptious granola that costs twice as much as commercial varieties.

Hot cereal is a very good, often ignored, breakfast food. Oatmeal, Cream of Wheat, and other cereals are extremely cost effective if you buy the boxed variety that takes up to five minutes to cook. (Don't buy the instant individual serving kind—it's far too expensive.) You can add cut-up dried or fresh fruit to add interest. If it'll be a while before the breakfast dishes get washed, soak the pan and rinse the bowls to avoid dealing with the "concrete" that forms from dried cooked cereal.

Eggs, much maligned by the media, are still one of the least costly sources of protein you can find. They are easy and quick to cook. If you're concerned about cholesterol, only eat a few a week.

Muffins, made the night before and warmed in the microwave, can be a part of a good, low-cost breakfast. Muffin mixes at stores (particularly store brands or generics) cost virtually the same as making homemade from scratch.

Pancake mixes cost more than homemade, but if you've always used frozen pancakes and waffles, you'll still realize a tremendous savings from starting with a mix. Simply adding water to the mix makes for very quick preparation.

For a real treat, if you have a bread machine, use the timer feature to have a fresh loaf of cinnamon bread, piping hot, waiting for you when you wake up in the morning. Don't do this, though, if you're on a diet. I've been known to devour most of a loaf by myself before anyone else could make it down the stairs!

—HSQ

Snacks and Sweets

Most Americans spend a fortune on junk food. Look at the amount of area in a normal grocery store that is allocated to soda, chips, cookies, and other snacks. That much space means it's a huge money-maker.

If you can't eliminate your soda, at least try to cut down on it. Try the generic equivalents and see if they'll satisfy. Try other drinks like iced tea (made from scratch) and lemonade (made from frozen concentrate unless lemons are really cheap in your area). If you don't want to give the kids caffeine, make iced tea from herbal teas.

Chips and other similar snack foods are not good for us. We all know that. They are full of fat and salt. Eliminating them from the diet is the best overall solution. If you can't give them up altogether, try to substitute popcorn. (Popcorn made from kernels is much cheaper and healthier than microwave varieties.) Making homemade pretzels can be a fun activity for the kids, but it's probably not something you'll want to do frequently.

Cookies may be the easiest snack you can make, and one of the lowest in cost. The simplest ones are "drop" cookies. Look for recipes in any basic cookbook. To keep the cost down, use margarine and generic chocolate chips. Besides "drop" cookies, look up "bar" recipes.

These are things like brownies that are low and flat and cut up into individual servings after they are cooked.

You may want to refer to the table at the beginning of Chapter 3 about comparison food prices. There are several snack foods listed.

If you are in the habit of buying a mid-morning snack and coffee at work, consider packing a snack from home and buying an inexpensive small coffeemaker to use personally at work. At the normal cost of a cup of coffee these days, you will recover the cost of your investment quickly.

Baby Food

I made my own baby food. No, I'm neither a hippie nor a fanatic. I was simply desperate. God gave me one of the fattest babies He's ever created. Most babies triple their birth weight in a year. My son tripled his in five months and then kept going! By the time he was close to a year old, diaper changes were a real challenge. His fat rolls had fat rolls—it was difficult to separate his legs far enough to clean him up. This child was enormous.

I bought the typical jarred bottles of food that were designed for the youngest babies. However, when it came time to graduate to the more advanced baby food, I discovered that all the manufacturers put tapioca in the food. Tapioca is a great thickener, but my kid certainly didn't need the extra starch. So, in desperation, I began to make my own baby food.

I was working part time and going to evening school while he was a baby, so I was leery of the additional time this effort would take. Surprisingly enough, I found it was neither difficult nor time-consuming. By the time my daughter came along four years later, I was working a very demanding full-time job and still finishing up my de-

gree at night school. But I made her baby food too because it was so simple.

—HSQ

To make baby food, take meat you've cooked for the family and
put a small amount with some water in a blender or food processor.
Blend until it seems the right consistency and pour it into an ice cube
tray. Freeze. Break out the cubes, once frozen, and pack them in a
marked plastic bag in the freezer. Do the same for cooked vegetables
(beans, peas, potatoes, etc.). Peel and microwave fruits like apples,
pears, and apricots and process them the same way. You'll end up with
a freezer full of little bags, but lots of variety. When you need to feed
the baby, pull out "cubes" of meat, vegetables, and fruit and warm
them up in separate dishes in the microwave.

My babies went to day care with packed lunches. Little
containers of the different cubes, one with cereal, and a
thermos of formula or milk were as easy to pack as they
were to make at home since I used the same containers
in both places. As the babies matured, I blended the mix
less and less to provide more texture. There was no big
transition to "home food" because my babies had been
eating it all along.

—HSQ

You might not want to make everything for the baby. Things like
baby cereal and teething biscuits are harder to reproduce at home. You
will definitely save money by making your own baby food. Bottled
baby food ranges in price from $.30 to $.80 for fruits and vegetables
(the more expensive ones are the larger bottles for older babies) and
from $.55 to about a $1.00 for meats. If you are already cooking for
a couple or a family, the little bit extra you'll cook for the baby food

will be almost imperceptible in the grocery bill. Even buying a small lamb or veal chop (normally considered very expensive meat but quite tender and therefore appropriate for little mouths) is cost effective because a small amount of purchased meat goes a long way when prepared for a baby. Portable, plastic baby food grinders are commercially available and make it easy to have a soft meal for your little one even when you're not at home.

It's worth trying! You can always go back to purchasing little bottles if you want, but you're missing a real money saver if you don't experiment.

Growing Your Own

People who lived through the Depression recall their backyard gardens as an important part of their food supply. City dwellers of that era will tell you about their trips to the country to pick fruit and wild berries; this was a serious source of food for the family, not a fun afternoon outing. A vegetable garden can be a money saver for you too, under certain circumstances.

Remember, the Depression era children had parents and grandparents who were probably farm dwellers. They were also raised by family members who had, most likely, been in that part of the country for a long time. They knew how to garden and what plants thrived best. That may not be true for people of our generation. Unless you have a good understanding of home gardening techniques that work well for where you live, undertaking a garden may prove to be an expensive, time-consuming, backbreaking, and futile task. Of course, real desire coupled with a willingness to invest the time and effort necessary can produce a fruitful backyard bounty, assuming your conditions are correct. You need space, decent soil, and sufficient sun and growing season.

Careful planning is essential. A good starting point is the cooperative extension run through your state college or university system. You should plant only what will grow well in your area and what your family will eat. Don't overdo it. Too much of a crop means you'll ei-

ther eat it until you can't stand it again, or you'll have to invest in canning equipment. Canning is long, hot, tedious work. It's worth it if
you want to do this every year, but otherwise, avoid the expense.
Don't count on selling an abundant crop. Unless you're very lucky, if
you have lots of something, chances are everyone else in your area
does too and the market will not be good.

Years ago, my husband decided to have a vegetable garden as a hobby. He had an area that was about twenty
foot square. This was when we had plenty of money and
he plowed lots of it into perfecting the soil. It produced
more food than anyone could have imagined. He didn't
have tomato plants; he had tomato trees that towered
over us and were laden with fruit. We had so many tomatoes that I spent the month of July boiling down huge pots
of tomatoes into homemade tomato paste for canning.
Our zucchini bushes were just as prolific. The freezer
was full of zucchini bread and grated zucchini for making more. We ate so much zucchini bread that summer
that I have never made it since. We had wonderful salads,
fresh berries, and many vegetables. We learned to plant
a greater variety and fewer plants of each type the following year.

—HSQ

If you live in a city, you should investigate whether a community garden is nearby. These may be run by a neighborhood association, a ten-
ants' association, or a community organization. Joining one costs
nothing or a nominal fee, but members of the community garden agree
to work a certain number of hours to ensure a good harvest for everyone. Community gardens are good places to meet people of diverse
backgrounds, share recipes, and exchange other services such as cooking, baby-sitting, and home repair.

Another option for those with a confirmed "brown thumb" is to
invest in a nearby farmer's crop. Some farmers will allow you to buy

shares at the beginning of the season and receive whatever is harvested each week. You will pay significantly less than grocery store prices for produce but will be limited in your choice to what the farmer has that week. If you choose this option, you should discuss your preferences beforehand to make sure the farm meets your needs. You should also plan to negotiate both the price and the amount of produce that meets your family's needs.

Making Cooking Easy: Forming a Cooking Co-op

In our neighborhood in Madison, Wisconsin, there were a number of cooking co-ops—families that had joined together to share cooking. Most consisted of two families that took turns cooking, but a few had three or more families. The cook for the evening would either deliver the food to the others or call and have the others pick up their meal when it was ready. This arrangement saved both money and time by allowing members to cook less frequently and in larger quantities.

Our co-op lasted six years, until we left for New York. It began when a friend's husband died after a long illness, leaving her the sole support of a five-year-old daughter. She had to increase her work hours to bring in more income and thus didn't have much time to cook; we wanted to save money because I had been unable to find a teaching job. Because each of us had only two people to cook for, this arrangement allowed us to take advantage of recipes for four or more.

Having the cooking co-op allowed us to share much more than cooking. I became the official photographer at her daughter's birthday parties. She took care of all the cooking after my son was born. We shared baby-sitting, taped each other's record collection, and exchanged books and videos. After the death of her husband, we served as an important source of support for her. She in turn helped

me find a part-time job and advised my husband and me
when we became parents for the first time.

—LML

Cooking co-ops offer a number of advantages to families who are
downsizing. Among them are economies of scale and the opportunity
to sample a wider variety of dishes. You will also save time by having
to cook only every other day. You can share cooking tips and learn
from each other. Cooking co-ops can form the basis for exchanging
other services, such as baby-sitting, automobile repair, and home repair, and you can save money by sharing videos, games, toys, clothing, sports equipment, and other discretionary items that you would
have had to buy yourself or do without. Finally, another family is an
important source of support in hard times. Single parents can especially benefit from having regular contact with another parent who's
trying to raise children alone.

You can locate another family for a co-op in a number of ways. If
you already belong to a support group—for widows and widowers, divorced single parents, or people who have been downsized—that
group is an excellent place to begin. Some communities already have
an active network of co-ops—not just cooking co-ops but co-op grocery stores, baby-sitting co-ops, and the like. If you are involved in
one of these other types of co-ops, finding a compatible family may
just be a matter of asking around. You should also look for notices in
the supermarket (or grocery co-op) and local "alternative" newspapers.
There's no harm in approaching friends, especially those with whom
you already share meals frequently. At least you know you like their
cooking and they like yours.

A successful cooking co-op requires planning and honest communication throughout. You need not be best friends but you do need
to trust each other and be compatible. You should also like each
other's cooking. No matter how friendly you are with the other family, if you think they are really bad cooks, your co-op (and quite possibly your friendship) will not survive the arrangement. If you think
your cooking needs help, be open with the other family and ask if they

can help you improve before working out a formal arrangement. Unless you work out alternative arrangements such as having one family cook more than the other, families should be similar in size. Your schedule should be predictable enough to make a regular commitment feasible, and all participants should be prepared to eat dinner at more or less the same hour. Your tastes should be similar or at least acceptable to the other. It would be difficult to have a co-op with a family of dedicated meat-eaters and one of strict vegetarians, or a co-op combining fans of international cuisine with a strictly meat-and-potatoes family. You should make sure all the participants can accommodate each other's special dietary needs. And you need to live near enough to each other so that the delivery of meals does not prove a burden.

As the co-op progresses, issues will arise. One of you may tire of constantly getting fried chicken. Or the meals may not be as balanced as you would like. A weekly meeting to plan meals will address these problems. Perhaps one of you may be going on a diet, or someone's elderly parent may be joining the household. As long as you communicate regularly, your co-op will survive these changes.

Chapter 6

Household Necessities for Less

Simply to maintain the house and the family, you have to buy certain items periodically. These aren't luxuries; they are the day-to-day things like laundry detergent, shoes, and electricity. A commonsense approach to these expenditures will be most helpful to you in the long run. You'll want to only buy what you really need and then purchase it at the lowest price possible.

There are many books and newsletters available that deal exclusively with ideas for saving money on these kinds of things. You may want to look these up in your local library. This chapter is meant to help shape your attitude toward these expenditures and offer ideas that don't demand you spend money to save money. Specifically, the topics covered are clothing, furniture, appliances, nonfood household goods, and utilities. Because many families include valued pets, this chapter also explains how you can cut back on supplies and other costs of maintaining a dog, cat, or other pet.

Attitude and Approach

In the chapter on luxuries, you read that those things needed to be cut out, cut back, or replaced with lower-cost substitutes. That seems logical enough when you are talking about entertainment and recreation, but does the approach to necessities differ? In a way, yes.

When you have money, it's easy to spend it on items that you define as necessities. Without money, you have to retrain your thinking and your definitions. Probably the best advice to follow here is to *slow down and think it out carefully.* Although your initial response to a problem will be to spend money, instead, ask yourself, "Can I live without it?" The answer may be, "No." If that's the case, then the next question is, "Can I live without it for a little while?" Often, the answer to this question is, "Yes, but only for a little while!" If you can postpone the expenditure, you should. That's how you will reshape your spending habits. Postponement of even a few days can be beneficial in this training process.

While you wait, you need to consider carefully the planned expenditure. Of course, you'll want to think about where you can purchase it at the least cost. Always shop for the best prices. Read ads, look through the Yellow Pages, use the phone to call places for comparison prices. Besides looking for the best price, you'll want to consider alternatives seriously. Worn-out shoes need to be replaced, right? Maybe not. Can they be repaired? If you can make do for a while, you can postpone the expenditure until your finances improve. In fact, you may not have to buy the item at all in the end. If you repair your child's worn-out shoes, for instance, you might be able to hold out until he grows into a new size. Think seriously about the way you are coping temporarily. Although it may be inefficient and inconvenient, is it enough of a solution to live with for a while longer?

For example, it's fall and your child has outgrown her lightweight jacket from last year. The first chilly morning, you layer her up with a sweater and sweatshirt and send her off to school. In bygone times, you'd go out that day and get her a new jacket. Now, you don't. Of course, you could look for an inexpensive jacket at a garage sale this coming weekend (postpone the purchase a few days—good!), or you could simply continue to send the child to school with a few layers of clothes until the weather changes enough to warrant wearing her snow jacket (inconvenient alternative without a new purchase—even better!). In this example, you risk your child losing some of the different layers. (The more pieces to keep track of, the greater the probability some will end up in the school Lost and Found!) However, this is still a viable alternative to spending money on this seeming necessity.

Postponing a purchase for a while, if there's any way you can, is a good strategy because many times circumstances change and the urgency of the need dissipates. The purchase may be postponed for a long time. For example, the air conditioner breaks in August. If you can live in agony for a month, the hot weather will be over for the year and the repair can be postponed until next spring. By next spring, you could be in entirely different circumstances. You may also be able to get your broken appliances fixed more cheaply in the "off-season." Deal with the problem then; endure the discomfort now.

The air conditioner in my husband's Toyota broke several years ago. The car was four years old, with 100,000 miles on it. Since it was already August, we decided not to fix the air conditioner. Except for one trip from Albany to New York City when we had to leave all the windows open, we experienced little discomfort that year.

The following spring, my husband collected estimates for the repair. The cost—$800–$1,000! Since I work at home, I let him use my car for his commute (which also involved driving the kids to summer camp). The few times I had to go anywhere, I went without air-conditioning, which didn't bother me since I'm from Houston, Texas, and used to a lot of heat and humidity.

We had planned on the same arrangement the following summer (at which time the trusty Toyota was six years old and had more than 150,000 miles on it), but my husband was able to find a secondhand air conditioner from a salvage yard. The total cost, including installation, came to $300. A year later, both car and air conditioner are still going strong.

—LML

Always ask yourself, "How would somebody who *never* had much money handle this problem?" People with little money define necessities differently from those who have had lots of disposable income in the past. If you have friends or relatives who have always lived on considerably less money, now is a good time to ask for their input. You're fortunate if you have relatives like this because relatives tend to offer blunt advice. (Just be prepared to hear things that you may not want to hear!) Ask these people where and how they shop for different items. Their input can be very valuable.

Now that your monetary resources have limits and funds have to be carefully allocated, your approach to spending money for necessities should be a slow and calculated one. Try to postpone the purchase and use that time to test the validity of the need. Once the need is truly determined, shop wisely to get the most for your money by keeping your eyes and ears open and learning from the experience of others.

Clothing

You or your spouse may have new wardrobe needs now. You may have a new office job that demands nice outfits. Or you may have have a part-time blue-collar job that means you need to put the suits in the back of the closet and wear something else, either more casual or more durable.

Even if your own clothing needs haven't changed, the kids' will. Their relentless growth and the inevitable seasonal changes will keep clothing needs high on the list of necessities. Averaged over the years, clothing may be the biggest category of expenditures for most families.

Clothing is a necessity, but it's also used by each of us to help define ourselves to the world in which we live. Our choice of clothes is a clear statement to others we meet. Adults are often amused by teenagers' hairstyles, jewelry, and clothing oddities, but actually, all of us tend to dress as our peers (or the people we admire) do, regardless of our age. Clothing is symbolic for everyone, and that adds a complicating dimension to purchases.

The best approach is to plan on buying clothes that last. In style, that means avoiding the fads and, instead, buying more classic types of clothes that remain in style year after year. For adults or children who are slow growers, you need clothes that will last in the sense that they are well made and durable. Sometimes, cheaper places, with cheaply made clothes, are not the best value over time. Of course, for the child who is growing so quickly he or she needs a new wardrobe every four to six months, you'll want to purchase the cheapest and fewest clothes you can get away with.

Once, several years ago, we decided to buy our son's new clothes at the local discount outlet. The jeans, sweatpants, and shirts we found there were half the price we paid at The Gap Kids, and Derrick liked the styles just fine. My husband and I thought we had gotten away with something until six months later, when all the clothes developed "ventilation holes." Derrick rarely grows out of anything; many of his things he's worn three years in a row. We realized that by buying cheap clothes that only last six months, we'd spend two to three times as much as if we bought more expensive but sturdier togs.

—LML

For the entire family, secondhand clothing may be the best tactic to pursue. Particularly in the suburbs, there is a surplus of (outgrown) children's clothing. You can find clothes for all tastes if you explore garage/yard sales or church bazaars. The bazaars are especially good places to find clothes because many people contribute, so the supply is large and concentrated and most people donate clothes that are in very good condition. Thrift stores (sponsored by the Salvation Army, Goodwill Industries, or religious orders) are also good places to find low-cost clothes. Bring the kids with you so they can choose clothes that fit and also are stylish enough to adapt to current school fashion. Of course, they won't find the latest fad items in secondhand places. Work with your child to find "classic" fashions that never go out of style.

The statement that one never finds the latest fad items in secondhand places isn't necessarily true. When we lived in Wisconsin, one of the hottest clothing stores for the teen set was a secondhand shop that specialized in strategically torn blue jeans. When my son lost his denim jacket last year, I refused to buy him another one, so he expropriated an old one of mine. Of course it was huge on his undersized nine-year-old body, but way oversized was all the rage last year. (At least he didn't wear baggy pants halfway down his hips to show off his printed boxer shorts!) Maybe you wouldn't like the latest teen and pre-teen fad items, but with a little creativity, secondhand and thrift shops are not only adequate but in many cases highly desirable places to shop.

—LML

If you have never shopped for secondhand clothes, this experience may feel extremely awkward initially. You may worry about "what people will think" if they knew you were doing this. However, after you visit a couple of garage sales, you'll quickly realize that this is an all-American custom, commonplace and accepted. Many people just like you—your neighbors, for instance—frequent them and save lots of money on various household items. It will teach your children how to save money, how to bargain, and how to pick clothes with lasting style and value.

Each year one of our neighbors holds a garage sale, where he sells the expensive suits he doesn't want anymore. And each year another of our neighbors picks up his entire work wardrobe there, at a quarter of the price he would have paid at a retail store.

Besides shopping for clothes at secondhand places, another way one may be able to save money on clothes is by sewing. This is practical only if you know how to sew, already own a sewing machine, and are extremely careful in shopping for patterns and material. Far fewer people sew these days and the fabric stores have become expensive places to compensate for that fact. It is easy to spend more money on homemade goods than you would if you bought them secondhand or even new.

To save money, as opposed to time, on clothes, take good care of them and repair them when needed. The old adage "a stitch in time saves nine" is still applicable today. Cleaners and polish can extend the lifetime of shoes. Dress shoes can be repaired and resoled. Tennis shoes can be repaired with products like Shoe Goo. Use common sense in wearing appropriate clothes for different tasks so you don't ruin good items. Don't paint your house in good clothes.

Avoid dry cleaning whenever possible—it's very expensive. Hand wash what you can. Men's dress shirts can be washed at home and carefully ironed. Practice and a little spray starch can produce fine results at a fraction of the price of a laundry service.

Whenever I shop for work clothes, I look for the three magic words that help me make up my mind—"Dry Clean Only." As soon as I see those words, the item goes right back on the rack!

—LML

One last piece of advice for saving money on clothes is to maintain your weight so you won't need to buy new clothes as your size fluctuates.

Furniture and Home Offices

In this category, the advice is to do without, repair what you have, or buy secondhand.

Furniture needs should be minimal at this time. You certainly shouldn't be replacing anything that is still functional; that is too luxurious for your present state. If you're concerned about worn-out furniture degrading a room while your house is on the market for sale, it would be better simply to take the piece out of the room rather than to replace it. (Real estate agents suggest that you remove furniture from rooms anyway to make them appear larger.)

If your downsizing situation has resulted in new additions to the household—such as parents, relatives, or others moving in to share expenses—and you really *have* to outfit a new bedroom, then you should consult your local paper and buy something secondhand from the classified ads or shop the garage sales. This will save the greatest amount of money in the long run. Don't get carried away, though; you should purchase only the absolute minimum you need to get by.

If you have someone working at home now (with a job or job hunting) and you feel the need to create an office environment, you have to approach this very conservatively. Does the family member *really* need a desk? Can the kitchen or dining room table suffice? If your house is not on the market, the dining room may be a perfect temporary solution. It will get messy with books and stacks of paper, but you probably aren't entertaining much these days, so who cares? A dining room table provides a lot of room and can even accommodate a computer and printer.

Other alternatives include taking over someone else's desk (even a child's) or using a card table or other collapsible table. If none of these exist, consider purchasing a used table from the classified ads. A table, instead of a desk, is usually much cheaper. Boxes can serve as file cabinets. Wood planks and concrete blocks make adequate shelving (remember these from your college days?). Or else, just stack your books.

This situation gets trickier if your house is on the market, because then you need to maintain a "pristine" looking environment. If this is the case, try taking over a closet. Move out what is normally there and stack your papers, boxes, and books in the closet. You will still probably have a desk or table by the closet; just keep it as tidy as you can.

The home office concept can get very expensive very quickly if you aren't careful. You may have always had access to a computer, printer, phone, fax machine, and all supplies and software when you had a job. If you don't have a home computer, the temptation will be overwhelming to go purchase one now. Try to resist this temptation as long as possible. Libraries generally have computers available to the public, as do many schools. Friends, neighbors, and relatives may be willing to let you borrow theirs—if not physically, at least let you have time on their equipment. More and more governmental agencies have computer and fax-equipped facilities designed for people out of work. You will have to put some effort into locating the resources you need, but you shouldn't assume you have to buy a computer.

Perhaps you have tried using these resources and for one reason or another, it just doesn't work. After considering your needs carefully, you feel that you really *must* buy a computer. You can save the most by buying secondhand (through ads in the paper or secondhand computer stores), or buying new through mail-order catalogs. Buy the minimum you need. If buying new, be sure to purchase a system that has upgrade potential (slots, memory, drive bays, etc.) so you can add on to the system later after you recover financially. If you are buying secondhand, this may not be possible because many older computers were not designed well for upgrades. Buy enough computing power to satisfy your present needs with the understanding that you will probably need to replace the entire system sooner than you'd want to otherwise. Get help from friends, family members, and faculty members at local colleges if you aren't very computer-literate, and consider getting software assistance through classes at a junior college.

Appliances and Gadgets

Appliances and gadgets are other household necessities. Things like washers, dryers, refrigerators, and dishwashers seem endowed with some diabolical spirit such that they only break or act up when the handy spouse is out of town or the finances are stretched to the limit. (Perhaps these are just the most memorable times because they are the most painful.)

If this happens to you now, approach the problem as described before. Postpone the repair or purchase and "test" the need. You can wash dishes by hand and utilize a commercial Laundromat. However, a broken refrigerator or stove will have to be dealt with soon. Call several places and try to get an idea of the range of costs that might be involved. (Be sure to check independent repair shops, not just the brand-name service retailers.) Look through the classified ads and see how much you'll have to pay for a secondhand one. Can you or someone you know repair it? You will have to weigh the options and decide accordingly. Take your time, and don't be pressured into an action with which you feel uncomfortable.

Seasons change and, with them, needs around the house and yard. Be on your guard against advertisers whose job it is to create "needs" so you'll buy their product. You may feel the urge to buy new tools to help you fix up your yard (in preparation for selling the house), but resist spending money and make do with what you have. Yes, an edge trimmer may be handy and fast, but old-fashioned garden shears (or scissors from the house) can also trim long grass effectively; it's just more backbreaking work! Gadgets that reduce labor are luxuries that you can't afford at this point.

When we moved from Wisconsin to Albany, our finances were especially tight. In our old house, we had shared a snowblower and a power lawn mower with our next-door neighbors. We took the snowblower with us and left them the mower. Since our new house had a small yard, we decided to get by with a push mower—initially much cheaper and far less expensive to maintain as well. If our neighbors could see us behind the trees, they probably would laugh at our little push mower and at us trimming the long grass and edges with ordinary kitchen scissors. More likely, they would see our children doing much of the work, since we don't use dangerous power tools.

—LML

This book may have already created "needs" in your mind. To utilize money-saving ideas from the prior chapters on food, you may want to buy a second refrigerator, a freezer, or perhaps a bread machine. If you're already downsized, don't. If you're reading this book in anticipation of such a happening, then you might consider a secondhand purchase. Saving money, however, is crucially important now, so spend your dollars wisely.

Nonfood Household Items

After gasoline and car insurance, the biggest price shock I had after I left home and started on my own was the cost of things like toilet paper and shampoo. It was staggering to me then, and it still is twenty years later with a family, just how much money can be spent on disposable, but essential, items in the home.

—HSQ

The first piece of advice is to not waste anything. Even very little children can understand this concept and can offer suggestions to reduce waste. Make this a topic for family discussion. Show them the difference between overuse (and waste) of items like shampoo, toothpaste, and dishwasher detergent. Not wasting means washing only full loads of laundry and running the dishwasher only when nothing else can be crammed into it. Be vigilant in turning off lights that aren't being used and never let the water run.

A second bit of advice is to find a nongrocery store as a source for purchasing these things.

When money got tight, I decided to try shopping at a large discount department store that I had heard my mom mention many times. I had never been in the store before, even though it is a nationally known chain. The Yellow Pages told me where to find it; it was about a twenty-minute drive on the interstate. Upon entering, I was struck by several things. The place was enormous—it took a long time to locate what I wanted. The store was full of people speaking in different languages—it seemed that every immigrant in upstate New York knew this place. Most im-

portant, everything there cost far less than my usual purchase price. The sales receipt was itemized, so I took it
back to my grocery store where I had traditionally bought
these items and compared the prices item for item. For the
twenty items I had bought, I had saved $8.40 at the dis-
count store. I was hooked! Now, I keep a separate list of
the things I plan to buy there and buy for a month at a time.

—HSQ

A warehouse discount store is the best place for large quantities and
cheap prices on nonfood items. Unfortunately, many have membership requirements, and you may not qualify. However, there are still
stores that will save you lots of money and are open to the general public. They may not be stores you feel very comfortable in at first, and
frequently checkout times are lengthy, but you *will* save a lot of money.

As you did with food and other household items, you need to consider each purchase carefully. Can you live without it? Reduce the
number of cleaning products you buy—try to move toward more
general purpose ones. Books are available in the library with recipes
for cheap, nontoxic, and effective cleansers you can make at home.
Are there reasonable substitutes that cost less? Try generic equivalents
available for most medicines, vitamins, and health care needs. Try
brands of shampoo and cosmetics that cost less. Do you have some
cloth napkins stored away that could be used so you don't have to buy
paper ones? How about rags for paper towels? Go back to the basics
and skip the cute marketing ploys. For example, toothpaste in an old-
fashioned tube is much cheaper than any other kind.

I have extremely sensitive skin, and I'm allergic to almost
all soaps, skin care products, and cosmetics. Years ago, I
discovered which products I could safely use. Unfortunately, most were extremely expensive. When money
got tight, I felt that I really needed to try again to find
products that cost less. Since new products are constantly
being introduced on the market, there were plenty to

choose from. I began the trial and error process. If it didn't work, I gave it to a family member or friend. I was able to replace my face cleanser, hand and face creams, and several cosmetic items with much cheaper products. The only thing I couldn't find a less costly substitute for was my foundation makeup cream. Each of us in the family has tried to do his or her part to lower costs on personal items. Every little bit helps the overall budget.

—HSQ

Utilities

We all know that lowering the thermostat in the winter and raising it in the summer can result in significant savings on the energy bill. Just "pushing the envelope" of comfort a couple of degrees in either direction will have consequences. In winter you can turn down the thermostat a few degrees more before going to bed and throw on an extra blanket or two.

Don't be foolish, however. One of my classmates in graduate school also had a young family. Money was practically nonexistent. In an effort to conserve, they decided to turn the heater off completely for the winter. They lived where it is fairly mild, so this was possible, but the house temperature still hovered in the 50s and 60s for months. Every single one of them got extremely sick and had a terrible time fighting off any infections. What they saved on energy was spent on doctor bills and medicine. The next winter, they opted for heat and there were no health problems.

—HSQ

Adding insulation to your roof is probably beyond your means now, but caulking and weather-stripping to seal walls, floors, and doors is worth considering. If you have a ceiling fan, use it year round to lower the energy bill. (You have to reverse the direction of the blades, if possible, in the summer and winter.) If your dishwasher allows it (check the specifications), consider lowering the temperature on your hot water heater a couple of degrees. Take shorter showers and fill the tub with less water for baths. Let the dishes in the dishwasher air dry. These are tips that will save you money without having to invest anything in purchases.

There are wonderful products like low-use shower heads, low flush toilets, programmable thermostats for the house and hot water heater, insulation blankets for the water heater, etc., but you shouldn't spend the money on these now. There's a good chance you will sell your house and you'll never realize the savings these items bring over the long run. The objective is to lower your utility bills from their previous level, and that can generally be accomplished by careful attention to and correction of wasteful habits.

Shop for the best rates from phone companies. Don't be afraid to change companies and try other services. Good deals exist, and trying a competitor can frequently result in substantially lower costs right after you change. (The first month or two may be extra cheap to encourage you to switch.) Savings in the short term is very important to you now. Of course, limit your long-distance calls. Be sure everyone in the family adheres to phone calling during the hours it is cheapest for your service.

Cancel your cellular phone service unless you *really* cannot live without it. If you need to be reached, consider a pager instead of a cellular phone; it is often more reasonable in price.

Consider using E-mail over the Internet instead of long-distance phone calls. This assumes you feel the need to maintain on-line services as an essential part of your existence and not a luxury at this point.

If it provides a cost savings, consider canceling your garbage collection service and take your own garbage to the local dump.

If you live in an area where competition exists for any of the utility services (gas, electric, water, phone, sewage, garbage, etc.), be sure to review the rates from all competitors and make sure the service you have is the cheapest you can find and realistically live with.

Home Maintenance

Here is an area in which you may not be able to postpone your expenditures, because even a day's delay may cost you thousands of dollars.

Some friends thought they would save money several years ago by clearing away the ice from the roof themselves. Every night, when the husband got home from work, he'd climb on the roof and chip away until it got too dark. He usually had no more than half an hour to work, and each time it snowed (a frequent occurrence that winter) he was back where he started. Unfortunately, the thaw came long before he had finished, and soon they had water coursing down the inside of their walls. All together, the ice buildup—only partially removed in his piecemeal effort—caused $40,000 worth of damage to the siding, ceilings, walls, and hardwood floors. Furthermore, since he did not know what he was doing, he tore shingles in a number of places, thus requiring an additional roof repair.

If the heat goes off, fix it—before the pipes freeze and burst. If the heat goes off at night or on the weekend (which it always seems to do!), pay the overtime charge. If you see termites or carpenter ants, call the exterminator before the pests reproduce and bring their friends; otherwise, they'll turn your most valuable investment, your home, into sawdust. If you live in an area with lots of snow, keep your roof swept and your sidewalks clear; the consequences of neglect far outweigh the costs. (Shoveling the sidewalk you can do yourself, but we don't recommend sweeping the roof yourself unless you know what you're doing.) If you're not handy, stick to minor repairs, such as replacing lightbulbs (contrary to the joke, you don't need a martini and an electrician).

A Word on Pets

Pets like dogs, cats, and birds are an important part of many families. It may not be prudent to get a pet now, if you didn't have one before, but you certainly shouldn't panic, overreact, and get rid of a pet because of the downsizing situation. Yes, they are another mouth to feed, but they also provide entertainment, diversion, and most important, love, at a time when it is greatly needed. Just as the family is now getting used to vegetarian dishes, soups and stews, and cheaper meals in general, your pets can adjust to cheaper foods as well. Making the switch from canned to dry foods is not only less expensive, it's healthier in the long run for your pet as well. Buy pet food at the discount warehouse store, try generics, and try mail order. Research pet food costs just like all other household items, with vigilance. Enlist the kids' help in this matter. If you have always used a grooming service for your pet, now is the time to learn to bathe, comb, and clip the pet yourself at home.

Situations may arise where you'll have to give up your pet in a downsizing situation. Some pets may simply be far too expensive to maintain (horses come to mind). If you have to move into an apartment, it may not be possible to find one that accepts pets. If you have a choice, however, finding an apartment that allows pets should be a high priority. Some landlords who don't permit pets may allow you to keep yours if you offer an additional security deposit to cover possible damage.

Another difficult situation arises if your pet requires expensive veterinary care. It doesn't seem right to sacrifice a beloved pet because it's old or sick and you don't have the money to pay for its care. Perhaps a relative or friend who knows the pet can help out. If the pet is suffering or the condition is incurable, you may well have decided to "put it to sleep" under normal circumstances anyway.

I adopted a beautiful collie mix not long after leaving graduate school and taking my first job. Although I thought the job would last, it ended four months later. I got a part-time position right away that paid the rent and not much else. With a lot of time on my hands, I started grooming the dog myself, but I lived in fear that he would get sick and leave me with vet bills I couldn't pay. Though I found a full-time job as a teacher in a private school not long afterward, it turned out to be more than full-time, with meetings and coaching duties into the night. Unable to care for the dog at that point, I ended up giving him to one of my students.

—LML

Whatever the reason, having to give up a pet will produce extra trauma for the entire family. Love and understanding is all that can minimally soften the grief.

Chapter 7

Child Care
Adjusting to Change

$\mathcal{I}$f you have young children and your income has been suddenly slashed, your child care needs will probably change. If there has been a layoff, then maybe the person now at home can become the primary caregiver. On the other hand, the death of a spouse, divorce, or other circumstances may force you to need child care for the first time. You may be caught in a situation where the child care you've always had is too expensive for you to afford now, or perhaps your employer-sponsored care has been lost.

The objective of this chapter is to explore options and open your mind to the many possibilities that exist. Of course, saving money is always high on the list of priorities!

The first section of this chapter is for those of you who have never shopped for child care before. It is meant to guide you toward the many resources available. The rest of the chapter is for those who have child care already but perceive a need to make it more economical, to "downsize" in this budget area as well.

Finding Child Care for the First Time—The "Basics"

Talk to ten working parents about their child care and you'll probably find close to ten different solutions. Ask a few parents of children in upper elementary or junior high to list all the different child care options they have personally used over time and, again, you'll be dazzled at the variety. These conversations are helpful because you need to realize that lots of options exist and you'll probably need to try dif-

140

ferent ones to see what works best for you and your children. You should anticipate that circumstances (or your own child's growth!) will force you to change caregivers. Don't be afraid of it—most kids adjust more quickly than the parents do.

There are many types of child care. There are "for profit" centers, locally owned as well as national chains. There are nonprofit centers. These tend to be parent co-ops, university-based centers, and centers sponsored by companies, churches or synagogues, and community organizations such as the Y. If you don't think a large center is the way you want to go, you'll want to consider family/home care situations (state licensed or not), the use of relatives to oversee your children, or hired sitters. Sitters could be nannies, au pairs, college or high school students, or other adults.

Costs vary tremendously. The only generalization one can safely make is that hired professional sitters (like nannies) tend to be the most expensive and costs are far more reasonable when one adult is overseeing multiple children, as is the case in a center or with a home caregiver who watches several children.

There are pros and cons for each type of child care. Any library will have lots of books and magazine articles on this subject, and they are a logical starting point. You will want to read descriptions of these child care options and pay close attention to the questions you should ask and the checklists provided for your use during your on-site interview and inspection.

Children differ in temperament. Their needs will vary and change by age as well. Books and articles will help here too, so you can anticipate how your child may adapt to the different child care environments.

Library books and magazine articles will give you the theoretical background, but in order to find out what is available locally, you will need to do more active research. Start with the phone book. Child care centers will be listed there. Also, look up the local and/or regional office of the 4C's (Child Care Coordinating Council), which serves as a clearinghouse for both day care centers and licensed in-home providers.

You should also start asking people for leads and ideas. Find parents whose children match the age of your children. For infants and preschool children, go hang out at playgrounds and wading pools and ask the adults you find there for advice. Local libraries are also good resources; ask your children's librarian. For older children, find parents at the baseball or soccer fields, playgrounds, and school functions. Call local churches and community organizations and follow up the leads provided. Look at community bulletin boards (try the library, grocery stores, etc.) and search for ads offering child care. Of course, check the newspaper classified section.

Many employers will help you locate child care. They often have referral services and ideas for initial contacts. Some companies work with day care centers that are nearby and you may even be able to obtain a discount rate.

If you have colleges or universities nearby, contact their Early Childhood Education Department. Through them, you may locate individuals or centers that provide care.

On a national level, you can contact the National Association for the Education of Young Children (NAEYC) at 1834 Connecticut Ave, NW, Washington, DC 20009 (800–424–2460), which provides lists of licensed facilities (centers, not family home care) that have accreditation through NAEYC. Or you can probably get similar information by contacting your county Department of Social Services.

It's important to keep an open mind as you go about your search. Preconceived notions may be very misleading.

The first time I looked for child care for my infant son, I was sure I wanted a home environment for him. I received a list of licensed homes providing such a service from the 4C's. With checklists in hand (to remember what to look for and ask), I went to house after house on the list. I came home in tears, unable to find any situation that I would even remotely consider for my child. The next day I set out to look at day care centers. I felt very negative about centers because the idea of rows and rows of cribs seemed entirely too institutional to me. Surprisingly enough, I was pleased with the facility requirements the state imposed (safety first!), and I liked the idea of parents coming and going frequently so the caregivers always had to be "on their toes." Multiple caregivers meant someone could watch the remaining children while another changed diapers. The advantages I found outweighed my abhorrence of the rows and rows of cribs. After checking several, I settled on a center and enrolled my child. No one was more surprised than I at the decision.

—HSQ

If you're new at child care hunting, it's extremely important to remember to obtain and check references. That can minimize unpleasant surprises.

Downsizing Child Care

You may already have your children in some kind of child care, so you don't need to deal with the challenges of starting that search. However, you do need to assess if it, like so many other things, must be changed to become more affordable. As with other budget items, you need to consider if it's something that should be cut out, cut back, or substituted with something less expensive.

Eliminating Child Care Altogether

There are two ways to remove child care from the budget. If the children are young, one parent stays home and becomes the primary caregiver. If the children are older (in school), you let them return from school to an unsupervised house, that is, they become latchkey children. Both options are explored here.

A Stay-at-Home Parent

A study in the early 1990s showed that in affluent, two-income families, 68 percent of the second salary was devoted to child care, household help, clothing, transportation, and other work-related costs (*Wall Street Journal*, 4/22/92). Although several years have passed, this statistic hasn't altered much. For the amount of effort involved in orchestrating two-income families' schedules, then, the rewards of the second salary are often dismally small. The decision to forgo the salary and keep one parent at home becomes one that must be considered logically. (Some reading this book may be downsizing for exactly that reason—to reduce the overall household budget so one parent can stay home voluntarily.)

Usually, there's more than just money that gets sacrificed with this decision. Benefits are lost. Experience, seniority, and continued professional growth in your field are cast aside when you decide to leave your job and become the caregiver for the children. These can have long-term, dramatic consequences for your future. Most professions, once dropped, are extremely difficult to reenter. Whether you're a man or a woman, the pace of business today makes it very difficult to get back into it—just ask any woman who has taken a few months off for maternity leave. When you return, the computers and software have changed, procedures and products are new, and catching up requires a monumental effort.

When I followed my husband to Wisconsin, I gave up my teaching job in New York City and was unable to find another one. After five years of unemployment, my New York State teaching license had expired, and I would have had to return to school for twelve credits to get a new license, with no job guarantee afterward. As a result, when my husband lost his job, I chose to go to library school, to start over in a new profession.

—LML

However, more and more people today are voluntarily making this decision and adjusting the rest of their lives to fit. Those who have volunteered to raise the kids are joined by many more who have been thrust into it because of layoffs. Reasons and motivations for these two new groups of caregivers are quite different. However, they will probably both go through many of the same "withdrawal symptoms" as they adjust to their new role.

Whether a man or a woman, this adjustment may be awkward. There's a lot to learn! The younger the children, the more there is to master. It's one thing to "watch the kids" for a few hours on a Saturday afternoon. It's quite another to shop for, feed, clothe, entertain, teach, and otherwise nurture children full time, every day. If you're grieving a job loss, those feelings will continue to permeate you constantly. You will probably miss friends and coworkers and stimulating, creative adult conversation. You may miss the prestige that went with your managerial position and the ability you had to delegate tasks to others. Now, *you* have to do all the dirty work. You may or may not find that you are suited to the task.

How you'll adjust to staying at home as a full-time caregiver is difficult to predict. I had always expected to continue to work full time, even after having children. However, the death of our first child as an infant changed my mind completely. My husband and I agreed that if we could have a healthy baby, I'd stay home with it. So I happily quit my job as I went into labor with my son. Although I cherished my baby more than anything imaginable, within a couple of months, I was miserable. I really missed my previous work. I started going to night school. It helped a little to provide distraction from baby matters, but before my son was a year old, I had returned to work.

On the other hand, I had a friend who was a stockbroker in the city. It was a physically demanding job and she had worked hard to achieve success in a profession where few women ventured in those days. She returned to work after a short maternity leave. After a few months, though, she quit and went into serious child production. I visited her once a couple of years later. There were kids everywhere, the house looked like a house with several preschool children, she wore battered clothes and a dirty apron—and the biggest smile you've ever seen. She was completely happy with her new station in life.

—HSQ

More and more today, *men* are discovering that they enjoy the role of primary caregiver. Recent statistics indicate that about 10 percent of the stay-at-home parents are now fathers. The percentage is on the rise as society, as a whole, adjusts to this concept. There are many positive aspects to a dad as the children's caregiver. Time and proximity allow a closeness to develop that may otherwise be difficult to achieve. It allows the dads to participate in after-school or early-evening sports coaching. Their perspective and assistance in school and community service is very important. (PTAs shouldn't be exclusively female groups!) Men around during the day offer a stable presence in the home and neighborhood. Being at home provides opportunities to develop new skills like learning computer software and time to keep the house and yard in good condition.

Our neighborhood features a family with a dad as the stay-at-home parent. I don't know if he feels self-conscious about his role, but both the kids and the other parents in the neighborhood love it and really appreciate his being there. Some of the moms who are home all day like the added feeling of security. When the family got a new computer so he could work at home, all his kids' friends were over there bugging him to let them play his large collection of computer games.

Another friend chose to stay at home when he was laid off from his management position. By taking care of the

household, he allowed his wife to pursue better oppor-
tunities with her company. He in turn coaches his kids'
sports teams, his favorite activity. More recently, he taught
himself some computer applications and now does con-
sulting on the side to finance the family's vacations.

Despite the advantages, men who choose to stay at home full time face unique challenges. Besides the potential lack of understanding on the part of in-laws and other relatives raised in more traditional times, there is the isolation of possibly being the only stay-at-home dad in the neighborhood. Men have to make a special effort to get out and meet other men in the same situation. You can seek out men who work shifts and care for the children part of the day. To meet other men, keep your eyes open on the playground, at the Y, or at library story hours. You can try to organize dads-only playgroups by posting notices at the supermarket, the Y, the library, and your church or synagogue. Some churches already have groups and programs to meet the needs of nontraditional families and families that have adopted nontraditional roles.

Both men and women have discovered the advantages of renouncing the outside career and caring for the kids. You finally get the time with them you've longed for, and the daily routine gets easier as the pace becomes more realistic. Confusion about whose standards and discipline methods will be followed are eliminated. Ending up in the role of primary caregiver, regardless of the circumstances that brought it about, can end up being surprisingly rewarding.

So, perhaps having one parent stay at home needs some serious consideration as you evaluate your future plans. Many things may be "in flux" for you now. You may need to sell your home and adjust to a less expensive existence. Can this time be an opportunity for changing child care needs for a while?

You may be able to say, "Yes, for a while." You may want to stay at home to help the kids adjust to their new circumstances before sending them to an outside day care center or making them responsible for their own care after school. You may need time to assess your new neighborhood—what day care facilities are nearby and if it is safe enough to leave kids at home alone—and, quite possibly, your kids' new school situation. If you have moved far enough away, you, too, will have to adjust to a new community.

For many, however, the answer to the question may be, "No." The budget, careers, or temperaments may mean that the parent at home is, at best, a temporary situation.

Depending on the age of the children, the stay-at-home parent who is also looking for outside work will face different challenges. Young children demand constant attention, and job search activities will be difficult to schedule into your daily routine. Realize this up front and set realistic personal goals. It's probably going to take longer to find new work if you can only get something accomplished during nap time. So, be easy on yourself. Cherish the moments with your children, and work hard to focus your attention on job search matters only when appropriate.

Latchkey Kids

The other way to eliminate child care is applicable to school-age children. You let them return from school to an unsupervised house, and they stay by themselves until the parent(s) return home from work. This solution is perfectly acceptable if the child is old enough and mature enough, and if the environment is safe. Usually, if you have an adult in the neighborhood available to the child for an emergency and the child can reach you by phone at work for consultation, then it ought to be an adequate solution. However, it may be difficult to predict how your child will react to the solitude and freedom. You may want to experiment and reevaluate after a given period of time.

A child left alone needs coaching on how to handle answering the phone, the door, and other intrusions. Also, be careful about an older child's ability to watch and care for siblings. There are good reasons why most people don't hire neighborhood baby-sitters until they are about twelve years old. Until then, the maturity necessary for this responsibility just isn't consistent enough for safety's sake. Furthermore, some kids simply do not have the interest or temperament to want to watch younger siblings.

A difficult aspect of the latchkey decision is what to do during school holidays and vacations. Leaving children alone for a couple of hours in the afternoon is quite different from leaving them alone all day, for several days. You have to plan, well in advance, for alternative care for these special times.

YMCAs and other community/church organizations often run special programs during school vacation days. The use of high school kids as baby-sitters at your home for these days is another option that shouldn't be too expensive. (They ought to have the same vacation days!) Ask around for referrals for sitters, or call your local high school and find out if it has a place you can advertise at the school. Many schools even assist their young people in locating part-time work. Another place you can look is the local Red Cross, since it often provides first aid classes for teenage baby-sitters. The teacher of that class may be able to recommend his or her outstanding graduates.

Cutting Back on Child Care

Reducing the total number of hours your kids are in child care is one way to realize some savings. Although it's extremely difficult to rearrange your schedule and give up some of your precious free time, it could be something to consider now.

One of my best friends took her twin sons to day care, then returned home to shower, dress, eat, and get off to work each morning. I've known others who left the children in day care a little longer in order to carve out some personal time to shop or exercise.

—HSQ

Many people leave the children at child care, then commute to work. Moving the care to a place near work would mean less time daily you have to pay for care. You'll save money, but now you'll have to commute with tired children in the car. This trade-off needs serious thought.

When my son was a baby, we traveled together in the car over two hours daily, commuting to his center and my nearby work. He was a wonderful traveler. We talked, sang, and really had fun together in the car. However, when his sister was born, our happy days were over. She screamed and cried nonstop for the entire trip, both ways. There was no satisfying her. Bumper-to-bumper traffic is bad enough, but to endure it with a crying baby day in and day out is absolute torture. After three months, I had to change child care and leave the kids near home. It was more expensive and I missed my son's conversation terribly!

—HSQ

So, circumstances vary. However, if you can reduce your child care needs even by one or two hours a day, that adds up to as much as forty hours over the course of a month. That translates into a significant cost savings!

Finding Less Expensive and Subsidized Care

If cutting out or cutting back your existing child care situation isn't possible or logical, you may have to switch your care to something completely different. Generally speaking, the more individually accommodating the care is, the more expensive it will be. The extreme example of this is the nanny or au pair. This kind of sitter lives in your home and adapts to the schedule you want. When you switch from this to home care or a day care center situation, *you* will be the one to adapt your schedule to the hours and rules that apply.

If you give up the nanny, au pair, or private sitter, you may worry about your child's loss of individual attention, or child care of lower quality. The truth is, your child will not receive as much personal attention in a group situation, but that is not necessarily a bad thing. Your child may come home with more colds from a day care center, but he or she will also come home with more social skills than if cared for individually at home. Most kindergarten teachers assume children have developed some social skills already, and a child who has not spent time in a group situation will be behind.

When our second child was born, I was working an evening shift. For that and other reasons, we chose to hire a nanny, a teenage girl from Idaho. She took good care of the baby, but by the end of her first year, our daughter was showing signs of boredom. Even more of an issue was the fact that the nanny, away from home for the first time, had become like another child and more of a responsibility than a help. We ended up sending the nanny home and putting Maddy in a day care center.

—LML

Furthermore, a licensed home care or day care center often provides superior care to a nanny in your house. Licensed day care providers are trained professionals. Especially in a center, they work under a great deal of supervision, not only from their superiors and other workers but also from parents who drop in unannounced. (If a day care facility does not allow parents to drop in and observe, you should avoid it.) As the recent controversy over the secret videotaping of nannies indicates, private sitters work under no such supervision, and far too many do an inadequate job.

If you have only used personal sitters in your home and now want to find more affordable alternatives, you should go back and read the earlier section of the chapter, "Finding Child Care for the First Time." Basically, your task is just like theirs. You'll need to consider the pros and cons of the different types of child care, the lists of questions to ask, and what to look for when evaluating places. You'll quickly discover the realities of waiting lists at popular places and the need to make compromises in many different areas of your life. Don't expect the adjustment to be easy.

If you're happy with your current child care but need to spend less, your first step should be to discuss your financial dilemma with the caregiver (or the director). There may be scholarship or subsidy money available of which you are unaware. You might see if a rate cut could be negotiated in exchange for volunteered time and effort. (For example, could you do the typing, filing, or phone calling for a center or lawn or facility care for a center or home?)

One of the most important considerations at this point is to find out if you qualify for any government subsidies. Don't get your hopes up for this assistance; the trend has been toward less and less money available. The federal government, though, does give some money to states to allocate on a per-need basis. The states decide. So, your best bet is to check with your local Department of Social Services (state or county level) and see if your income or status qualifies you for aid. Single parents—especially "displaced homemakers" and those earning the minimum wage or slightly more—have the best chance of receiving aid.

You may want to locate a book at a library entitled *Free Money for Day Care*, by Laurie Blum. This book is a listing of thousands of sources of financial aid from government, private foundations, religious institutions, and corporations. Each type of funding is covered in a separate chapter, and within each chapter the resources are listed in state order. If you think you might qualify because of marital status, income level, religious affiliation, ethnic background, or disability (yours, a spouse's, or a child's), follow the directions carefully for applying for the aid.

The day care my two children attended was affiliated with a Jewish community center. A number of the children there were refugees from the former Soviet Union. Local synagogues sponsored their immigration, and the Jewish community centers subsidized the children's day care while their parents attended school to train for new careers.

—LML

Financial aid through the government may be decreasing, but the trend of private companies providing assistance is increasing. If you haven't checked on child care assistance at your company in a long while, it may be worth a visit or phone call now. More and more companies are offering employees the opportunity to elect child care benefits in lieu of something else. Some companies provide vouchers for child care costs. Some even underwrite company-sponsored or nearby private day care centers so the employees can save money. Increasingly, Child Care Reimbursement Accounts are available. These are reservoirs of tax-exempt funds that come from your paycheck but are used to pay for child care costs. It's the tax-exempt status that provides an overall savings to your budget, as child care costs come from pretax rather than after-tax dollars.

Many school districts, community organizations, YMCAs, and church-related centers offer child care with sliding scale rates based on need. Rates are calculated according to your income and family size. Frequently, these facilities offer a package if you have more than one child enrolled. These are all worth investigating.

If a neighbor or friend has a sitter at their home for their child, you could suggest that your child, too, be watched by the same sitter. Sharing the costs of a sitter may be more economical for both of you.

Baby-sitting co-ops may be the least expensive possibility. However, they are very difficult to organize for full-time workers. In a co-op, every family in the group takes care of all the kids during a fair percentage of the time. If you're lucky enough to have differing hours and days that you work that mesh well with a couple of other parents, this is a feasible way to go.

A variation of this would be, "You watch my kids after school and I'll watch your kids on the weekend." Fair trades can eliminate or reduce costs and grant some free time or worry-free time for all involved.

Conclusion

My children are now nine and thirteen years old. Over the years, I have utilized a day care center, care at someone's home, live-in nannies, a preschool (for morning)/sitter (for afternoon) combination, junior college students as after-school sitters, Mom at home, and most recently with the layoff, Dad at home. Along the way, we have had a few bad experiences, but by and large, the different care situations have been fine, and the children have thrived. I have learned to trust my instincts in the decision-making process. Moreover, I have also learned to trust my child's response to caregivers and groups of kids during the evaluating phase.

—HSQ

As parents, we want the very best for our children. With effort, even in a downsized situation, we can provide a safe and nurturing environment for our precious little ones.

Chapter 8

Transportation
Getting Around for Less

$\mathcal{I}$n America, the car is the symbol of independence and freedom. For many, the kind you drive is also an indication of your tastes, values, and level of success in our material culture. Your choice of models and colors helps define your role. But all cars (whether they are luxurious touring cars, sport utility vehicles, minivans, or sport cars), have similar needs: payment, insurance, gasoline, maintenance, and registration requirements. The vehicles you have must be operated now as economically as possible. In the short term, you will have to set realistic expectations for your car's usage and consider alternative transportation methods. In the long term, you may have to consider selling your current status symbol and adjusting to a sensible, good quality, but inexpensive performer. All of these topics are explored in this chapter.

Car Payments and Leases

If you own your car outright, you can skip this section.

If you're paying on a vehicle, you have the loan principal, plus interest to pay each month. You need to do some thinking and research now. How much money have you already invested in paying it off? Are you close or are there still years of paying left? How much is the car worth, right now, if you tried to sell it?

In general, the initial payments on a loan are for interest only. If you have recently taken out the loan, that means you have paid off little or none of the principal. Thus, if you sell the car, you still have to pay back most or all of the price you negotiated when you bought the car. With a recently purchased car, you will probably have a loss, since a car loses much of its value the minute you drive it off the dealer's lot. If you sell the car under these circumstances (people in the finance world call it being "upside down"), you will have no car and a big debt to pay still.

Some cars hold their value well and can be sold with little or no loss. For example, sport utility vehicles have held their value very well in recent years. If this is the case, then selling the car, paying off the debt, and purchasing a more economical car makes a lot of sense. Unfortunately, this will only apply to a lucky few. Most people buy cars that lose a quarter to a third of their value in their first year. If this is your situation, then you may want to hold on to the car and consider debt consolidation schemes that combine all your fixed debt and lower the necessary monthly payment. This is discussed in more detail in Chapter 12.

If you leased the car and the lease payment is no longer affordable, then you may have fewer options still. Pull out the lease agreement and read all the fine print. Is there a mechanism for terminating the lease early? Under what circumstances can you return the car? It's time for a frank discussion with the lessor. Being up front and honest with your situation and showing genuine concern about trying to meet your debt obligations should help you in your effort to negotiate an alternative payment plan.

Car Insurance

A detailed discussion of car insurance is taken up in Chapter 11, along with all other types of insurance most Americans carry.

In a nutshell, if you have few assets, you can reduce your coverage in all areas (Bodily Injury, Property Damage, etc.) to the state's minimum requirements. You may even drop Collision and Comprehensive coverage on older cars. These moves will reduce your overall insurance bill but could potentially put you at high risk if you are severely underinsured and involved in an accident. If you cannot afford to take the risk—you have assets that you want to protect, for instance—insurance may not be a very good place to trim the budget.

On the other hand, if your downsizing situation is the result of a layoff, you may not have as much need for a car right now. If the vehicle isn't being used much, is it possible to alter schedules enough to eliminate its use altogether? If so, you could take the car "off road" and cancel the insurance. If the usage is necessary, but minimal, look into a low mileage policy, which can cost significantly less.

Gasoline

Those who experienced the gasoline shortages in the early 1970s learned the tricks to conserve gasoline. However, supplies are now more plentiful, and we all adjusted to the higher cost for fuel, so the tricks have fallen into neglect. Those too young to know those days may never have had an opportunity to learn money-saving tips, so they are reviewed here.

Ask the service people at your dealership if your vehicle can safely use a lower quality of gasoline. If so, start using it, or perhaps combine expensive and cheap varieties at the same fill-up. Purchase fuel in the cool morning hours when vapor pressure is lowest and the gasoline is the most dense. This will minimize the vapor (which isn't burned) and maximize the liquid (which is). Improve your miles per gallon by keeping your tire pressure correct, removing the roof rack, using cruise control, and turning the engine off rather than idling more than a minute. More significant savings can be realized by driving at lower speeds (the optimal speed is 50–55 MPH), avoiding fast accelerations and brakings, and shifting gears at lower RPMs with manual transmissions. If you have more than one car, utilize the most fuel-efficient one whenever possible.

Maintenance

Maintaining your vehicle properly is always important. The wise individual will continue to keep up-to-date on maintenance even though
expenses are being trimmed as much as possible elsewhere in the
budget. Changing the oil as often as the dealer suggests is probably the
easiest and least expensive way to keep the car in good running condition. Whatever you spend on the oil change is far less expensive than
buying a new engine. Oil additives really aren't necessary if you use a
reputable oil. To save the most money, change the oil and filter yourself and dispose of the used oil responsibly.

I once bought a two-year-old vehicle that had undergone
very little preventive maintenance; in fact, in its first
18,000 miles, the previous owner had changed the oil
and filter only once. Even though I changed the oil regularly after that, the vehicle went a mere two years and
30,000 miles more before the engine cylinder warped
and cracked. In the middle of winter I was without a car
for two weeks and had to pay $2,000 for the engine to be
partially rebuilt.

—LML

Keep your tires in good condition for the safest driving. Shop
wisely for tire replacement and purchase moderately priced, reputable
brand names.

My husband's car for commuting to work was overdue
for all new tires when he got his layoff notice. We quickly
discovered that, without his daily commute, the car really
doesn't get much use. Rather than replace the tires, we
have just stopped using that car at all. Adjusting to using
only one car hasn't been easy, but if we can continue to

do it successfully, then we can minimize the insurance and fees on it and reduce upkeep costs to almost zero. This is the current plan. If we find that we have to use his car, then we will have to buy new tires right away.

—HSQ

If you decide to put a car aside and not use it, then there are some things to keep in mind. Cars that are stored and never run begin to deteriorate. You should start and run the car weekly until the temperature gauge registers "warm" in order to keep it in good condition. Storage for a long time can result in flat-spotted tires and brake corrosion.

You can take care of the physical appearance of your car inexpensively by washing it yourself. Use liquid soap (not detergent) and old rags. There's no need to buy fancy products. Wipe off and vacuum the interior. If you've been paying others to wash your car for years, it may come as some surprise that the job really isn't very difficult or time-consuming. (By the way, this is an excellent task for young hands around the house!)

Rust is a big enemy of cars, especially in regions with snowy winters. Just because you paid an outrageously inflated amount for "rustproofing" when you bought the car doesn't mean you can rest easy. Frequent washing in winter—even once a week—to get off the dirt and road salt will prolong your car's life significantly. Keep in mind that rust doesn't just ruin the appearance of a car; it can compromise its structural integrity and put your life at risk in an accident. You should also repaint any "dings" or scrapes as well before rust gets into them. In checking for and eradicating rust, don't forget to look at the doors, trunk, and undercarriage of the car; often cars rust from the inside out. For that reason, too, make sure your floor mats are in good condition, and try to keep the floor dry.

Keeping your car clean, inside and out, will mean better resale value or a higher trade-in credit if and when you decide to turn it over. Meanwhile, you'll feel better about driving it as it ages; it'll be an "old friend" rather than an "old junkheap."

We owned our first car for seven years. The body had rusted through, but we hung on to it because every year we didn't buy a new car we were saving thousands of dollars in interest and depreciation. Because our family had grown by two, we finally sold it to some friends and bought a new car.

That was more than six years ago. Having learned from our mistakes with our previous car, we wash this one regularly and repaint the scratches right away. Aside from the financial considerations, we wouldn't consider trading it in. We couldn't bear the idea of anyone else driving our faithful flivver around town (and getting another 175,000 miles out of it)!

—LML

State Safety Inspections/Licenses/Registration Fees

If you keep up-to-date on your car maintenance, then your Safety Inspection fees should be minimal. You may be lucky enough to live in a state without these annual inspections. All states, though, have license and registration fees. There is no way to save money on these expenses. However, you'll want to stay current and avoid any late fees or fines. If you are not using a car, check with your state regarding its laws about licensing and registering a stored vehicle. Don't assume there isn't anything to pay; you could end up paying fees as well as penalties.

Parking Costs

Parking costs in downtown areas can be exorbitant. If you have this problem, you might consider parking farther out at a cheaper lot, perhaps even taking public transporation into town. Remember though, be safe. It's not worth risking a long walk through an unsafe part of

town. Perhaps you can ask someone else at work to join you in the farther lot so you can walk in together. As you consider parking areas,
of course, you need to try to minimize the chances of your car being
vandalized or stolen.

Many people we know who live in the outer boroughs of
New York City and on Long Island avoid paying Man-
hattan parking fees by parking on streets near (safe) sub-
way stations and taking the train in. One of the "regulars"
who parks in front of my mother-in-law's house in
Queens comes from Oyster Bay, some thirty miles further
out on Long Island.

—LML

Alternatives to Cars

We are all aware of the benefits of using other modes of transportation: saving energy, preserving the environment, and lowering our
transportation costs. However, it's almost always more convenient to
drive than to adjust to the mass transit, train, or bus schedules. But
convenience isn't as high a priority as saving money is now. So it's time
to reconsider the alternatives. If you have public transportation available to you, go pick up the published schedules and really put an effort into trying it. You may discover some advantages, such as being
able to read while you travel and not having to hassle with traffic and
parking.

Biking and walking to work are wonderful exercise if you can do
it, if it's not too far, and if weather permits. Check and see if there are
showering/changing facilities at your work site to make the effort
more feasible. Encourage your older kids to ride bikes or walk more
frequently for short trips around the neighborhood. Every little bit
helps. If you bike or walk instead of drive, it saves on car-related
costs.

Don't forget carpooling. This is a wonderful alternative and can result in tremendous savings. Advertise in your local paper or in company newspapers around where you work to locate others who have similar commutes.

At one time, I carpooled with a man I had nothing in common with except that we both lived and worked in the same cities. Our politics, religion, child rearing philosophies, and music preferences were complete opposites. There were no topics, other than the weather, we could discuss without ending up in a fight. The commute was an hour and a half each way, which is a long time with someone you don't like very much! So we settled into a routine where we didn't talk, the person driving that day chose the radio station, and the passenger rested with closed eyes. Believe it or not, we carpooled that way for several years until his job changed and he moved away.

—HSQ

Should You Sell Your Car?

As you downsize your lifestyle, it may be possible for you to eliminate the need for a car. Of course, then it makes sense to sell it and reduce your budget on transportation costs. Many families have multiple cars; getting rid of at least one can really help.

If you own a very expensive car and the payments, insurance, and upkeep are exorbitant, then you should investigate what you could make by selling it. It might be a wise move to sell it and get something far more economical in the long run. A cheaper, less "trendy" car will be less of a target for vandalism or theft. Lower-priced cars usually carry less expensive license and registration fees in addition to lower insurance premiums.

If your expensive car is paid for already, selling it may be a quick way to raise cash, even if you have to buy another car. For instance, if you replace a high-priced Mercedes or BMW that you own free and clear with, say, a Tercel or Geo Metro, you'll have tens of thousands of dollars left over.

I learned some interesting lessons a few years ago when we sold my luxurious, high-powered, gas-guzzling car and bought a tiny, diesel VW Rabbit. The miles per gallon tripled and all costs fell dramatically. The biggest surprise was my need to relearn how to drive. On the Los Angeles freeway system, I went from being a predator to being the prey. My new car had no pickup at all. I had to choose my on-ramps carefully, or I couldn't get up to speed fast enough to merge with the flow of traffic safely. I could no longer intimidate other drivers by revving the engine and making aggressive lane changes. It was a real eye-opening education and quite an adjustment! It seems that whenever we downsize, there have to be adjustments!

—HSQ

On the other hand, I went from predator to prey several years ago when I *upsized* my vehicle in the city. My boxy, battered Isuzu Trooper developed multiple system failure and, reluctantly, I replaced it with a shiny new Jeep Grand Cherokee. With my old Trooper in New York City, I was a psycho driver with nothing to lose. Everyone feared me and got out of my way. My Grand Cherokee, though, got no respect at all, a behavior I reinforced by driving timidly, afraid of getting a scratch. Ultimately, the Grand Cherokee was stolen and stripped, something that would have *never* happened to that beat-up Trooper.

—LML

When you're buying a new car, do your best to anticipate family growth and changing needs. (For example, buying a four-door, instead of a two-door, car makes more sense for a young couple planning to have children someday.) Forget the status symbols. Choose a moderately priced, high quality car that will be functional over the long run.

That's exactly what it should be now—a "long run." The days of purchasing a new car every three to four years are behind you. You'll want to maintain your car with religious fervor and hang on to it for many, many years.

Implementing this advice will require some serious attitude adjustment for lots of you reading this. The automobile is so integral to our American psyche that it has become a "sacred cow" and is very hard to alter. However, the focus right now is to reduce the monthly cash flow. If changing your attitudes about the car can result in significant savings, then it's time to do just that.

Before we moved to New York, my husband sold his twenty-eight-year-old VW Beetle. He still regrets it. It was such an economical car to operate, and maintenance was so simple. There was nothing in that car that couldn't be fixed with a set of wrenches, a screwdriver, and the owner's manual. His recommendation to anyone looking for a way to save on car costs is to find an old, rust-free Bug, fix it up, and "putt-putt" your way down the road forever.

—HSQ

Chapter 9

An Education for Less (Doesn't Mean Less of an Education)

$\mathcal{E}$very generation tries to "pave the way" for the next. Most parents strive to provide their children with the same educational opportunities they had, if not better ones. There is no way that you want your current financial crisis to jeopardize your children's educational future. You must approach your children's schooling with a positive and determined attitude. It is, and will continue to be, a top priority.

This chapter will look at the educational challenges and options for kids of all ages: preschool, grade school, high school, and college. Both public and private schooling is discussed.

Preschool Children

Present family economics may mean you need to withdraw your child from preschool, reduce the number of hours he/she attends, or cancel your plans to start in the first place. Don't despair. Your child's future success in graduate school isn't going to depend on what happens in preschool. Besides, it's important to remember that *you* are your child's best teacher.

Nowadays, most children do have some preschool experience before they begin kindergarten. That experience is beneficial. However, you can provide much of the same experience without taking on the financial burden of the formal school setting. The important things taught in preschool are: socialization skills; an introduction to the

165

alphabet, numbers, colors, and shapes; vocabulary; and observation skills. Children also receive opportunities to express themselves in music and art. They are read stories; this experience teaches them to sit still, pay attention, and let their imagination soar. You can provide situations for your child, daily, to teach the same things. Socialization skills require other children, so you'll need to locate playgroups of similar-aged children for your child. Put up notices, if you have to, but your best bet is locating other kids at your local playground. Playgroups (in homes, backyards, and at the playground) are important for children to learn how to share, take their turn, help each other, and simply "get along." The other things taught primarily in preschool you can do one-on-one with your child. You can also bring him/her to the local public library for story hours and other activities.

To provide the basic foundation crucial for future educational success, you must prepare your child consistently and frequently. Basically, you are "home schooling" your preschooler, and you must provide a regular, consistent structure with a variety of activities. If you do these things, your child can enter public kindergarten and fall in step with the other children with few difficulties.

If your child is handicapped or has special needs that make preschool essential, you should locate the book *Free Money for Day Care* by Laurie Blum, mentioned in Chapter 7. This book lists thousands of resources that provide money for educating special-needs children. Alternatively, check with your local Department of Social Services for leads to publicly funded programs for which your child may be eligible. If your child has a physical disability or is hearing- or speech-impaired, for instance, you will probably qualify for a special program.

Grade School (Kindergarten–8th Grade): Public School

If your children are in public school, then you are already taking advantage of the least expensive type of schooling available. Basically, this education is free. (Of course, we still have to pay our property taxes, which generally fund schools, but at least you aren't paying additional tuition on top of this.) Although there has been much public debate on providing "vouchers" to parents to help underwrite the cost of alternative educational opportunities, as this book goes to print, vouchers don't exist.

Today, although the education is essentially free, most schools require you to provide basic supplies for your children at the beginning of the year: paper, notebooks, pencils/pens, rulers, glue, crayons, etc. Then come the additional requests: please join the PTA, please donate a box of tissues, please buy a school T-shirt to show your "spirit," please buy books from the book club, and (by the way) please contribute to the teacher's end-of-year present. Of course, you will probably have to provide additional money for field trips throughout the year. Even with one child (let alone several in school!), requests for money constantly show up in the backpack.

It's important to do two things. First, make sure your children realize that you cannot purchase everything that is offered. They may have to resist pressure to buy the school T-shirt, books at the fair, or other items to help the student council or PTA. Yes, these are worthwhile causes, but you'll have to let others do the giving right now. In any case, resisting the temptation to buy will give your kids valuable lessons on resisting peer pressure. Explain how and why you weigh the importance of each request so your child understands your thought process and can learn to do the same. Items essential to the educational process ought to be much more important than items for recreation and extracurricular activities.

Field trips can be especially expensive. Everyone enjoys them, and they often provide special childhood memories. So the second thing you should do is contact the school and find out how you can tap into the special funds that most schools have available to help parents like yourself who could use some help underwriting costs of expensive trips. Usually, the principal is the one in charge of these special funds.

About two months after my husband lost his job, my third-grade daughter arrived home very upset. The biggest field trip of the year, a day-long bus trip to New York City to visit the zoo, had been announced. She had gotten all excited about going until the teacher explained it would cost about $50. At that point, she realized it might not be possible. By the time she arrived home, she was full of ideas about how she could earn some of the money to help pay for the trip. We were dumbfounded by her understanding of our financial situation and her willingness to work and sacrifice to try and resolve the dilemma. We assured her that we would accept her help and that, somehow, we would all come up with the money to pay for the zoo trip. As it turned out, we didn't have to ask the school for assistance, but I would have before I would have allowed my daughter to be singled out and denied the opportunity to participate. She had a wonderful time on the trip!

—HSQ

If you receive some aid from the school, you may feel more comfortable if you can volunteer your time or effort to help the school or teacher in return. A stay-at-home parent may be able to spend time during the school day assisting in classes or the library. A working parent can still volunteer to make phone calls in the evening or do sorting, cutting, or some other classroom preparation.

Regardless of whether you receive financial help from the school, you should always try to play an active role in your child's school. Don't let your lack of property or financial resources intimidate you.

At a community meeting one parent described the change that occurred after her husband lost his business and the family had to move from their home in a subdivision to a mobile home park. The mobile home park had a bad reputation among the suburb's wealthier residents.

"I have a master's degree and a responsible job," the woman, an arts administrator, explained at the meeting.

"At work, I'm in charge of programs and a lot of people. Before we moved to the park, I used to go to my kids' school all the time, and I felt I was important there too. But now every time I have to walk into the school, my head's down. I feel like everyone's looking at me and thinking I'm uneducated and a bad parent because of where I live."

She went on, "There are plenty of people with college degrees, even master's degrees, living at that park."

Hers is a normal reaction to a financial crisis. Furthermore, some people will look down on those who have less money or live in a "bad" neighborhood. You must see it this way: Money, cars, houses, and jobs are all things that can be lost, due to events beyond your control. But no one can take away your education and the value you place on your children's education. A bank or creditor cannot foreclose on your college degree. Thus, you must see yourself as your child's advocate at the school. Get involved in the PTA and other parent organizations. Your physical presence at the school is extremely important over time. If you can't be there during the day, take advantage of all the evening activities to make your presence known. It gives you the opportunity to know teachers, administrators, and staff, and the overriding philosophy of the principal.

By all means, acquaint yourself with the counseling opportunities the district provides. There may be some program or support group that your child can benefit from to help with the adjustment at this time. One example is Banana Splits, a nationally known support group for children whose parents have gone through a divorce.

Grade School: Private School

If your child attends a private school, then you have to deal with this financial burden. You have some serious thinking to do. It's time to evaluate the reasons why you chose private school in the first place.

At the grade school level, reasons for choosing a private education are probably one of the following: You need a full-day program, with after-school child care. The public school in your area has a poor academic reputation. The public school may be overcrowded and you feel your child needs more individualized attention. You may want religious training for your children during an impressionable time in their life. You may want your child to associate with others of the same gender, religious, ethnic, or cultural group. Or, you may feel your child needs to learn in a special environment that the public school cannot provide.

You may also want to think about why you chose *that* particular private school. Will a less expensive private school meet your needs and still be affordable? Catholic schools and other schools affiliated with religious institutions—commonly called "parochial" schools—are generally cheaper than nonsectarian private preparatory schools—known as "independent" schools. Granted, classes will probably be larger and facilities more spartan, but you may very well cut your tuition bills in half.

It would be wise to reevaluate the public school system now if it's been some years since you did it, if at all. Visit the neighborhood school, talk to the principal, and try to envision your child there. Does the district have magnet schools or special programs?

If your child needs extra help and attention, is a private tutor, coupled with a public education, a cheaper solution than the tuition at the private school? If religious training is the primary concern, can you send your child to public school, but enroll the child in other church or synagogue programs to supplement your training at home?

If no other options are acceptable and a parent plans to stay home full time on a long-term basis, home schooling is also an option. Most often identified with conservative Christians, home schooling is in fact practiced by families of diverse beliefs and philosophies and for a variety of reasons. In most states, you will have to apply for permission and follow some sort of curriculum. Your local school district may also be required to furnish textbooks to help you along. Some supplemental materials may be obtained from local libraries, but depending on what you teach and how you teach it, you may have some out-of-pocket costs. If you choose to home school, you should think about providing social experiences for your children through sports, scouting, or other community-based activities. You can also find lists of support groups through books on home schooling or through your church or synagogue.

If it looks as though you cannot afford your private school tuition and you don't want to transfer your children, you should definitely investigate to see if any aid is available. Make an appointment with the Headmaster or school director and discuss the problem openly. There may be scholarship money or perhaps work opportunities for an adjustment in tuition. If this has hit you mid-year, try to work out a plan to complete the term or school year. Keep your child informed about what is happening. Even at an early age, children can learn that tough decisions have to be made in life, the process often takes time, and it's frequently hard to live with the consequences.

> *A neighbor lost her state job when her political party was voted out of office. Her oldest child had been attending a private school known for its small classes and individual attention. With great trepidation, she enrolled him in the local public school. In the meantime, the private school, which she had informed of her situation, offered her a part-time job that would have defrayed most of the tuition costs. At that point, however, she had already prepared her son to attend public school, and she didn't want to burden him with any more changes. Even though the classes are more than twice as large as what he was used to, he's enjoying public school, doing well academically, and making more friends in the neighborhood.*

Moving your child to the public school may not appeal to you, but try to look on the positive side. Even if your children don't share the same racial, ethnic, religious, or socioeconomic background of most of those at the public school, the diversity may actually offer them an advantage in the long run. They will grow up with a much better appreciation of the "real world" and will therefore be better prepared for the workplace of the future. If they attend a neighborhood school, they will make more friends locally, and you won't have to drive them clear across town for a play date.

Helping your child adjust to the public school environment should be a top priority. Most private schools are quite small, so the neighborhood school may seem overwhelming. Visit the school (perhaps several times), meet the new teacher, be sure the teacher and school staff are aware of the transition, and enlist the aid of the school or district psychologist whenever possible. The chances are good that your child will already know some children if it's a neighborhood school. Do your best to facilitate your child making friends—encourage your child to invite friends over after school. As parents, get involved with the workings of the school as soon as possible so you begin to feel a sense of ownership yourself. Your acceptance of the public school should provide a good example for your child to follow.

High School: Public School

As before, if your children are in public school, you are already taking advantage of the least expensive type of schooling available. However, just as with grade school children, you will generally be expected to provide the basic supplies and pay for field trips. In addition, your child will be barraged with opportunities to spend more of your money on sports, clubs, or other extracurricular activities. The cost of band suits, football uniforms, club outfits, hockey gear, prom tickets, sports tickets, graduation gowns, etc., can be astronomical even to those with lots of discretionary income. Particularly in upscale suburban areas, the schools seem to take for granted that all parents have "deep pockets." Even if the schools don't feel that way, most of the kids do! Since these extracurricular activities are so central to your child's social life and his/her role at school, it's very difficult for parents to curtail the excitement, "clip the wings," and crush the hopes of your teens by denying the funds to make their participation possible.

What can you do? Start by planning ahead as much as you can. Based on the child's interests, you need to find out how much money you might expect to spend in the upcoming months for the activities involved. Call the school, find out who runs these activities, and talk to those persons directly. Ask the activity sponsor for names of people currently involved and call them too to get their input on what to expect. Ask other parents about how much time is involved, how it might affect the child's homework, etc., and then question them about costs.

If you can get an approximate idea of the costs involved, then you can start setting expectations right away. What can your child do to help contribute to the expense? Discuss what is reasonable and what isn't. A person of high school age is old enough to understand what you are going through with your downsizing. Some kids, however, are more mature than others. The attitudes about money with which you have raised your children will also affect their reaction. Don't be too surprised at the range of emotions you might be faced with over this issue. No matter what they say, the fact remains that you don't have the monetary resources you used to, and everyone in the family is going to have to adjust to that reality, no matter how difficult it is.

Check with the school and see if financial assistance is possible to underwrite some costs. Districts vary tremendously; all you can do is ask. If aid doesn't exist for extracurricular activities, it still might be there to help with the cost of things like field trips. (Some high school trips can be unbelievably expensive!)

One of the biggest dilemmas for parents of teenage boys involves participation in sports, especially in football. Many boys see football as not only a ticket into the social elite of the school but also as a means of getting a college scholarship. Yet football is both an expensive and a dangerous sport, and the possibilities for a scholarship are, at best, uncertain.

One family lost its health insurance when the father lost his job. The son played varsity football, but he had broken his wrist the year before, and the parents knew if he were to get injured again, they could be faced with thousands of dollars of medical bills. They considered pulling him off the team, but he enjoyed the sport and had already received recruitment letters from colleges. A scholarship was a real possibility. In the end, the parents approached the school district and found out that the district subsidized an insurance plan, limited to the sports season, to cover its many student athletes in this situation.

Another family of limited means had invested several thousand dollars over the years in football camps and clinics for their son, in the hope that he would receive an athletic scholarship. By his junior year, it became clear that, while he had some athletic ability and enjoyed playing, he would never become an outstanding player. After a frank discussion, the boy and his parents agreed to pull back on the outside training, even though it meant he would spend most of his senior year as a backup player. Fortunately, the boy had maintained an almost perfect grade point average, and with the extra time he had over the summer he was able to apply for and win an academic scholarship. He says that wherever he goes, he may try out for the team as a "walk-on," and he may settle for intramural sports, but in the meantime he'll enjoy just being on the high school team with his friends.

As you are anticipating future expenses for your high school student, you should also begin thinking beyond high school to the upcoming college years. Encourage your son or daughter to take as many Advanced Placement courses as possible in high school. With enough credits from AP classes, it may be possible to cut down your college time by a semester, or maybe even a full year. College time saved translates into huge savings.

After her husband died, leaving three children under the age of thirteen, my future mother-in-law knew both a private high school in New York City and college would be a tremendous burden. Since her husband had worked for the United Nations, she negotiated for her children to continue attending the United Nations International School at a substantially reduced tuition. The U.N. School also followed the rigorous International Baccalaureate curriculum, which entitled each of the children to a year's advanced placement in college. All three children finished college in three years instead of four, which amounted to an instant 25 percent reduction in tuition.

—LML

High School: Private School

Reasons for choosing a private high school can be quite different from reasons for choosing a private elementary education. It may be traditional in your family to attend a certain private school. Your adult peers may have their children in elite private schools, so you feel compelled to as well. You may feel your child needs the extra structure and discipline provided by a military school. You may wish to have your child in a religious school. There may be more opportunities for your son or daughter to participate and excel in sports in a smaller school. You may feel the public school in your area is too unsafe an environment due to violence or drugs. The private high school may have tougher academic requirements and will provide a better preparation for college. In fact, several of these reasons may apply in your situation.

Regardless of your reasons, the decision to put your child in a private high school was a major one, and the decision to remove him or her will also be a major one. As you evaluate your finances now, if you decide that the private school education has to be sacrificed, the adjustment process you and your child experience may depend on your reasons for choosing the private school in the first place.

If your child has been attending a boarding school or independent day school, again, you might want to investigate nearby parochial schools. In general, the tuition is less than half of that at exclusive preparatory schools. The drawbacks are: generally larger classes (often larger than at public schools); fewer science labs, computers, and other amenities; less well-appointed buildings and grounds; and, if you don't share their beliefs, mandatory religious classes. Or your teenager may not fit into the more rigid environment of a parochial school. On the other hand, parochial schools are an alternative if the neighborhood public school is unsafe, magnet schools are not an option, or if your child needs a more structured environment to succeed. Parochial schools, like independent schools, offer more sports opportunities to kids who would not make the team at a large public high school.

If family tradition or peer pressure was your primary motivation for sending your child to a given private school, as you reverse your decision and enroll your child in public school (or even a less expensive parochial school), you will have to absorb or deflect the criticism you encounter from family and friends. If you feel that the discipline or religious training is essential for your son or daughter, to use the public school means you will have to provide additional structured activities to compensate for what you lose from the private school environment and curriculum. This will probably entail more meetings or classes, which will complicate the weekly family schedule. If sports opportunities were at the center of your private school desires, they may have to be sacrificed with a move to the public school. You may have been counting on a scholarship in a sport to fund college; that may no longer be possible. However, the realistic chances of this happening may also be low.

Fear for your child's safety at a public school is a much more difficult issue. You can provide transportation to and from school for your child. You can be sure your child is fully aware of the potential problems, understands the vocabulary that might be encountered with other students, and is knowledgeable about how to defuse arguments and tensions. Classes in self-defense or martial arts can provide a basis for self-confidence. Excellent communication between you and your child is important so you can provide coaching regarding the situations that may be encountered.

Parents attracted to private schools for the advanced academics available there may feel very unhappy with what is perceived as a "watered down" curriculum at the public school. It's important to remember that a good education really *is* available at virtually any school and the dedicated student can achieve it despite the many social and budgetary problems the public schools deal with constantly.

I am a product of the Los Angeles public school system. When I was in high school, overcrowding was the biggest issue. My high school had over five thousand students in facilities built for less than half that number. As an adult, I taught in both public and private high schools for several years. There was an astonishing disparity between the two. The students at the private schools got more attention (fewer students per class), more homework, more daily hours devoted to the "solids" (math, English, social studies, science, and languages), and covered more material per year than their public school counterparts. Their academic education was significantly more demanding than what I had personally experienced. However, the tuition was staggering. Few people can afford to send their children to schools like this. I have always wondered exactly how much difference it eventually made in the lives of those children to have attended this kind of high school. Yes, a handful went on to the prestigious Ivy League colleges, but most didn't. They went to colleges and universities filled, primarily, with public school graduates.

—HSQ

I, too, taught in both private and public schools, including the New York City Public Schools. I had the privilege of teaching at Brooklyn Technical High School, one of the "academic-specialized" public schools in New York City.

Not only were the students more highly motivated (and more interesting, because of their diverse backgrounds) than those at the "exclusive" private school, but I found out that many had attended private and parochial schools in earlier grades. For many of the struggling working-class and middle-class families of New York's outer boroughs, it was common practice to send younger children to nonpublic schools and then have them take the test for the academic-specialized high schools. If they passed the test, they went to public school, and their families saved a lot of money. If they didn't pass, they stayed where they were or went to a private high school.

—LML

As you evaluate the public school situation in your neighborhood—as well as the existence of magnet or specialized schools further afield—and weigh the financial restraints you are under, you must also factor into the equation the effect the transition will have on your child. The closer to twelfth grade he/she is, the harder the move will be. Teens have their social circles set in concrete often before high school even begins. Breaking them away from their friends and thrusting them into a foreign environment will be very difficult on them emotionally. Emotions *will* affect their academic performance. It's hard to predict how the young person will adjust over time. You know your child better than anyone else. Hopefully, you can successfully communicate your concern for his or her welfare as you struggle with this decision process.

As with private schools at the elementary level, scholarships and work opportunities may also be available, especially to students with high grades and/or significant participation in extracurricular activities. Most private schools will be reluctant to let the star student, in line for admission to Princeton, or the quarterback of the football team leave for economic reasons. Even if your child is only an average student and a mediocre athlete, the Headmaster, director, or financial aid office may be willing to accommodate you, particularly if your hardship seems temporary. In the end, you may decide to pay the full private school tuition, even it means selling your home and moving to an apartment and/or a cheaper area. Only you can grapple with all the factors involved in order to reach a decision on this complex matter.

Planning for College

If your downsizing situation has hit you while your high school senior is planning for next year's college or university experience, you may have to reexamine your decisions carefully. You are going to have to be realistic about what is affordable and what isn't. Look for scholarships that make sense. Athletic scholarships go to only a select few; avoid "pie-in-the-sky" plans. (If your child is a gifted athlete, you should also be aware that colleges often withdraw the scholarship if he or she fails to make the team or is injured.) Having your income slashed may actually benefit you in your search for financial aid. Many affluent families make too much money to qualify for any assistance programs. That's no longer a problem!

However, the expensive private colleges you had hoped for may really be beyond your means at this point. To save money, you should consider your state university system or a community college that can lead to a transfer to a four-year institution or a technical training program.

No matter what school you choose, you can still hunt for financial assistance to help out. (All colleges are expensive!) There are many, many little-known scholarships. How do you find them? There are professional services available to help with this; you can always call one or two and see whether or not their fees are affordable. In general, you'll have to make a risky up-front investment to get information you might be able find yourself. Don't be deceived, however; digging up information on scholarships requires considerable time and effort. Your teenager should do most of the legwork; after all, it's his or her future at stake! To research this yourself, try your local library, a nearby college library, your counseling office at the high school, the Internet, and the financial aid office at the school(s) of your choice. In looking for scholarships, you should explore those available on the local level. For example, fraternal organizations such as the Rotary or the Elks offer college scholarships to high school students in their community.

Don't forget the military as an option. It's not for everyone and you'll need to examine the pros and cons carefully. (A few years ago, a lot of young people who thought they'd get a free college education found themselves getting shot at in the sands of Kuwait!) However, many young people get a fantastic education, an opportunity to travel (of course, you don't get to choose where you'll go!), and a chance to explore fully their skills and capabilities while letting Uncle Sam pay their way.

In 1993 the federal government funded the Americorps program for those who wish to serve their country and earn money for college but don't want to (or can't) join the military. Americorps "volunteers" generally work in inner-city projects in return for up to two years of college tuition. Most Americorps projects are run through community agencies; if your teen is interested, he or she should contact the principal agencies in your area. Your church or synagogue may also be a good place to start.

Those who join the military or Americorps receive another benefit. Since you work in your area of interest and expertise and then get further training in addition to college, you end up highly skilled with real-world work experience on your résumé.

If the prospect of taking time off to enlist in the military or Americorps doesn't appeal, your best alternative is the typical package of grants, interest-deferred loans, and work-study employment. This is, of course, not an ideal situation. The direct grants, such as Pell Grants and scholarships offered by the college, aren't usually substantial, and your child will face a big debt upon graduation. In addition, work-study jobs do take time away from studies, socializing, extracurricular activities, and the general enjoyment of the college experience (even though most students these days seem to have jobs). Your teenager should be aware of his or her responsibilities and have the discipline to manage time effectively.

Faced with these prospects, your child may want to take time off to live at home and work before college. This solution is best suited to youngsters who could use the time off, who lack the skills and maturity to manage a tough class and work schedule effectively. He or she can pick up credits and experience the requirements of college-level classes at a local community college in the meantime.

My brother-in-law chose to take time off before going to college. With great effort and federally guaranteed student loans, his widowed mother could have paid the tuition, but after thinking hard about it, David realized he wasn't ready for college. His grades in high school hadn't been that good, and he couldn't honestly say he enjoyed school. He moved to South Carolina and worked as a cook for a year and a half; then he returned to New York City and worked in restaurants for another two and a half years. One day he wandered into a class at New York University and thought, "This is easy. I could do it." He applied to colleges and was admitted to Boston University, where he graduated three years later with a degree in philosophy and a perfect 4.0 average.

—LML

For young people who are ready to go away and want to get on with their life, the "time off" option really doesn't pay. Most jobs for high school graduates pay little more than minimum wage. Even if your youngster lives at home, he or she will barely clear a year's tuition after a year of full-time work, even after putting every penny away. (This doesn't include transportation costs, clothing, meals at work, and taxes, and it assumes your teen can *find* a full-time job.) Better to take out interest-deferred loans and pay them back at a college graduate's salary than to "prepay" with the meager earnings of most high school grads.

Already in College

The further along your child is in college when your income drops, the better off you'll both be when it comes to finding the money to finish. With a decent "track record" (grade point average), financial aid *will* be available. Have your child make a beeline for the financial aid office to find out what options exist for finishing the current term and going beyond. While your son or daughter is searching on campus, you can investigate other financial agencies for rates on loans.

This is a time to go in debt, not to pull your child out of school. Your income may rise again someday and make it easier to pay back the loans. Your son or daughter can pay back loans with money he or she earns in a job obtained because he/she *has* the college degree. If you disrupt the continuity of your child's education at this point, it may be harder for him/her to get back into the "swing of things," or to fulfill prerequisites for postgraduate study. Many students who drop out of college never return, or only return years later, at which point they may have to retake required courses. On the other hand, if your child has not done well in college and/or lacks direction and motivation, the time off to earn money may provide a valuable learning experience.

In his first three years of college, Dan, an architecture student, spent far more time skiing than studying, and his grades showed it. Then his father lost his job. Unwilling to take out loans to finance a C- average, Dan's father suggested he leave school and work for a while to learn about the "real world."

His party over, Dan moved back home and worked as a draftsman during the day and at a discount store at night. He saw how little money and opportunity for advancement he had without a degree. After a hard year, he returned to school, more appreciative of what his classes could offer. He quit the fraternity and hit the books, finishing his senior year on the Dean's List!

By all means, make this a partnership endeavor. It's your child who benefits from the education, not you. Your child should be accepting some responsibility for the repayment of these loans. An education that is fought for is appreciated more than one that is handed out on a silver platter.

My mother came from a very poor family. No one had ever gone to college, but she was insistent on finding a way. She won a full scholarship for her freshman year at a religious school. She took it although she was not of that religion. The scholarship was not renewed for a second year. She enrolled in the city's university and began the arduous task of working during a term to earn money to attend school the next term and then stopping again to work until she had the money to attend again. There is no harder way to earn a degree! No one values an education like my mom!

—HSQ

Conclusion

Yes, Bill Gates dropped out of college and still became a multibillionaire. However, for the vast majority of us, we have achieved a comfortable existence by hard work—before, during, and after long years of education. Hindsight has shown us just how valuable our education has been to our success, even if we may have suffered a setback now. It's a primary responsibility for us, as parents, to instill this same value system in our children. Amazingly enough, passing this on to the kids is, in itself, a process without a price tag. Consider struggling immigrants to these shores who quickly discovered that the opportunities for their children were virtually unlimited because of the availability of free and universal education in this country. Countless uneducated immigrant laborers and freed slaves passed on a reverence for education—as well as positive attitudes, strong values, and high expectations—to their offspring. Yes, your monetary resources are not what they used to be. There's no reason why this should become an insurmountable barrier. Others have succeeded, and so can your children. As your child's first and best teacher, you merely need to set the example!

Chapter 10

The Costs of Getting a Job

Chances are pretty good that you have a new line item on the monthly budget plan—job hunting costs. If you have been laid off, you'll be looking for a job. It doesn't matter whether you look for a job similar to your old one or whether you want to use this time to investigate entirely new career opportunities. There will be costs involved in the search. If you are newly divorced or if your spouse has been laid off, you may be looking for work for the first time, for a second job to help make ends meet, or for a higher-paying job. This chapter examines the typical costs entailed in this process, considers the hidden costs of interviews, and helps you analyze a job offer to see if it makes financial sense. Finally, this chapter looks briefly at the promise and pitfalls of starting your own business.

Job Search Costs

You'll probably need to write a résumé, make copies, and mail them. You'll need to use the phone to contact possible employers. These costs can add up quickly. By all means, utilize an outplacement agency if you can. If you are anticipating a potential layoff, think seriously about negotiating for outplacement services in your severance package. An outplacement agency provides a place for typing, faxing, phoning, and getting assistance on many aspects of the career search. It can save you hundreds, or even thousands, of dollars.

Finding potential employers will also cost you money. There may be listings at the outplacement center, unemployment office, or public library—computerized or not. However, much of the time, it's your own hard work, ingenuity, and searching that ferret out the real

185

possibilities. It takes time, effort, and money. You'll want to locate newspapers from major cities; subscribe, find a library that carries them, or get friends or relatives who live there to mail them to you. Search through the professional journals in your field. Look for these at a library, if you can, to avoid high subscription costs.

You may be in a situation where retraining and/or additional education would be beneficial. Many people want to become proficient in basic computer skills and software packages (word-processing, spreadsheet, and database usage). Besides computers, other skills or subjects may also need review, practice, or mastering for the first time.

The good news here is that the federal government has been increasing funding in this area. You might be able to get Uncle Sam to defray all or part of retraining costs. If you qualify, you should definitely take advantage of this program, because it is a good way to learn new material and network with other people, and the schooling will provide needed structure in an otherwise out-of-control existence for the newly unemployed. You can find out about retraining from the U.S. Department of Labor, your state Department of Labor, or the local office of your congressional representative.

You will probably consider using employment agencies or executive search firms (known as "headhunters"). Employment agencies tend to specialize—you'll need to research this. Some prefer to deal with temporary or part-time workers; others deal primarily with full-time, permanent placements. There are agencies that place technical people, others that deal with accounting or administrative support jobs, and still others that specialize in a profession such as nursing or teaching.

When my husband lost his job, I was working a part-time job out of my home. A year earlier, when we moved to New York from California, I had left a high-paying, full-time technical sales position. Since we didn't know which of us would have the best chance of finding a lucrative position, we both decided to pursue full-time employment. A publication from the Chamber of Commerce

in my area contained an article on the specialties of the
employment agencies in our area. Using that, I was able
to contact the three of them that spent most of their time
placing people with my background.

—HSQ

You'll want to utilize agencies that get their payment either
from the employer that hires you, or from money earned (from you,
in your first year of employment) once you have been placed. Be
wary of agencies that expect you to pay any kind of application fee.
Some states set a maximum percentage an employment agency can
take from your salary. If the state doesn't set limits, be sure that
amount isn't excessive, because once you go back to work, you'll have
plenty of other expenses and perhaps some unpaid bills stemming
from your time of unemployment as well. If the agency takes a percentage for placing you, you'll also need to maintain that budget
item for the next year.

Headhunters are utilized primarily by businesses seeking to hire
top people in a given industry. A headhunter is paid by the employer
to locate an individual—usually an executive, high-level manager, or
someone with a specific professional or technical background—to fill
a particular position. They'll look for the key individual wherever he
or she can be found. Their job is to woo the targeted person to leave
his/her present position and take the newly offered one. If you are
lucky enough to be the one recruited, you shouldn't have to pay a
penny for the service. Although you may want to leave your résumé
with such an agency, expect not to be called. For the most part, these
firms are looking for a specific person and will find him/her on their
own. Most of the time, the person in whom they're interested is already employed and will be "stolen away," though a call may come out
of the blue even if you're unemployed. Most books on job-hunting,
including the respected and best-selling (you should get it from the
library, though!) *What Color Is Your Parachute?*, recommend alternatives to the common strategies of checking the classifieds and registering at employment agencies. Many of these alternatives, such as

targeting a couple of firms you'd like to work for and establishing connections there, joining a self-help group for networking purposes, contacting friends and relatives for leads, and contacting your college alumni association or job placement office, cost relatively little.

A recent economic trend in this country is the rise in temporary and short-term work. Whether you are a laid-off secretary or a former top executive, you may be faced with the decision of taking a short-term job. Many agencies specialize in temporary placements, and a reputable one will not charge you if it places you. Of course, you will make significantly less than a regular employee under this arrangement, and you will probably not receive benefits. You will want to consider whether a short-term placement pays, given child care and other expenses, and whether the promise of a full-time, permanent job once you "get your foot in the door" outweighs the drawbacks of temporary or part-time employment now.

When I first moved to Albany, I registered with several nearby school districts to be a substitute teacher. Many of the teachers who worked for those districts had put in years of substitute teaching before a permanent job opened up. In the most popular districts, substitute teaching within that district was a virtual prerequisite for new hires.

In my case, the cost of child care was a major factor to be weighed before signing up. I had no guarantee that I would get a job on a certain day, but I had to arrange for child care all the same. Child care cost so much, and subbing paid so little, that I figured I'd have to work at least four days a week just to break even. I went ahead and arranged for the child care because I wanted to teach, and on my days off (which was most of them, because I got called only once in two months) I searched for jobs in other fields. After two months, I found a job as a librarian and removed my name from the substitute lists.

—LML

All of the costs incurred by you or your spouse in job hunting should be meticulously recorded and tallied. They are tax-deductible once you have located a job.

What if you've never worked, haven't worked for many years, or don't have enough work experience to write a résumé? Where do you look?

If you have any secretarial skills, you may be able to get hired by a temporary secretarial service. You'll probably be given a typing test and possibly a general test to ascertain your reading and filing capabilities. If you qualify, you'll be hired by the agency and sent to various companies for short stints to replace people on vacation or out on leave. You may also help in situations where a company needs lots of people for a short time only (like inventory time). Without keyboarding or typing skills, you may still qualify for answering phones, filing, or stockroom work. After some experience, you can look for other, higher-paying jobs. This is simply a place to start.

Another place to look for work (when you lack experience or no other opportunity is available) is at stores, as clerks. If you're hired, the store will train you on the cash register or in whatever skills are necessary. Of course, fast-food places have a high turnover rate, so they are generally in a "hiring mode." Retail and department stores hire many people for the Christmas holidays, but don't expect to be kept on much past the first of January. Still, this might be a good place to look for a second job to help with the holiday bills.

You might think it's ridiculous to work for minimum wage. However, just because you *start* there doesn't mean you have to *stay* there. If you've run a home for twenty years, raised children, and orchestrated a family's activities and finances, you have many skills that are directly applicable to work situations. Your maturity counts a lot. Your basic intelligence will take you much further than you may think.

One summer, during college, I had a good-paying job that ended early, leaving me with four weeks to go before my classes resumed. I went to a nearby amusement park and got a job in its fast-food area. I was given a kiosk and taught to sell ice cream and pretzels. At the end of the first week, I was brought into a large snack bar area and put on one of the cash registers. By the end of the second week, I was being trained to open and close all the cash registers in our area of the park. During my third week, I was moved into the office to work on the payroll. During the fourth week, I was offered a job to assist the Concession Manager for the entire park. The job paid considerably more money and eventually offered the chance to become eligible for salary and benefits. At that point, I explained that I was planning on quitting at week's end to travel back to college.

My skills weren't really that great. My success was more a function of the high turnover in these jobs and the fact that most of the teens who worked there couldn't follow directions and really didn't try very hard.

—HSQ

Without work experience you'll have to start at the bottom. However, don't despair. You can prove your worth. You can learn what you need to know. Remember, "cream rises to the top," and so can you!

Cost of Interviews

It's exciting to get an interview with a potential employer, but you have to get to it and be dressed appropriately. Both can mean money out of your pocket.

If your interview is in a distant place, you'll have travel expenses. Often, it is unclear as to who is expected to pay these expenses. You also may feel that it's an awkward topic to discuss. If you've been using an agency as the go-between, leave it to the agency staff to clarify this for you. If you're on your own, try the subtle approach first—ask where to stay, the best way to get there, etc., and see if, in the answers, anything is clarified. If a particular hotel is mentioned, you could make a comment like, "Oh, I usually try to stay somewhere more reasonable," and see if the response indicates who is paying. If all else fails, ask directly: "What is your conventional practice in covering the cost of travel for someone interviewing?" It's important to know up front. Chances are, even if the company ultimately pays, you'll be expected to pay now and be reimbursed later.

You may also need to buy a new outfit for the interview.

When I left the teaching profession and entered the business world, I bought one suit, which I used for interviews. I eventually got a job in a company where I spent the next fifteen years. I moved about in the company and had several different jobs. The dress code at this company was extremely relaxed for everyday routine, but it was expected that a suit be worn for an interview. So I wore the same suit for the first three positions I held. After that, I started having children and could never fit into it again. I ended up getting rid of the suit I had worn a handful of times over the course of several years. It seemed like such a waste!

—HSQ

If you think you might be headed for such a situation, you may want to borrow an outfit from a close friend or relative or perhaps purchase just a jacket to formalize an existing outfit. For women, investing in a nice scarf to dress up an outfit may be all that's necessary to add "class" to your look. If you don't feel competent with scarves, go to an exclusive store and ask for assistance from the sales staff. They are usually quite knowledgeable and helpful with accessories. You don't *have* to purchase something there, but use the advice offered.

It's important to feel comfortable with how you've decided to dress for the interview. Don't let it "unsettle" you if you are dressed up more than the interviewer. That's common and perfectly acceptable. Everyone you meet will know you are interviewing; at this point, you aren't expected to be "one of them." Generally speaking, you'll want to be neat, uncluttered, and conservative. This can be attained with careful spending.

Costs of Taking a Job—Evaluating an Offer

As you plan to accept a potential job, be sure to recognize and factor in what it may cost you to take the position.

Calculate new child care expenses (see Chapter 7) if your child care needs will change. You may decide to look for child care near your new employer. If an offer arrives, you'll have to investigate your options quickly so you can accurately estimate this expense before you accept.

Do you have to purchase a new wardrobe if you take the job? If so, it's time to window-shop and plan your clothes purchases as accurately as you can. Minimize what you start with; plan on using separates to mix and match. Once a paycheck comes with regularity, you can slowly add to your wardrobe, but right now, you're trying to minimize up-front out-of-pocket expenditures. As you buy clothes, avoid ones that need dry cleaning if at all possible.

My last full-time job demanded that I be dressed in a suit, good blouse, and high heels. Since I was genetically endowed with the *no grace* gene, I spilled things on my outfit with regularity. I think I must have spent more on dry cleaning each month than lots of people make! I was never able to find suits that didn't require dry cleaning, but I quickly discovered that polyester blouses, instead of silk, saved me at least some cleaning costs.

—HSQ

You'll need to factor in transportation costs. Go back and review Chapter 8 to help you keep your initial costs down. Hopefully, you can get creative, use alternative transportation methods, and avoid buying an additional car, at least for a while. If a car is necessary, you'll need to estimate all the costs involved with it—loan or lease payments, gasoline, parking, etc.—on a per-month basis.

Relocation expenses are, by far, the most significant expense you may have. Negotiate this with the employer before you accept a job that necessitates a move to a new home. Beware of an employer that won't pay for the majority of the moving expenses. It might be indicative of their commitment to you. Don't, however, expect the new employer to bail you out if your current home won't sell in a poor market. That, unfortunately, is *your* problem.

If you are considering a move to another state, be sure to investigate what the cost of living is there. What are the housing prices? Are the public schools acceptable, or will you have to consider private schools for your children? What is the quality of the state universities? (Even if your children are young now, anticipating future needs is very important.) Be sure to find out about the state income and property tax burdens in the area you are considering.

We knew a senior executive from a prestigious research institute in the East who accepted a job offer in the San Francisco Bay Area without thoroughly exploring these issues. He was shocked to the core when he ended up having to buy a house that cost twice as much when it was half the size of his old one. It didn't even have a basement! On the other hand, when we moved from the Bay Area to upstate New York, we were able to buy a large "dream" house. However, we had greatly underestimated the taxes in the state. Property taxes are almost three times what we had paid in California!

—HSQ

You *have* to know these things before you can adequately evaluate a job offer that requires a significant relocation. By all means, build time into the interview trip to meet with a local real estate agent. Call a national chain in your hometown and ask them to locate an agent for you where you are going. (You don't have to let the potential employer know you are investigating this aspect of the offer.) It doesn't cost you anything to look around, and it will provide an opportunity to get a great deal of local information.

Once you think you have a fair idea of all the costs involved, you should put together a monthly budget plan that you would use if you accept this job. Go back and review the many different line items in the typical American budget as listed in Chapter 2. Look again at the job offer from a purely financial point of view. Does it make sense from a monetary perspective?

If it seems to, then start considering the other factors. Look carefully at the benefits package and make sure it's what you need. Is this a job you want, or are you considering it because nothing else has come along? Are there any guarantees about the longevity of your employment?

If there are substantial risks involved, it's probably a bad idea to consider relocating the family right away. You should think seriously about living apart for a while until you make sure it's going to work out. To keep costs down, you might be able to rent a room in someone's home as opposed to setting up an entire apartment. If you can make it work financially, and the emotional burden on you and your family is not too great, taking a job in another city may serve as an option to provide an income while you continue to look for a more appealing opportunity.

Starting Your Own Business

America is the land of opportunity. One of the dominant images in our culture is the entrepreneur or tycoon who started out with nothing and attained fabulous riches. For many, starting your own business and being your own boss is a very alluring concept. For those who have been "burned" in the corporate world, the idea of making it on your own, with your success determined by your own skill and effort rather than by the whims of those "higher up," seems especially attractive. Indeed, for many, starting a business can be a realistic and successful way to go. However, the risks are very high, and you should not pursue this path unless you've considered it before your downsizing situation and/or have *really* done your homework since.

Go to the library and check out a few books about starting your own business. (Every library has lots of books on this popular subject!) Look for at least one that provides questions to help you determine if your personality and aptitudes would make you a likely candidate to succeed with your own business.

When I first moved East, I had no job at all. For years, I had dreamed of opening my own coffee shop and I thought that perhaps now I could do it. When I began to research what was involved, I came across a book, *Starting Up Your Own Business: Expert Advice from the U.S. Small Business Administration* compiled by Dr. G. Howard Poteet, that provided a questionnaire for me to check my ability to be a sole business owner. I failed, miserably, to match the profile of the typical entrepreneur. Of course, I ignored that. The book couldn't possibly be accurate! I read further. Other books provided similar questions to test my suitability. I continued to come up with a mismatch. Although I work independently quite well, I lack many of the skills and personality traits that successful business owners generally have. I don't think I would be patient with employees, and I'm not sure I could hire people I could trust. I also have neither the interest nor the expertise to maintain the books for a business. Although I didn't want to admit it, I finally became convinced that unless I had a partner to compensate for skills I lack, I was simply setting myself up for a fall—not to mention a serious financial failure. I put the dream aside for the time being and returned to my former line of work.

—HSQ

Of course, a sole proprietorship is not the only opportunity available. There are different kinds of businesses: consulting, independent partnerships, and franchises. Each has different start-up costs and risks associated with them. Read carefully about each of them to see if you "fit."

Franchises have tempted many people who have been laid off, especially those receiving generous severance benefits. Franchises are not cheap, and the more established the name, the higher the cost to get in. Basically, franchisees pay a set amount—which could range from a few thousand to a few hundred thousand dollars—for the name and a standardized product. Rent, utilities, equipment, and labor costs are on top of the franchise fee, and franchisees often pay a percentage of their gross sales to the franchise owner as well.

Franchises may look like an easy path to a business, but there are two pitfalls for those who do not do their homework. You may go broke, or the franchise may go broke, leaving you high and dry. Some unscrupulous franchises sell licenses for locations that are too close together, and you may find yourself chasing the same customers as the guy a half a mile away.

Paul looked forward to retiring from the military after his twenty years of service, but he knew he would have to look for another career; his pension wouldn't cover the living expenses for his wife, himself, and their two children in New York City. A franchise of indoor play spaces for children had just spread to their area, though not to New York City at that time. He figured this franchise would be a good bet; city kids never had enough places to play, especially in the long, cold winter months. Business plan in hand, the Gulf War veteran approached several banks for a loan. All turned him down.

He confided his frustrations to a friend, who suggested he go into law instead. Paul had one year of college left, and then he'd have three years of law school until he got his degree—all the while, still having to support his family. But when he started looking at the numbers, law school became more and more attractive. He was eligi-

ble for a number of grants and federally guaranteed loans, which made the cost of four years of schooling significantly lower than the franchise fee alone. Since most new businesses don't earn enough to support their owners for several years, he realized he wasn't worse off going to school, where he could qualify for loans and possibly find well-paying summer jobs.

Today, Paul is in his last year of law school. He's interned at major law firms and is confident of getting a good job when he graduates. And the franchise? It recently declared bankruptcy. Hundreds of franchisees lost their investments; others are barely hanging on.

Be careful! Avoid the impulse to sink your life savings into a business unless you have spent a long time researching it, have written a business plan approved by a bank, and know you have expertise in this area that would give you a distinct advantage. In addition to the library, you should check with the Small Business Administration. It provides an information packet for prospective entrepreneurs, and you can discuss your plans with retired executives who volunteer through a Small Business Administration program called SCORE (Service Corps of Retired Executives). Be wary of any opportunity that demands you spend a lot in start-up costs. Distributorships will do this. You may never break even, let alone realize a profit. Watch out also for "business opportunities" that are advertised in the newspaper or for which you get a cold call over the phone. People in search of meaningful employment and/or income opportunities often become the victims of scams. You would be far smarter to start small with something you have researched well, to work "on the side," and to see if your talents are what you think they are.

Chapter 11

Insurance
Could You, Should You, Downsize?

This downsizing situation has resulted in stress. The stress has made you ill. Even on days when you're feeling halfway decent, the stress can cause distractibility. You find yourself driving along, thinking about your problems, and realize you can't even remember the last ten miles you drove. You try to concentrate on driving for a while, but soon your mind is wandering again. All of a sudden, you rear-end a Lexus with your BMW. Your neck is already hurting as you climb out of the car to see the extent of the damage. Maybe this *wasn't* a good time to have canceled your medical and car insurance. . . .

Your current financial crisis may be temporary or permanent. At this time, it's hard to tell. Insurance exists to cover you for losses you cannot afford to cover on your own. This principle remains the same as you downsize. Yes, you have less money to pay for insurance, but at the same time, you can afford fewer losses as well. What are the strategies for coping with this dilemma? How can you save money but still provide the protection your family needs? These are the topics discussed in this chapter.

Medical Insurance

Nowadays, there are two general types of medical insurance plans: fee-for-service plans and managed care plans.

Fee-for-service plans can vary, but in the most common type, you pay a deductible, then anything beyond that you split with the insurance company—usually you pay 20 percent and insurance pays 80 percent. With this kind of insurance, you can choose any doctor, hospital, or specialist you want. However, your out-of-pocket costs are high. Many preventive things are not covered (like checkups and immunizations), and usually prescriptions aren't either. These plans are costly for employers and are therefore not as widely available as they used to be, even a few years ago.

Managed care plans include HMOs (health maintenance organizations), PPOs (preferred provider organizations), and POSs (point of service) plans.

In an HMO, you get all your medical care from a network of doctors, hospitals, and specialists working with the HMO. You choose a primary care physician who decides which hospital and specialists you will use. HMOs cover (and stress the importance of) preventive care. For services and prescriptions, you pay a small co-payment, and there is virtually no paperwork for you.

A PPO or POS functions much like an HMO. However, you *do* have the option of going to out-of-network caregivers. When you use services outside the network, you meet a deductible, and then the insurance company and you split the rest (usually 80/20).

When you are assessing the needs for your family in this area, you'll need to think about how often your family gets sick. Is there anyone with a continuing condition (like diabetes or asthma) which requires constant attention and, even with fastidious care, can still end up with expensive complications? What are the ongoing prescription needs in the household? Is psychiatric counseling necessary? Are your children cavity-prone and therefore require constant dental attention?

I specialized in high-risk pregnancies and premature babies, and then produced children with severe asthma. When the kids were little, they saw doctors several times a month, and every pharmacist we've ever used has known me on a first-name basis almost immediately. Understanding different medical plans has always been of major importance in our family!

—HSQ

You need to know about the quality of care that your local managed care plans provide. This is best attained by talking to many people in your community who utilize doctors extensively. Generally, any doctor should be able to easily diagnose an ear infection in a young child or athlete's foot in an adult. You want to find people who have had a challenging disease to diagnose—how did the managed care plan handle the situation? How long did it take to get referred to a specialist? Was the specialist and/or hospital able to deal swiftly and correctly with the problem? Different managed care plans will carry a local reputation, and reputations are generally based in truth.

Managed care plans are less costly than fee-for-service plans. So if you feel comfortable with the network of doctors used by the managed care plan, you can save substantial amounts by changing in that direction. On the other hand, if choosing your own doctors (and timetable for seeing them) is a major priority, then you'll need to use a fee-for-service plan. You can still try to save money this way, by taking out higher deductibles. Also, check to see if your coinsurance ratio is as high as is allowed. The more you pay for medical care each doctor's visit, the less you'll pay in monthly insurance payments. Another way to reduce these costs is to move to a bare-bones policy that doesn't cover dental, prescriptions, immunizations, psychotherapy, cosmetic surgery, physical therapy, etc. If you and your family are very healthy and rarely see a doctor, you can use such a fee-for-service plan and save a great deal. It is not, however, applicable to everyone.

A word to the wise: The downsizing situation you have experienced has produced an incomprehensible amount of grief and stress. Stress is major contributor to illness, both physical and mental. Conditions can take months to show up and many more months to treat and resolve. The stress-related illness can hit *any* member of the family, maybe several. Our advice is *not* to cut much from your medical insurance at this time.

In the couple of months that followed my husband's layoff, we all experienced multiple illnesses. (It was a lot, even for our family that always seems sick!) My husband

got kidney stones. I had pneumonia three times, once requiring hospitalization. My son was absent from school
fourteen days for sickness in seventh grade, more than all
his other years combined. My daughter had a higher than
normal number of cases of bronchitis and strep throat.
Were they related to stress? Who knows? The fact remains we had a greater incidence of medical problems.
We were very grateful for COBRA.

—HSQ

COBRA stands for Comprehensive Omnibus Budget Reconcilia-
tion Act of 1986. It requires companies with more than twenty employees to continue to provide group health insurance for up to
eighteen months for terminated employees. For widows, divorced or
separated spouses, and dependents of active employees, the coverage
is up to three years. The cost is up to 102 percent of what the company paid for the employee insurance. At the end of the eighteen
months (or three years), you have to purchase your own insurance if
you don't have an employer with benefits by that time. COBRA is designed to protect you after an initial shock and give you time to "shop
around" for medical insurance. If you have questions about utilizing
COBRA, contact the employer who last provided you with medical
coverage. A recently enacted law also allows you to use money from
your IRA, without incurring any penalties, to purchase medical insurance if you are unemployed.

What do you do if your medical insurance has run out and you
aren't eligible for COBRA? Check with alumni or professional organizations to see if group rates exist that you can use. If you can't afford even an HMO, you will have to assume the additional risk of
getting ill and having to pay as you go. If you are in this situation (or
if you have taken on a high deductible or high co-payments in order
to obtain a cheaper plan), the first thing you should do is take care of
yourself and your family to avoid costly medical procedures. If you've
been lax in taking care of yourself in the past, now is the time to
change your ways. For instance, if you brush and floss your teeth reg-

ularly, you probably won't need expensive dental work. Make sure your kids take care of their teeth too, and cut back on sugary snacks. Not only should the kids wear a helmet when they ride their bikes, you should wear one too. Depending on the ages and situation of your children (are they realistically "in the running" for an athletic scholarship?) and the availability of individual insurance for them through your school district, you might want to pull them out of sports, such as football, that carry a high risk of injury. All the members of your family—except young children—should also consider getting flu shots each fall, particularly if anyone has asthma or other health problems, or if you can't afford to miss work. Many public health departments offer flu shots for a nominal fee. You can find other tips on basic preventive care in any medical reference book.

If someone *does* get sick, you need to know how to decide if you can take care of the problem at home, or if professional attention is needed. You will probably have had a relationship with doctors in the past, so you might be able to use advice over the phone from nurses in the office to help you diagnose the severity of an illness. (Unless you tell them, they shouldn't know you don't have insurance.) It would be useful to have at least one good reference book on self-diagnosis of medical problems. But as we mentioned earlier, health care is no place to skimp. (Most families have Dr. Spock's book on baby care, and others like it exist for adults as well.) If you can't buy a book, use ones from the library. A particularly useful book for emergency treatment of illnesses and injuries is *Take Care of Yourself,* by Donald M. Vickery, M.D., and James F. Fries, M.D. This best-selling book offers illustrations, diagrams, and text to help readers understand their symptoms and determine whether they can treat the symptoms at home or should see a doctor. *Take Care of Yourself* covers emergencies and items essential to a home pharmacy. While we do not recommend ignoring a serious problem (or a minor problem that could become serious), this book can help you to make more informed decisions.

Private physicians probably won't treat you without medical insurance unless you pay up front. Since they are very expensive, you might do better looking for a hospital that also runs an out-patient clinic. These clinics are used to people with limited financial resources, and they can actually help you tap into local, state, or federal assistance for which you may qualify. Some states, such as New York, have a subsidized program for uninsured children. If you meet the income qualifications, your children can receive health care free, or at a nominal charge. Contact your local Department of Social Services for more information. If you are in severely dire straits, particularly if you're a single parent, you may also qualify for free health care through Medicaid (again, contact your Department of Social Services). Your local public health department also provides children's vaccinations and sometimes basic checkups for free. Call the public health office to see what services are available and if there are any free clinics scheduled in your area.

A truly acute emergency means you need a hospital that will care for you without insurance. Some states demand that any hospital treat an acutely ill or injured person without first ascertaining whether they can pay for it; other states don't have such generous guarantees. Before you have an emergency in the family, look around and find out which facility you can count on if you need an emergency room. "Not-for-profit" hospitals are more apt to accept people without insurance, but even "for-profit" hospitals might. If a hospital has obtained federal loans for building, the loan often comes with a provision to provide a certain amount of charitable care. City, county, and state facilities are usually under obligation to take anyone, no matter what the circumstances, but not all places have such a facility close at hand. If you live in an area without such hospitals, look for a facility that runs an out-patient clinic. Chances are, that's a hospital that would take you, and a simple phone call should confirm that fact. By all means, think this through *before* you need to react in an emergency situation.

Medical care costs are shooting out of control in this country. Unfortunately, you will bear the brunt of it if you have a dire emergency without any medical insurance. If this is your situation, this is one place where it's appropriate to use a credit card.

Auto Insurance

Auto insurance policies have many different line items, each one re-quiring choices on your part. States differ, too, in certain require-ments. If you haven't done so recently, pull out your policy and call your agent to discuss each item individually in an attempt to reduce your cost. Once you have determined what you must have, by law, and what minimum coverage you think you can afford to carry, call several other insurance companies and make sure you've got the best deal around. Most people rarely think about their car insurance un-less they buy a new vehicle or have an accident, so this could be a worthwhile exercise.

Most policies contain Bodily Injury, Property Damage, Unin-sured/Underinsured Motorist, Medical Payments, No-Fault (or Personal Injury Protection), Collision, and Comprehensive line items.

Bodily Injury liability covers the cost of medical expenses and legal fees if you're at fault and you injure or kill someone. Some states permit you to carry this at very low limits that don't adequately reflect health care costs. If you drop your limit too low, you risk being sued to bankruptcy.

Property Damage liability covers the cost of someone else's property if you're at fault (or if you've given permission to someone to drive your car). If you drop this to its lowest level, pray you don't hit a Ferrari!

Uninsured or Underinsured Motorist coverage pays your expenses if the other party can't. It also covers you if you are injured while riding in someone else's car or if a car hits you while you're walking or biking. This isn't required in all states, so it might be optional on your policy. If your state requires insurance in order to drive and if the uninsured accident incidents are low where you live and drive, then you might consider dropping this line item in order to reduce your premium.

Medical Payments coverage pays the medical costs of anyone hurt in your car regardless of whose fault it is. If your health insurance is good, you might consider dropping this to save some money. But if you do, you'd better stop driving the soccer team to the field because then your insurance won't cover people beyond your immediate family.

No-fault, or Personal Injury Protection, is required in states with no-fault insurance programs. It is a broad-based coverage to pay for medical bills, lost wages, funeral bills, and personal care payments. In states that have this, it replaces all the liability line items and you have limited ability to adjust it.

Collision Coverage pays for your car damage when you are at fault or if you're a victim of hit-and-run. The cost of this line item will depend on the year, make, and model of your car. (The newest and most expensive cars cost the most.) If you own your car outright, this is usually optional. If you're still paying on a loan, there's a good chance you'll be required to carry this. The higher the deductible you carry, the lower the premium will be. Check to see what flexibility you have. On an old car, you could drop this altogether.

Comprehensive coverage covers oddities like fire, hail, falling trees, breaking glass, theft, and vandalism. Costs will vary by where you live, or perhaps where you drive. Like Collision, lenders generally demand you carry it. If you own your car, if your car is old, and/or if you habitually keep it in a garage, you could drop it or at least increase the deductible significantly in order to save money on your premiums.

There are a couple of other things you can do to keep your car insurance low besides taking more risk and increasing your deductibles. Having a good driving record keeps your rates low. Taking a defensive driving course, using the same insurance carrier for auto and home, being a nonsmoker or a student with good grades, and reducing or eliminating insurance on vehicles not being used can also lower costs.

Homeowners Insurance

Homeowners insurance is designed to rebuild your home if it's destroyed. Generally, you are supposed to carry enough insurance for

100 percent of the home's replacement value, but you must cover at least 80 percent while you have a mortgage. Many policies cover the actual cash value of the property (cost minus depreciation). This is different from replacement cost coverage. You should check your policy and make sure that what you have is what you really want.

The different types of homeowners policies are named HO1, HO2, HO3, etc. HO1 protects you against eleven common calamities (like fire, lightning, hail, smoke, theft, etc.). HO2 protects you against seventeen. HO3 is the most common type and doesn't try to name all the possible calamities; instead, it carefully enumerates what it *doesn't* cover (like flood, earthquake, termites, landslides, tidal waves, nuclear accidents, etc.). HO3 also protects your home contents against the common seventeen. HO4 is for renters. HO6 is for condo owners, and there are others with slight variations.

Besides the normal homeowners insurance, if you own property of significant value (paintings, jewelry, fur, antiques, etc.), you probably carry additional insurance for them in the form of riders or floaters to the policy.

As long as your home holds its market value, there isn't much you can do to reduce the policy expense. Check with your carrier to see if you can lower costs by having your vehicles and home insured by the same company. Will the installation of smoke alarms, dead bolts, or a theft alarm system reduce the premium? (Smoke alarms and dead bolts don't cost much and you might come out ahead by installing them. Most burglar alarm systems cost too much to be a viable option at this time.) Taking higher deductibles may very well be the only thing you can quickly and easily do to reduce your cost. If you sell collectibles to raise needed cash, be sure to remember to drop the additional insurance you had covering them.

Life Insurance

Whereas your home insurance needs tend to stay constant with time, life insurance needs change dramatically as you age, raise your family, and eventually retire. This policy should be reviewed every few years to make sure it's adequate to your needs. Life insurance is meant to protect against the loss of income from the death of the insured person and the resulting financial burden of the mortgage, loans, children's education, burial costs, and estate taxes. Some people carry separate mortgage insurance to supplement the life insurance. Mortgage insurance is generally much more expensive than life insurance. It would be wiser to increase your life insurance policy to cover this eventuality if this is a concern to you.

When trying to determine your needs in this area, think about how much money is needed to cover the bills if you die. Looking at it like that, it's easy to see that children don't need life insurance and a retired person only needs enough to cover debts and burial costs. Single persons without dependents likewise need very little. The greatest needs exist with young and middle-aged families.

There are two general types of life insurance: term and permanent. Term life insurance is the least expensive. In its simplest form, term insurance is renewed every year and you have to meet minimum health requirements at each renewal. Costs can increase with age and with long-term health problems. People who can qualify for this kind of insurance generally choose it because they want the less expensive option and prefer not to have an investment option attached to their insurance plan (as is the case with permanent insurance).

Some term policies do *not* have to be renewed yearly, nor require constant health checkups. You can purchase a limited number of years with consistent payments and if your health changes, it does not affect your coverage. These policies, though, still don't have any "cash value investment" associated with them.

Permanent life insurance (whole life, universal life, modified life, limited payment life, etc.) *does* have an investment aspect. It is a long-term contract with a company. You pay over many years and the insurance company covers you regardless of future health changes. The premiums with permanent life insurance are more expensive than term; they can stay the same or sometimes decrease with time. This kind of insurance pays out a death benefit, but it is also an investment account because it builds up a significant cash value over time with tax-free interest (unless you withdraw it).

If you have this kind of insurance, you might be tempted at this point to convert it to term for the savings on your premiums. However, read the fine print carefully. Many permanent policies charge significant penalties for such a conversion and you might not gain anything. It may be more advantageous to investigate loan possibilities against the cash value in your policy or an outright cash withdrawal from the account.

Disability Insurance

This is a frequently ignored insurance and one you probably would be willing to drop to save money while you are between employers. However, people aged thirty-five to sixty-five are six times more likely to be disabled than to die. If you end up starting your own business, this insurance is worth remembering.

Disability insurance is generally paid for by employers. The cost is based on age, sex, smoking habits, and occupation. For highly paid professionals, there is often a ceiling. To purchase your own, bear in mind that the longer you wait for benefits to begin, the lower the cost. Policies exist that start out low in price and increase as you get older, and plans that don't cover your entire life cost less than ones that do. If *you* have paid for this insurance (not a company), then benefits paid out to you are tax-free.

Conclusion

Insurance exists to protect you from financial losses you cannot afford to cover on your own. This principle becomes even more significant as you downsize because you have far less discretionary income to bail you out of a bad situation. You may have to pick and choose carefully where your insurance dollars will go right now. Accepting more risk in some areas may be a necessity even though it makes you quite uncomfortable. If you have to take higher risks temporarily because you are struggling to make ends meet, remember to readjust these later as you settle into whatever permanent condition you eventually attain. Over time, as you exchange your expensive home and cars with much more affordable ones, your premiums will more appropriately match your income, making monthly payments a lot more reasonable.

Chapter 12

Fixed Debt
Credit Cards, Loans, Taxes, Housing

$\mathcal{H}$ow deeply you were in debt before your income loss is critically important. In fact, this is what will probably make or break you. If you were previously living at or near the limit of your indebtedness, you have very little to cushion you now. Hopefully, even if you have a great deal of fixed debt, you've paid your bills on time and kept up a good credit rating. That helps—perhaps more than you think.

This chapter looks at the limited ways you can reduce your debt liabilities temporarily. We first look at some general guidelines for dealing with creditors. Credit card usage needs to cease. It may be possible to reduce loans, taxes, or rent. For most people, however, the largest fixed debt is the monthly mortgage. One has to be realistic. If, despite all your belt-tightening efforts, it is still impossible to meet the mortgage payment, then you will have to sell the house. How do you prepare a house for sale on a shoestring budget? How do you decide where to live next?

Dealing with Creditors in General

Ignoring a bill that needs to be paid is a lousy idea. If you know you can't meet an obligation, the sooner you contact the company you owe, the better. The general advice in this circumstance is to write a letter rather than make a phone call. A letter has the best chance of ending up on the proper desk whereas on the phone you may be passed around aimlessly and never speak to the person who has real authority to make decisions. A letter also serves as tangible (and often legal) proof that you have taken responsibility for your situation and are seeking a solution. The same methodology is suggested for dealing with *any* of your bills, from utility bills to credit cards to the mortgage company.

In the letter, you need to explain your situation briefly and matter-of-factly. End with the fact that you can't pay the creditor right now, or can't pay in full. Offer suggestions for dealing with the payments— what you *can* pay and *when*. If possible, explain your general plan for getting yourself financially stable again. For instance, "I expect to be working full time again in six months . . ." or, "The real estate agent says it should take four to eight months to sell the house, after which . . ." Your tone should reflect your genuine concern and willingness to discuss and negotiate an equitable payment schedule.

Writing such a proactive letter demonstrates several important things. You are mature, responsible, understand you have a commitment, and plan to live up to it as soon as possible. You care about your credit rating. You are a solid citizen, not a deadbeat. It's important to deal with this issue right away, before you start to miss payments. Your account will be turned over to a collection agency by the time you are three or four months overdue. You have *no* ability to negotiate other payment terms once your bill is in the hands of a collection agency.

If you want to talk terms over the phone, include that in your letter. If you do so, it's still wise to reiterate any agreement reached by phone in a subsequent letter so no misunderstandings exist on either side.

By taking this approach, you stand a very good chance of getting the reprieve you need from the company. They are interested in getting paid—better late than never. If you have several companies with which you are negotiating, be sure to plan out correctly what you can afford to pay. Trying to *re*-negotiate may not be so successful!

If you have a lot of loans and credit card bills, you will want to investigate various debt consolidation plans. Many different types of financial institutions offer these, but rates and terms vary tremendously. Simply put, a debt consolidation scheme puts all your obligations together and gives you a loan to cover them. You pay off the individual debts and pay a lower monthly fee on your new loan. Of course, your interest will be high, and your term will be long. If you don't have much or any income, getting loans will not be easy.

Whether or not you seek debt consolidation, you should meet with a counselor from your local or regional Consumer Credit Counseling Service (CCCS) as soon as possible. The CCCS is a free service available to anyone who has problems with excessive debt. The CCCS counselor will discuss with you your past spending habits and current indebtedness, show you how to budget, and help you to create a plan for paying off your debts and spending more sensibly in the future. Even if you haven't been a big spender in the past—if you've experienced a drastic loss of income or racked up huge medical bills, for example—the CCCS can help you with a strategy for paying off bills incurred due to circumstances beyond your control.

Though they lived two thousand miles apart and didn't know each other, Vicky and Chantal were two typical customers of the CCCS. Vicky and her husband came in on the verge of bankruptcy. Though he had a well-paying job, she was a compulsive spender. She took advantage of every credit card offer—from department stores, oil companies, and, of course, the major banks. Then she'd go shopping. When she liked an item of clothing, she didn't just buy one; she bought one in every color (and matching ones for their three girls!). She hid her purchases from her husband, and since she paid the bills, he never found out.

Things went from bad to worse for Vicky and her husband when he quit his job to start his own business. He knew nothing about her habits, but when he didn't bring in much income during the start-up phase of his business, the creditors came calling. Soon they realized her habits not only had destroyed the household budget but were also threatening the future of his start-up enterprise.

The CCCS saved their finances and their marriage. The counselor told Vicky to cut up her cards and close her accounts, and she worked out a repayment plan for the couple. *Through the counselor's intervention, Vicky joined a local group of Debtors and Spenders Anonymous. Vicky now has a job of her own, her husband's business is thriving, and they're almost debt-free.*

Chantal, on the other hand, encountered trouble through no fault of her own. *In college, she resisted the credit card offers, preferring to pay her own way—with cash. Shortly after graduation, however, she developed an allergic reaction to a friend's medication (which she had taken for an infection instead of going to the doctor) and then, two months later, contracted a nasty case of pneumonia. Since she had been unable to find full-time work after graduation, she was completely uninsured. The two visits to the hospital left her with close to $15,000 in bills, on top of her student loan.*

At this point, with no credit history and lots of debt, *Chantal couldn't even get a credit card, except for one with high up-front fees and astronomical interest. Friends urged her to forget about the medical bills and declare bankruptcy (which would have wiped out the medical bills but not the student loan). Being a responsible young woman, Chantal instead went to the CCCS.*

Her counselor helped her to approach the hospital and to negotiate a reduction in the bill and a repayment schedule. *On both counts she was successful. The hospital reduced her bill by more than half, and she was able to pay it off in two years.*

Credit Cards

Cancel most of them. The temptation to use them is overpowering for most people. Breaking this habit may be the hardest thing you do as you adjust to living on less. You should carry one for *(true!)* emergencies and identification purposes. But make no more charges on any cards unless it truly is a life-or-death situation.

As was mentioned in Chapter 2, the road to financial ruin and bankruptcy is paved with credit cards. Most people in our society blame the credit card companies for making cards so accessible today. However, it's not the company's fault if you misuse the cards, it's yours. *You* have to be responsible enough and mature enough to "just say no." You cannot see the cards as a means to tide you over until your situation corrects itself because you have no guarantee of how long that will be. You have to work out a better plan to deal with your overall situation and reserve that one credit card for the dire unforeseen emergency that may occur.

Many affluent people today are barraged with credit card offers. They arrive in the mail daily with preapproval and, often, very low interest rates for six months or so. Some of these cards will allow you to transfer the existing balance on another card to their card. This is something you could do right now to lower your monthly payment on the card. You can save substantially. Be careful, though. If you're late on a payment or run the balance too high, your interest rate may immediately revert to the normal high prevailing rate. Pay attention to how long you keep the card, too; for many of them, the interest rate jumps to 20 percent or more after only six months.

As you are debating which credit cards to keep and which to cancel, consider the annual fees charged as well as the interest rate. Some cards have hidden costs that cover things like life insurance on airline tickets or simply prestige. These aren't necessary anymore.

As was mentioned in the prior section, to deal with credit card payments that you can't afford, contact each company by letter to work out a more realistic payment schedule.

Loans

People generally have loans either for luxury items like boats or furniture or for essential items like a car or education. The two should be handled differently.

If you're strapped for funds, you have to try to deal with the burden of luxury items you bought in better times but can't afford now. What are your choices? You can surrender the item back to the lender for repossession. A repossessed item will be sold at an auction. If it's sold for less than the loan balance, you're still liable for the remaining balance. Alternatively, you can sell the asset yourself and pay off the debt and/or work out a deal with the lender for settling the remaining debt. Remember to keep discussions and negotiations in writing as much as possible when you deal with lenders.

You'll need to maintain the loans on essential items. Keep them as "bare bones" as possible (an economical car, the minimum possible for an education, etc.). Try to work out a reduced payment plan with the lender. You could suggest partial payments or interest-only payments for six months as an alternative.

Taxes

Death and taxes, the two sure things in life, right? There are a lot of taxes to consider: local, state, and federal taxes, payroll taxes for Social Security, and Medicare, and property taxes. If your income has fallen substantially, so have your taxes, with the exception of your property taxes. But it's important that you are properly withheld. Check your withholding (W2) and make sure it's appropriate for the income you have now. If your or your spouse's employer withholds too much, you'll get a refund check when you file your return in the spring. But you need the money now. Keep in mind also that when the government holds your money, it doesn't pay you interest. (If you, on the other hand, owe the government back taxes, you will also have to pay interest!)

If you receive unemployment compensation, be aware of the fact that it is taxable. You are responsible for filing a quarterly payment for it.

Property taxes will stay the same. You'll have to anticipate this payment in your financial planning. This tax can be a significant burden when your income has dropped. It's one more incentive to consider selling your expensive home.

If you owe income taxes, because you are self-employed, have income from other sources besides employment income (royalties, income from investments, spousal support, etc.), or are in arrears for any reason, you should contact the Internal Revenue Service or your state's tax office as soon as possible if you can't pay right now. Contact these offices in writing, just as you would any other creditor. You will probably be able to work out something with the I.R.S. or state tax officials—of course, you'll have to pay interest on your outstanding balance—but if you do nothing, you'll face serious legal problems. Keep good records of all letters and other correspondence with tax agencies.

If you owe property taxes, you may also get the local government to work out a repayment schedule with you. Local governments have the right to repossess your property to pay back taxes, but this creates trouble and expense for them.

Rent

If you are renting and can't afford it, move immediately to a more affordable place. Breaking a lease early usually involves stiff penalties, however. Read your lease and see how expensive it is to leave; it still may be worth it to get into cheaper housing as soon as possible. You may be able to sublet your place and avoid the penalties.

The landlord wants payment. If you know it's going to be a real challenge, contact him immediately (by letter) and explain your situation in an effort to work out some reasonable payment option. The advice here is not to say you've had a loss of income; instead indicate your funds have been directed to some other emergency. Landlords are the least likely to show leniency; you have to pick and choose your words carefully.

If your income is *really* low now, or if you lost your place due to a fire or other disaster, you may qualify for housing assistance. Rules and availability of assistance vary from state to state, and in most areas of the country (particularly urban areas), there are long waiting lists for public housing slots or housing subsidies. It doesn't cost anything to ask, though. Contact your local Department of Social Services and/or the local office of the U.S. Department of Housing and Urban Development for more information.

Mortgages

Many people maintain an escrow account that accompanies the mortgage. It can cover the cost of property taxes, hazard insurance, mortgage insurance, and other such items. Often, banks set these up to hold more money than you really need in them. If you have such an escrow account, you should look at it carefully now and make sure there's no extra "padding" in it that you could use at this time.

The largest and most important bill people pay every month is the mortgage. What happens if you can't pay it? The lending institution "forecloses" on your house, takes possession of it, and resells it. Foreclosures are troublesome and expensive, so the lending institution doesn't usually make money on it. Therefore, avoiding foreclosure is a high priority for them as well as you. This is particularly true for small banks. Less leniency can be expected if your mortgage is held by a huge mortgage company, but you at least have a chance to work something out.

Acting responsibly is the key to being taken seriously. This kind of negotiation is done on a case-by-case basis. In the long run, expect it to be financially painful for you—you are "bucking the system" and you'll end up paying a premium for the special attention and any dispensation you receive.

Some of the things that you might suggest are setting up partial payments or a repayment plan, obtaining a modified loan, or tapping into the equity of your home.

A partial payment is where you suggest paying something like half or a third of your normal mortgage payment for two or three months and then making up the difference in the following yearly payments. Repayment would be where you've already missed some payments and you agree to repay them by doubling up the next few months.

Modifying your loan might be possible. One modification that might be acceptable is to agree to skip "X" number of payments and extend the length of the loan to compensate for those months, plus penalties. You might be able to negotiate a modified loan that reduces your interest payment. Another possibility is to change to a subsidy loan in which the interest rate starts low and increases with time. A financial institution may charge you several hundred dollars just to consider these options, and your application may be turned down.

There are three ways to tap into the equity you have in your home: refinancing, taking a second mortgage, or getting a home equity loan.

Refinancing your mortgage is a possibility if your credit is good and if you have a job. (It's extremely doubtful that an unemployed individual will be approved for a refinancing package.) When you refinance, you take out an entirely new loan and pay off the old. If the house has significantly appreciated and/or if interest rates have gone down, refinancing can reduce your monthly payments substantially or convert equity in the home so it can be used to pay off other debts that carry a much higher interest rate.

If your current lender still holds the mortgage, you might be able to refinance without rewriting the loan. However, you will still have to pay for a home appraisal, legal fees, document preparation, and recording fees. If your mortgage was sold (to the secondary market), refinancing will entail going through another mortgage closing. This means closing costs (generally 2–3 percent of the loan), bank fees, and paying for an updated credit report, title search, and title insurance.

Another way to utilize the equity in your house is to take out a second mortgage. You'll receive a check for the full amount borrowed, minus fees. Expect the loan to have a term of five to fifteen years. Alternatively, you can apply for a home equity loan. Here, you receive the money in small amounts (by writing a check or using a credit card) and this loan can run many years as well. Both of these plans will also cost money. Up front, you'll be expected to pay 2–3 percent of the amount of the loan and there will be various fees as well as interest. However, the interest you pay on a second mortgage or home equity loan is usually only 1–2 percent higher than on your primary mortgage; thus, it's a far better bargain than the 18–21 percent interest on most credit cards. If you qualify for a second mortgage or home equity loan, a good strategy is to use them to pay off any credit card balances or loans at higher interest. Then, cut up the credit cards before you feel tempted to splurge again.

While you are trying to come up with money to meet your mortgage payment, you might consider renting out a portion of your home to bring in some needed cash. This may violate zoning laws in many suburban communities, so it would be best to check with your local city hall.

Keep, Sell, or Abandon

There is little as gut-wrenching as the idea of having to give up your home. You worked so hard to get it. You've invested so much time, effort, money, and love to make it distinctly yours. But no matter how much you have poured into your home, no matter how much you love your neighborhood, the unfortunate fact for many reading this book is, the time has come to seriously consider selling the house. It's hard enough to tread water; you don't need the ball-and-chain of a large mortgage attached to your ankle while you're struggling!

How do you make this decision? There is no easy answer. There are entirely too many factors involved for any person or any book to tell you how to make the correct decision. A bank wants you to borrow money from it. A real estate agent wants to sell a house. You can ask their advice, but their answer is prejudiced by their self-interest. However, both sources can give you important facts that will factor into your decision. The banker can tell you about the interest rates and the projected strength of the local economy. The real estate agent can tell you the current status of the local housing market and how much you can realistically expect to get for your house. Once you know this, you can calculate the equity in your house. The equity is the difference between the selling price (including the costs of selling your home) and the outstanding balance on your mortgage loan.

With this knowledge, there are some "rules of thumb" to help you decide if it makes sense to sell your house. You might want to take out a sheet of paper and make three columns: Parameters, Sell, Keep.

Under "Parameters," list the various factors that are discussed below. For each one, think about your situation and decide, based on this parameter alone, if the facts indicate you should "Sell" or "Keep" the house. Put a checkmark in the appropriate column. At the end, look at your sheet and see where most of the checkmarks lie. It's one way to help you make your decision. It's by no means foolproof. Only you know all the factors involved and can weigh them in terms of their importance.

You can start your sheet by considering purely financial parameters: carrying costs (mortgage, taxes, maintenance), the real estate market, interest rates, and the equity in your home.

Carrying costs include three major categories of expenses. The first is the burden of your mortgage payment. If your payment is a low percentage of your (current!) income (generally less than a quarter of your current pretax income) and/or you have a low outstanding balance, then your carrying costs are low. Under these circumstances, you should be able to keep the house. The second category of carrying costs is taxes, and the third is the amount you spend annually to maintain your house. If your property taxes are low or reasonable in relation to your current income and the house is in good repair, again, your carrying costs are low. These low costs indicate this is a house to keep, not to sell. On the other hand, if the mortgage is staggering to your current income, if you are having trouble keeping up with the tax bill, if the house needs repairs, or maintenance is high, these high carrying costs indicate it's time to sell.

The status of the local real estate market is crucially important. The housing market tends to follow the fate of the local economy. Are the major employers expanding or cutting back? If the market is sluggish, with declining home prices (because the economy is weak or declining), then selling your house is indicated. In fact, sell as quickly as possible before it loses any more value! On the other hand, an active real estate market with stable or rising home prices means you have a choice. Selling should be easy and you'll get a fair price for your home. But you don't *have* to sell because the house continues to appreciate the longer you hold on to it.

We sold our house in Wisconsin because we *had* to move; my husband had found a job in upstate New York. Although we didn't have to arrive until August, we put the house on the market in April so we'd be able to buy a new house right away. In a very hot market, we sold the house without an agent ten days after we put it on the market and, after expenses, we realized a 15 percent gain on a house we owned seven years.

Some friends who lived down the street were also moving to upstate New York at the same time. But they waited until July to sell, and they used an agent. Their house also sold within ten days. They had paid the same amount we had originally, but had only owned the house four years. Prices had gone up so much between April and July that their house fetched $20,000 more than ours, and after paying the agent's percentage and expenses, they realized a 30 percent gain.

—LML

The prevailing interest rates will influence your decision. If interest rates are stable or declining, keeping your house is indicated. This is particularly true if you have a variable interest rate loan. If interest rates have dropped at least two percentage points since you took out your mortgage, refinancing may be a great option. You can lower your monthly payment and pull out money to pay off other debts. On the other hand, unstable or rising interest rates point you in the direction of selling your house. This is because as interest rates rise, fewer people can afford to borrow to buy your house. Demand for your house decreases, and your only alternative is to lower your selling price. Alternatively, if you can offer an assumable mortgage at an older low rate at the same time as prevailing interest rates are rising, your house immediately becomes one of the more attractive prospects on the market.

The equity in your home is also important. If the equity is high, you probably want to keep your home. As was mentioned earlier, there are several ways to use home equity to retire debt and tide you over until your situation improves. If the equity is low, there is little help available from this source, and selling your home may be the best way to raise cash and/or get out from under your mortgage.

The extreme case regarding equity is when the house isn't worth enough on the market to pay off the outstanding mortgage balance. This occurs in communities that overbuild and/or the local economy collapses when the primary employer in town closes down permanently. The market falls, and you're left holding a house that can't pay for itself (even if you can find a buyer). This is a situation where abandoning the house altogether may be an option. There are a couple of things to note, however, if you are contemplating such a foreclosure. It's a severe mark on your credit rating and may make it virtually impossible to get a reasonable mortgage again. Also, states differ on laws governing what assets mortgage lenders can go after in their attempt to have you repay the balance. Some states protect you by allowing lenders to take only the house and no other personal property; other states don't. Be sure to investigate what laws are in effect in your area.

If you don't want the credit stigma of a foreclosure, you might want to try and negotiate a "short sale" with your mortgage lender. An example illustrates this best. Assume you have a mortgage of $175,000, but the house is now worth only $100,000. You offer to pay the bank $25,000 and return the house to them. The bank loses $50,000 in this deal. But if you foreclose, the bank will have lost $75,000. From the bank's perspective, a short sale is better than nothing at all. Of course, the difficulty here is for you to come up with a significant amount of cash right now. However, it may be a possibility for some.

We found ourselves in a situation in which the carrying costs were very high, the local real estate market was sluggish and housing prices were falling rapidly, the interest rates were unstable, and we had virtually no equity in the house. All factors pointed to our selling the house and taking at least a $50,000 loss. The house, however, would take a long time to sell because it's an upscale contemporary style in an area where traditional homes are more popular. We were faced with having to come up with the mortgage payments for a long time.

—HSQ

As you are filling in parameters on your sheet of paper, you now need to consider your personal financial situation. How much money in savings do you have that you can cash out to help pay the mortgage each month? Is the house worth depleting your savings for? If you have some savings, then you may be able to keep the house for a while. If you don't have much, it indicates a sale.

What is the level of your fixed debt? If you are burdened under credit card purchases and loans with little savings to draw on, you'll probably need to sell. Otherwise, you may be able to keep the house for a while.

If you've been laid off, can you realistically find employment in your area? If the chances are low, then it indicates a sale and relocation. (Of course, due to Murphy's law, the week after you sell your house, you'll get a local offer!) How does your spouse's job factor into all of this? Is it transferable? Do you need to stay close by to preserve your spouse's income?

One last financial parameter needs to be considered—the capital gains tax you'll have to pay within two years if you sell an expensive home and buy a much cheaper one or don't buy one at all. The capital gains tax may be as much as 28 percent, depending on your income. (If your income has dropped substantially, your tax burden may be lower too.) You may not be able to avoid it, but you certainly don't want to be unprepared for it! The calculation is fairly complex; you should get the appropriate forms from the I.R.S. so you can calculate it accurately. Then if you sell, set aside the amount you need to pay this bill and don't consider it part of the earnings on the sale. Put the money in an interest bearing account or a CD if you know when the bill will be due.

After these financial parameters, you need to consider the personal and emotional parameters as you decide whether to keep or sell. If you move, do your children change schools? How would this affect them? Usually, the older they are, the more difficult the adjustment will be, both academically and socially. Are you tied to the area due to family, friends, neighbors, community, or religious involvements? List the other factors that you can think of that affect the overall decision. Open this exercise to family discussion to get all the different perspectives.

With all the factors listed, you get some direction on whether the parameters as a whole suggest selling or keeping your home. The most important aspect of this exercise is that you must be *painfully realistic* about everything. If you're unemployed, you don't know how long it will take to get another job. You never know how long it will take for a house to sell. These facts may mean that even your best-intentioned decision will backfire on you. You will have to make your decisions on a month-to-month basis, continually evaluating your financial situation as circumstances change or stagnate.

Preparing a House for Sale—Cheaply!

Any real estate agent will tell you that the most important thing you can do to ready your house for sale is to clean it. Cleaning takes effort and time, but luckily, very little money. Cleaning means getting rid of all clutter—it's time for a garage sale or charity giveaways. It means restoring order to all closets, garages, basements, and storage areas. Remove excess furniture from all rooms to make them appear larger. If you can't afford a storage rental stall, it's time to impose on family or friends and store the boxes and furniture at their place. Store rarely used kitchen gadgets so you have cabinet space to clear the countertops of things you use frequently. Empty countertops make the kitchen look spacious.

Cleaning also means washing everything: windows, walls, mini-blinds, floor corners, and carpets. Rent a carpet cleaner. Do all the work yourself. Pack away personal items like photos, memorabilia, and the kids' sports ribbons and trophies. After doing this, the walls will be full of nail holes. Fill them in and paint the walls.

Evaluate existing wallpaper critically. If it's in relatively good shape and is unobtrusive, repair any loose areas and lightly wash it to restore "newness." If it's a mess or likely not to have universal appeal, then it's best to pull it off, clean the walls, and paint them.

Painting isn't expensive and it brightens up the house better than anything else. Pick a light, neutral shade. It's actually the last step in cleaning, because it makes any room look fresh and inviting.

The outside of the house also has to be cleaned. Get rid of spider webs and insect nests. Trim all bushes, and clean out all flower beds. Edge the beds and grass. Mow the lawn. Get rid of all lawn clutter, just as you did house clutter. Put a major amount of effort in the front yard. If you can afford a few flowers, put them in at the entrance of the house, the sidewalk approach, or on the porch. You want the first impression to be a positive one, and that impression is reached before the door is ever opened.

These efforts to prepare the house cost very little but can make a huge difference in your ability to sell the house quickly and get the price you want.

Selling and Moving

Coming to grips, emotionally, with selling the house may be the hardest thing since the event that produced your loss of income. If there's been a long time between the two events, the separation from the house may likely produce the grief all over again. For the entire family, this will be the most tangible example of what downsizing means. Children who haven't been affected by much yet *will* feel this.

No matter how long you have to get used to the idea of selling your house, there's nothing like the initial shock of seeing the For Sale sign stuck in the front lawn. I knew that the real estate agent planned to put it up, but it did nothing to stop the sick feeling in the pit of my stomach when I saw it for the first time. Up to that point, it seemed so hypothetical. Now, it was very, very real.

—HSQ

For us, and especially for our son, who was three years old at the time, the hardest part about selling our house was when the new owners came to cut down the trees the day after the closing. (Because we had to wait until I graduated from library school to move, we rented the house back from the buyers for two months.) We lived on a heavily wooded lot that bordered a rarely used railroad spur. Two large evergreen trees stood on either side of the front door of the house. In an afternoon, the evergreens and most of the other trees were gone, and the house looked so bare. For years after that, our son talked about how "his" trees had been cut down.

—LML

A chapter of your life is ending and you have to turn the page and start a new one. Where do you live once you've sold the house? Your options probably include a smaller house, a rental house or part of a house, apartment, mobile home, or perhaps moving in with a relative. If you have an income that you can count on (albeit less than you had originally), then you may want to try to qualify for a mortgage on a small house, town house, or mobile home. If you are unemployed, you won't get a mortgage, so you'll need to consider renting or staying with relatives.

As you contemplate your next housing option, remember it's for an indefinite amount of time. Since you might be there longer than you anticipate now, choose as carefully as you can. You may be miserable, but you can't let that numb your common sense as you make this important decision.

Home ownership is often a critical priority for people. So if you can buy one, consider the size, condition, and type of house carefully. Even though the house is worth less than your old one, you still want something that is fundamentally sound, well built, and with resale potential. Regardless of whether you are buying or renting, location is important. Know what school district you're moving into and its general reputation. Don't ignore this if you don't have school-age children or if your children attend private school; it affects the value of your home in the long run. Look carefully at the condition of the house and yard. How difficult will it be for you to maintain this property? Consider the general amenities available nearby (playground, pool, etc.) as well as your potential neighbors. A move to an extremely low-income area may carry significant liabilities.

Joe and his wife had a new baby and wanted to rent a house instead of an apartment. With Joe having recently left his job and returned to school, the only thing they thought that they could rent was on the "wrong side of the tracks." The second time the house was broken into, they decided the crime risks were simply too great and moved again. This time, their house literally backed up to the railroad tracks. During commuting hours, the trains sounded and felt as though they were going through the living room, but the trade-off for personal safety made it worthwhile.

If you have always lived in a white-collar, professional neighborhood, there may be some differences if you move to a working-class area. Don't assume, though, that the differences will all be negative!

My parents were outraged when I moved to a racially mixed area while in graduate school in New Haven, Connecticut. In the two years I lived there, the apartment (the first floor of a house) was never broken into, nor was I personally threatened. On the contrary, I made many friends among the diverse residents of my closely knit block. I spent way too much time gossiping, cooking, and playing softball with my neighbors and not enough time studying. I still remember those years fondly.

—LML

What you're looking for is a place where you and your children can feel safe. As you adjust to a downsized lifestyle, the objective is to find a comfortable place where you no longer have to live "hand-to-mouth" but can enjoy a few luxuries, where you can plan for your kids' education and your own retirement, where you can still save a little every month, where you can maintain a good credit rating and have ample insurance. These objectives can be met in many different places and income levels. Your old neighborhood did not have an exclusive hold on them. It's crucial to keep this in mind.

I was concerned about how the children would react to our moving to a smaller and more affordable house. Our first serious house-hunting expedition substantiated my hunches about the kids' reactions. My eight-year-old daughter was completely open-minded about the transition; her teenage brother was highly opinionated, antagonistic, and disgusted with aspects of every house we saw. (I had assumed that youth and innocence would help out.) Personally, I was surprised by how nice several places were. Smaller, yes, but that meant fewer bathrooms to clean and less lawn to maintain, so the trade-offs weren't completely bad. The neighbors reflected pride in home ownership, so that made me feel more comfortable. I began to see that I could move there and eventually find happiness with the new home and neighborhood. It would be different, yes, but I tried to concentrate on the overall important things.

—HSQ

Chapter 13

Reassessing Your Financial Situation
Can You Climb Out of the Hole?

*W*hen your income plummeted, it's as if you fell into a deep financial hole. This book is designed to be a ladder giving you direction and a means to climb out. Many ideas and strategies have been suggested. You can look at the climb up the ladder as a time when you are "robbing Peter to pay Paul," a transitional time when you deal with the bills and at the same time work to establish a new, downsized lifestyle. Getting to the top of this financial hole occurs when the finances start to settle because you have found a new job, sold the house, and/or cut back enough in other areas.

Finally, you climb out of the hole altogether and get back on level ground. One of two things has happened to make this possible. Your former income has been restored, or you have established your lifestyle, permanently, in a far less expensive manner. Either way, you'll never be the same again. The scars will last; the fear of a repeat performance will hang on forever. It's crucially important to protect and increase your savings for the future.

This chapter explores this progression, beginning at "the bottom of the hole" and continuing until you are on "level ground" again. If you are at the bottom, you can read how to prioritize bills and use your assets to raise needed cash. If you have not managed to climb out of the hole, the "contingency thinking" ideas presented in Chapter 2 must now be acted upon. You may need to consider bankruptcy as an option.

As you start to climb out of the hole and reestablish financial stability, you may have debt repayment plans to consider. The money you borrowed to pay bills, the bills you didn't pay, and the plans you worked out with creditors will have to be addressed. You will be making huge adjustments at every stage. It's important to stay focused on the ultimate objectives that will help shape a positive attitude.

At the Bottom of the Hole

In Chapter 2, you were encouraged to look at how you used to spend money. This allowed you to see where you spent discretionary income that could now be cut, to point out your spending weaknesses and priorities, and to help you begin to formulate a budget for your short-term future. A target budget was supposed to be the end product of that endeavor. But this target budget was also supposed to be a starting point, a tool that could evolve as you read the book and began to implement some of the ideas and strategies suggested in order to save money. If you have started to implement these ideas, you should be realizing significant savings over your old ways.

But is it enough? Can you make ends meet without selling the house? If the answer is "No," then it's pretty clear what you have to do. You must sell the house and/or get more income. You can work on accomplishing both tasks simultaneously. Houses take a while to sell, and the final closing can take even longer. If you are currently unemployed and looking for work, employed at lower-than-desired pay, or in school for retraining, then you are hoping and planning for the picture to improve. You are counting on the fact that this will be a short-term situation and actively pursuing the means to increase your income. Unfortunately, you don't know how long "short-term" might be. If your current financial situation is, for all practical purposes, permanent, then at least you can make final plans regarding the extent of your downsizing.

Recent government statistics indicate that most down-sized executives, managers, and professionals are finding new jobs within six months, but the jobs pay, on average, 10 percent less than their old jobs. William's situation was pretty typical in this respect. A senior loan officer at a bank, he found himself out of work after a merger. He sent out résumés and after four months received an offer. The position represented a demotion in terms of position, responsibility, and pay; in fact, his new bank offered a salary 15 percent lower than his previous one. But since he had no other possibilities and didn't want to see his savings vanish while he pounded the pavement, he took the job. At this point, he could make final plans, knowing his modest downsizing was permanent. He and his wife sold their house, which had very high maintenance costs, and the family moved into the slightly smaller house nearby where her parents had resided before retiring to Arizona.

Betty faced a similar situation. As an executive at a large publishing house, she had made more than $100,000 a year but was forced to take early retirement after a restructuring. Faced with a long job search in her field, she dusted off her teaching credentials and almost immediately found a less stressful position as a school library media specialist. The career change cost her more than half her salary, and even though her husband's job remained, the couple had to cut back drastically. They sold their pricey Manhattan co-op and moved to their country home, near the school where she worked. Fortunately, her husband was able to telecommute, which made this move to a less expensive rural area possible.

You're at the "bottom of the hole" when you've accurately assessed your financial situation. It takes some time and a great deal of effort to research all that you need to in order to get an accurate picture. Be careful about letting it take too long. You can't afford to procrastinate. Depression and grief may seem insurmountable to you now, but you only hurt your family more by delaying actions that you know are inevitable in the long run. On the other hand, you don't want to jump to hasty conclusions. Be sure to devote enough time to understand thoroughly your financial position.

You may find yourself in the undesirable position of having to make important financial decisions for the first time. Perhaps your spouse always took care of this and now he or she is gone or disabled. Hiring an accountant may be a logical first step. Accountants generally work on an hourly basis, so be sure your initial phone contact makes the fee perfectly clear. An accountant can help you understand your overall worth, assess current tax liabilities, and put investments into perspective for you.

If you have investments, another individual who can help you evaluate your estate is a financial planner. A financial planner may have up-front fees, but more frequently makes his or her living from commissions on investments you make. If you don't have an income or only want to liquidate investments, you probably won't be well received by a financial planner. At this point, you may have to rely on knowledgeable friends and relatives for the information and advice you need.

Eventually though, you come to the point where you understand both your assets and liabilities and you know what you have to do. That's when you have to take a deep breath, take the bull by the horns, and start the uninviting task of climbing out of this hole. You'll have to juggle resources to make ends meet during this period of transition.

Robbing Peter to Pay Paul

You can prioritize your debts in terms of urgency to be paid. Generally speaking, the basic necessities top the list—housing (mortgage or rent), food, and utilities. After that comes child care, transportation, insurance, and your fixed debt (credit cards, loans, and taxes). The rest comes in last. Unfortunately, all are important and need payment. You should (literally) prioritize your own bills. Number them in the order of importance to pay each month.

In Chapter 2, the different types of savings that people have were briefly reviewed. These can also be put in order based on the penalties and difficulties involved in liquidating them to raise cash. Cash savings have no penalties and Certificates of Deposit have minimal ones. You'll suffer from the cost of sale by selling stocks and stock mutual funds; even more expensive are bonds and bond mutual funds. You'll also have capital gains taxes to deal with on these. Your worst penalties lie with liquidating annuities and other pension plans—401Ks, IRAs, Keoghs, and SEPs—before you reach retirement age. (The penalty tax on withdrawing pension plan funds early may be waived if you are paying for medical expenses.) If you don't have a choice and need to use these savings to keep the family going, choose wisely. List them in the order that you decide makes the most sense to liquidate and use.

Rather than deplete your savings and retirement (if these investments are increasing in value), you may choose to borrow money. Family members may be an option here. Do you have any inheritance due to come to you that you might talk the givers into bestowing early? Is there a cash value to your life insurance policy? This can either be recouped or borrowed against. In the last chapter, utilizing the equity in your home was discussed. Refinancing, a second mortgage, or a home equity loan are the three ways to do this. If you have certain investments with a brokerage firm, your account may be a source from which to borrow as well. If you've done your homework, you should have a pretty clear picture now of how much money you might be able to generate by borrowing from various sources.

If you had a lot of debt before your sudden income drop, you may not have much in the way of resources (savings, investments, or borrowing ability) to draw on now. If this is the case, you probably need budget and debt counseling. This is available, free of charge, by contacting Consumer Credit Counseling Service (CCCS). As described in the previous chapter, this is a nationwide, nonprofit organization that is regulated by the banking industry in your state and funded through voluntary, tax-deductible contributions from corporations and employers. Its goal is to prevent debtors from declaring bankruptcy. If someone declares bankruptcy, creditors can only expect to recoup cents on their dollar, and only after years of proceedings; thus, banks and other companies have an incentive to sponsor such a service. Counseling is free, and if you need to establish a debt repayment plan, a small monthly fee is charged based on what you can afford. Usually, debt repayment entails your paying CCCS and it, in turn, pays your creditors.

If you can, now is the time to sell things in the house to raise cash. Start with a garage sale. You'll probably be surprised by how much cash you can generate just by getting rid of the junk in your home cluttering up the closets. Also, start advertising to sell the cars, jewelry, antiques, artwork, etc. These will take some time to sell, and advertising costs will be involved. You may want to use some of the proceeds from the garage sale to fund advertisements for your collectibles, which can bring in substantial amounts of revenue.

When Angelique's husband took off, he left her and the kids with nothing except the house, his collections of antique beer mugs and musical instruments, and a pile of unpaid bills. Knowing she could never afford to keep the house on her own, she put it up for sale almost immediately and made plans to move in with her mother. In the meantime, she and the two kids cleaned out their closets and held a garage sale, which netted over $1,000. With that money, she set about trying to sell the beer mugs and instruments. Within four months she had made another $20,000 from the collectibles. Though unable to sell the house during this time for the price she wanted, she rented it out while staying with her mother. Taking into account the tax advantages of the mortgage and depreciation, she actually came out ahead with this arrangement!

As you move money around to keep the creditors at bay, you have to keep meticulous financial records. You've made decisions based on certain suppositions, like how long it will take to sell the house or find new employment. It's important to reevaluate these suppositions weekly or bi-weekly in your family discussions. You need to "stay loose," or financially flexible. If what you're trying isn't working, try something else.

Emotionally, this is going to be a very rough time. Keep reminding yourself that this is a temporary situation. It's only a means to an end; you won't be living like this forever. Work hard to maintain some perspective, and try to keep an open mind.

Diary Entry, March 13, 1996: Month after month goes by, and we keep dipping into our savings to pay the mortgage and supplement my husband's unemployment compensation. My part-time job has been expanded, and I'm allowed to work as many hours each week as I want, but I've been so sick with pneumonia that I haven't been able to take much advantage of this generous offer from my employer. Our son has grown another two inches and just announced he needs new slacks again. Our daughter wants money for the big field trip of the school year. Another whole week has gone by with no phone calls or new contacts in my husband's job search. I'm worried about what this loss of self-confidence will mean to him in the long run. I hear that another big snowstorm is on the way, and the house is very cold. Needless to say, the mood around here is quite somber. I thank God daily that we have savings to live on now. There are so many people who are in far more desperate straits than we are. I just have to keep reminding myself of this fact.

—HSQ

Bankruptcy

If you suspect that bankruptcy is your only alternative, consult an accountant and a lawyer for advice. (Don't, however, ask a bankruptcy lawyer; the advice will be biased.) There are self-help books on this topic, and you'll probably want to read a couple from the library to help you in the assessment. Generally, it's suggested that if bankruptcy really is necessary, then you should hire an attorney specializing in this field rather than trying to do it by yourself.

There are two types of bankruptcy procedures. If you have an income and can maintain a payment plan, you can file for Chapter 13. This is the "wage earner plan." It stops the letters and calls from creditors and allows you to keep much of your property. A court reviews your income, assets, and expenses and assesses your potential for paying. Then, if you qualify, a defined payment plan of two to four years is established.

If you can't qualify for Chapter 13, the alternative is known as a "straight bankruptcy," "liquidation bankruptcy," or Chapter 7. This is used when you have no other income or income that is too low to pay your debts within a reasonable amount of time. Chapter 7 provides for the sale of your property to pay your debts. States differ, but generally you get to keep only your furniture and household goods worth less than $200 each, clothing, life insurance, IRAs, and equipment so you can continue to earn a living. Some states allow you to retain some specific amount of the equity in your house and car. Basically, everything else is sold to pay your debts. Any remaining debts not covered by the sale of your estate are canceled. There are some debts, however, for which you remain responsible. These include spousal and child support, state and federal taxes, student loans, traffic tickets and other fines, debt for credit card purchases of $500 or more for luxury goods, and credit card purchases or loans of $1,000 or more made within twenty days of filing for bankruptcy. In some states, however, you are responsible for credit card purchases and loans made up to six months before filing for bankruptcy.

Chapter 7 and 13 bankruptcy have certain things in common. Once you file, you can't declare bankruptcy again for six years. The fact that you have declared bankruptcy stays on your credit rating record for ten years. It can keep you from obtaining any future loans. If you can qualify for a loan, you will have to pay significantly higher interest rates. Some potential employers use credit ratings to screen applicants, and in these cases, filing bankruptcy will probably cost you a job. Declaring bankruptcy is a process that takes about six months to finish. Be careful of the implications of these facts.

One last word regarding bankruptcy when coupled with divorce. A bankruptcy declaration (by either party) halts any divorce proceedings that may be underway. The bankruptcy issue is dealt with first. There may be some advantages for you and your "ex" to file jointly for bankruptcy before the divorce is complete anyway, because of issues related to the distribution of property. If the divorce is final and then your "ex" declares bankruptcy, you should be immune to any involvement in it.

At the Top of the Hole

Eventually, things begin to work out. The time involved may be far longer than you wanted or expected, but eventually, the finances begin to settle. This may come about after the house finally sells. You may have found a new job so you don't have to sell the house. You may have been able to cut back enough to make the situation manageable.

Often in a layoff situation, finding another job that matches financially what you had before may be very difficult. You may have to settle for less just to keep the family going at all. Even with multiple jobs (on the part of both spouses), the combined income may not be what it used to be, and the job-related expenses may be significantly more than they were in earlier days.

As you plan your housing and level of lifestyle for the future, you'd be wise to be especially conservative at this time. Rather than find housing that costs up to a third of your present income, aim instead for spending a fourth. You probably have debt to repay. Your debts may include capital gains tax on the big house you sold at a profit. You'll want to replenish (and probably expand) savings. You need some "breathing room" in your finances. You've lived hand-to-mouth for too long. Don't make the mistake of making yourself "house poor" at this point.

Many people make the assumption that salaries will continually rise and therefore they can take on a greater and greater debt burden, always expecting that the future will take care of itself. Unfortunately, that just isn't true in today's American corporate culture, as you now sadly know. Since you know that downturns can exist around any corner, it's important to prepare for that by investing and saving at a high rate. Then, if you should be blessed with making lots of money again, you will be prepared. In the end, you may even find true freedom—the freedom of not having to work for a living at all! But it's difficult to save significantly when you are living at, or near, the extent of what you can afford for a home. That's why it makes sense to scale back just a little more than seems comfortable now.

Your attitude about finding your next, more affordable, home will improve if you remember what the objectives *are* for a house. The home is where you can feel safe and comfortable, where you have enough money to enjoy a few luxuries, where you can save some every month, where you can plan for the higher education of your children and secure your own retirement, where you can carry a good credit rating and provide ample insurance. Although your income may be far less than before, others having your current income have been achieving these same objectives quite successfully for a long time. You can too.

Back on Level Ground

You get to this point by one of two routes. Either your former income was restored, or you are now permanently settled in a downsized existence.

If your former (high) income was restored, depending on the length of time it took, you may or may not have had to sell your house. Some may sell, live in an apartment for a while, then buy a comparable home and try to "pick up where they left off." Others may have been able to stay in their house, managing the finances somehow. They may shift back to the old style of life fairly quickly.

If your income has stayed low, then you reach the end of this nightmare by settling into a smaller, more affordable house and car. You replace fancy vacations with less expensive and less frequent ones. You eat out less, dress more economically, do most of your own work around the house. In other words, you've adjusted to a downsized lifestyle.

In either case, you have some things in common. You need to pay off debts that were incurred during the difficult months. You need to replenish the savings and investments that were liquidated to pay the mortgage. Set realistic goals for yourself. You and your family have suffered a great deal. In your attempt to replenish the coffers, don't make the suffering continue. Allow yourself some luxuries and enjoy them!

The kids may immediately assume that the old ways have returned. Family discussions are still important to set their expectations correctly. Gently remind them that the lessons they have learned about money being a scarce resource are still relevant and applicable.

Whether you are permanently downsized or have had your income restored, there is one more thing you have in common. You have gone through dark times and the emotional scars will stay with you the rest of your life. The individual who has had the income restored sees it as a near-death experience. The unfortunate fact in today's world is that the drastic drop can happen again.

We lived in one neighborhood in California for eight years. During that time, one neighbor lost his job twice, and another lost his job three times in the high-tech companies of the Silicon Valley. It got to the point where they had to base their lifestyle on the wives' incomes, which were in more stable fields.

—HSQ

In our house, my husband's income, as a tenured college professor, stays the same while mine, as a writer, fluctuates wildly. We've learned to use his income for the basics, and if I do well, we get some fun stuff too. An especially lucrative contract allowed us to finish the basement. An unexpected royalty took us to Disney World. But there have been years in which we've gone nowhere, all year, except to visit our parents (who pay for the trip).

—LML

The toll that multiple layoffs have on an individual is devastating. No one ever gets used to being kicked in the teeth. The loss of self-confidence and self-worth is terrible. The only thing you can do is continue on the best you can. Save money when times are good in anticipation of the bleak days that may lie ahead.

Conclusion

Some friends had a near-death experience, both literally and financially, when he was diagnosed with cancer at the age of twenty-eight. Their second child had just been born (six days before he received the diagnosis), and they were in the middle of building their dream house. A professional musician, he was unable to work because of the treatments. He and his family moved in with her parents; they had to sell their half-built house just to pay the medical bills.

The support of her family played a major role in their survival, as her parents, siblings, and assorted relatives offered emotional support, housing, child care, and a job for him in the family-owned business as he recovered. When my husband and I visited them, he had been cancer-free for three years. While still working for the family business, he was also performing and recording music. He and his wife had almost finished building a

new, smaller dream house, much of which her father
had built with his own hands. As she said to me about her
father, "He isn't the kind of father who'll tell you 'I love
you.' But he shows you how much he loves you by the
things that he does."

—LML

Most people reading this book are either in the midst of coping
with a sudden drop of income or are anticipating such a dilemma. If
so, it's hard to imagine that life will ever be normal again. Indeed,
when you're in a hole, it's very dark.

It will help your overall attitude to focus on the important things
in life. Important things include spending quality time with your
spouse and children, expressing your love through actions and words,
not material things. It means setting an example for your children to
emulate—coping in an admirable manner. Your desires are to raise
your children successfully in an unfriendly world. To do that, they
need love, discipline, encouragement, confidence, challenges, and
role models. The size of your house or the model car you drive don't
teach these lessons. You do. All parents, regardless of their income or
social status, strive for the same objectives.

If nothing else, this financial nightmare for you provides a means
to teach your children that life is not like a game of Monopoly in
which he who acquires the most, wins. A downsized lifestyle can help
the entire family to rediscover what really counts in life—the value
that lies in the worth of each other. Those who undergo this type of
crisis often discover, or develop, the inner strength to help them get
through other crises in life. Marriages that survive are stronger for the
experience.

Chapter 14

Preparing for a Drop
If You See It Coming

$\mathcal{I}$n Aesops's fable "The Ants and the Grasshopper," the ants work hard all summer piling up food stores in their underground home. The grasshopper ridicules their efforts and encourages them to take some time off, relax, and join him as he plays his violin and frolics in the summer warmth. The ants refuse his offer. A few months later, winter sets in with a vengeance, and the ants take refuge in their well-supplied home. At that point, the grasshopper, now cold and hungry, comes to their door and begs for some food. An ant tartly replies that the grasshopper can go away, play his violin, and frolic. The ants want nothing to do with him and scoff at his inability to plan ahead for the winter snow. How many of us need to be Ants and not Grasshoppers at this point in our lives!

Often, the inevitability of a loss of income looms over us for some period of time before it finally happens. Marriage instabilities that portend divorce usually take time to develop. Certainly divorce proceedings do. Many times, a corporate reorganization and/or downsizing is announced months before it happens, even if it's only the numbers of people and not the specific individuals to be affected. Election results or the passage of a budget bill may portend job losses for those who work for the government. An individual employee may have problems with a boss or receive an unsatisfactory performance review. The declining health of a spouse may indicate that plans need to be made for a potential death.

It's crucially important to look at the time element as a blessing. You have been given the opportunity to plan ahead and you *must* take advantage of this time to make preparations. Denying what could

242

happen is childish and foolish. Being prudent and financially conservative can only benefit you in the long run. If you get lucky and you don't have to undergo a job loss, divorce, death, and subsequent income drop, at least you may be able to sleep better at night knowing that you have a contingency plan in case one is ever needed.

This chapter explores the things you should do while you still have adequate money to prepare for the lack of it: in the house, regarding the family in general, and the financial decisions you should consider. You'll want to save, modestly invest in what will help you survive on less in the near future, pay off debts (and not incur more), look for a second income, and begin training for a new career. Anticipated divorce and death have some special implications that are also considered.

The House and the Kitchen

You want to be able to run the household as economically as possible. Enlist the kids' help in lowering utility bills by reducing waste. You might want to give the kids a portion of the money saved the first time they make a concerted effort to lower a particular utility bill. Target one at a time. This may provide enough incentive for you to see dramatic results!

Make a conscious effort to replace lightbulbs as they burn out with lower wattage and/or fluorescent bulbs. Fix water leaks promptly. Be sure windows are caulked and well sealed. You might consider buying a small space heater to heat one room of the house rather than heating the entire home if only one person is home many hours of the day.

There are some more expensive investments you can consider depending on the level of your savings and disposable income now. These include things like an insulation blanket for the water heater, a programmable thermostat, low-flow showerheads and toilets, and ceiling fans. These will help lower your utility bills, but probably aren't worthwhile investments if the odds are high you'll need to sell your house if you experience a drop in income.

Anything you consider doing to the house should be done with the understanding that you could soon be trying to sell it. You don't want to put any serious money into the house that can't be recouped in a sale price. On the other hand, small amounts spent on things like paint, repairs, and carpet cleaning can be prudent investments.

In the kitchen, you can buy some low-cost items that will help you save lots of money on the food budget as you move away from "instant" meals and move toward cooking from scratch. These possible purchases include a good basic cookbook, a set of knives, a large soup kettle and strainer, and thermos bottles for packing lunches. Now is a good time to scout garage sales for things like a Crock-Pot, a bread maker, and possibly a second refrigerator or a small freezer. These last items shouldn't be bought new. One can easily exist without them, but if you have an opportunity to pick them up "on a steal," then you should consider taking advantage of the opportunity. This is *not* a time to spend very much money (it's far better to save it!), but careful planning now can help you if and when you need to make all your food from the basics and buy large, economical amounts of meats.

The Family

Now is the time to get caught up on your preventive medical and dental checkups. If your medical insurance covers annual physicals, child immunizations, and flu shots, get them scheduled immediately. Be sure the dental exams and cleanings are up to date. Fill cavities, seal the molars, and generally take advantage of whatever insurance you're carrying. Get eye exams and new glasses if they are necessary.

If child care changes may occur as a result of losing a substantial portion of your income, now is the time to do your homework. Go get those books at the library and read, in depth, about your options and what is important to consider in this decision. If you don't do it now while you have the time, you will be tempted to skip it later. Not giving it the time it needs can compound the guilt and stress later when you have to leave your children. In addition, many day care centers have waiting lists, and the earlier you get on them, the better the chance you have of getting your child into the program of your choice. Visit day care facilities, talk to friends, and make contingency plans. Experiment with older children to see if leaving them alone is a realistic option—just how responsible (and comfortable with being alone) are they? You can begin by leaving them home alone for up to an hour while you run errands and move on from there.

Find the warehouse discount stores in your area and get a membership with one if you can. Don't make assumptions about membership. Many of these stores have fairly odd rules.

My friend, Janet, shopped a well-known discount store in our town. I wanted to, too, so I went in and asked for a membership form. The rules precluded me—but Janet should have been precluded as well. I asked her how she got her membership card. She replied that a friend of hers was a member and members were allowed to have two "other" people on their card and had offered it to her. She would ask her friend if I could join under her name too.

—HSQ

If you are a legal resident alien, you should seriously consider getting your citizenship. Government benefits apply only to citizens. In fact, without citizenship, circumstances can even lead to your being deported from the country if you are left destitute or without insurance.

When Mario, a citizen of Spain, was hired by a major midwestern university to teach Spanish language and literature, the university had to certify that it could not find a qualified American citizen for the position in order for him to receive his "green card" (legal residency permit). Mario had no intention of renouncing his Spanish citizenship, and so things continued happily along for six years, until his department turned him down for tenure.

He had one year left on his contract in which to look for another job, but the job market had tightened considerably in the six years he had worked in the U.S., and he was unable to find another full-time position. Though he could collect unemployment for six months, he, his wife, and their toddler had to move in with friends because he had lost his university-subsidized housing; had he applied for government-subsidized housing or any other benefits, the government could have deemed him no longer "necessary," revoked his green card, and deported him to Spain. He thought about becoming a citizen so he could receive assistance and perhaps go back to school to retrain in another field. Nine months after his university teaching job ended, however, he received a comparable offer from a university in Europe and left the U.S., disillusioned but wiser for his experience here.

Begin to discuss the possibilities of an economic downturn with older children at home. This will help prepare them mentally for what may lie ahead. You don't need to make this formal and strained; the objective is to reduce, not increase, the stress level in the household. You do, however, want the children to understand that difficult times are met together, as a family team. Just as everyone in the family participates in the fun of a family vacation, everyone will be needed to participate and help in a family crisis. Supporting each other is a concept that can be taught, and it will help everyone cope more effectively. Solicit their money-saving ideas, acknowledge their attempts to help, and, if at all possible, try out the children's ideas. Positive reinforcement will stimulate continued creativity on their part. If you "squelch" all their ideas, don't expect them to be enthusiastic about your own plans.

The most important lesson everyone in the family needs to learn and practice now is *how to save money.*

Financial Planning

You need to save money every month—more money than you think you possibly can save. How? By utilizing ideas suggested throughout this book. Just altering your cooking style may save you $100 a month. Substituting cheaper luxuries for your favorites can save even more. "Tightening the belt" should be a calculated, aggressive effort by every member of the household. Put the money away in a savings account on payday and then adjust to living on less the rest of the pay period.

Add up the bills you need to pay every month and add in an amount for food and general living expenses. Now multiply that number by six. That's how much money you should have in a fairly liquid account in case you experience a downturn. That may seem like a pretty staggering goal, but in reality, it is what you can expect to need (on the average) until you can stabilize your life by finding new work or a new home. A buffer of six months will mean all the difference in the world in your mental stability if and when the crisis strikes.

If you have high credit card debt, you'd be better off paying this down first, before you start saving cash. A liquid account won't earn you much interest, and if you're paying 17–20 percent interest on revolving debt, it's smarter strategy to clear that up first. By all means, stop charging things! Put the credit cards away, except one for identification and emergencies. The ideal way to use credit cards is as a convenience, but only charge what you can pay off each month. If you can't pay off the entire charge, then you aren't living within your means, and you need to forgo all charging until you are fully out of debt. At that point, you can permit yourself to use credit carefully, but if the temptation is more than you can handle, get counseling from CCCS (see Chapter 13) and stop using credit cards forevermore. Just as a recovering alcoholic can't taste any alcohol ever again, the credit card addict shouldn't carry *any* charge cards.

Before you experience an economic downturn, it would be wise to have your house and valuables appraised. Appraisals usually cost money, but the knowledge of exactly what something is worth can be extremely valuable later if you need to sell the artwork, antiques, jewelry, etc. in order to raise cash. Rather than getting a formal appraisal on the house, meeting with two or three local real estate agents can be very enlightening to update you on the current market value of your house, how long it may take to sell it, and what improvements should be made to ready it for market. The reason you want to meet with several is to make sure you are hearing a consistent story and not just what you want to hear. These meetings don't cost you anything, and they will also provide you with the opportunity to evaluate which agent you'd potentially prefer to handle the business.

Appraisals are important for up-to-date insurance policies. This is a good time to review your insurances and make sure they are adequate and you've got the best rates you can find. Sometimes, you can get lower car insurance rates by taking a defensive driving course. This may be something to consider now, while you have the money to pay for such training if the savings is significant.

If a layoff looms on the horizon, be sure the medical insurance is the one that covers you the most at the least expense. Your insurance will continue for up to eighteen months under COBRA protection (if you're coming out of a big company), but you will need these payments to be as manageable as possible. Many companies only permit you to change your medical and dental insurance during one month of the year, so plan accordingly. If you are offered COBRA insurance, don't assume that its rate is the lowest you may find. It would be wisest to "shop around" and make sure that you are getting the best deal available.

It's time to rethink all your outstanding loans. Perhaps you've purchased a large-ticket item recently, such as a boat, an expensive stereo system, or a fancy sports car, and you're paying off a large credit card balance or a loan. Can you pay it off easily? If not, you might want to sell the item and pay off the balance. If you lose your job, you don't want a big debt weighing you down. You also don't want to risk a foreclosure, with all the damage it can cause to your pride and your credit rating. Do you have any ongoing expenses for luxury items, such as lease payments for a luxury car, an expensive club membership, or the maintenance of a horse? If it's at all possible, and the penalties aren't too great, you might want to get out from under these obligations as well. Expensive luxuries and toys are not compatible with serious plans to save money.

You should look into the possibility of refinancing your home. If a job loss is anticipated, this option will disappear at the same time as the job. (Without an income, you can't refinance.) If you have accrued equity in the house and if interest rates have gone down since you got your mortgage, this may be a smart thing to do. It's always worth looking into different loan packages; it's possible that a variable rate mortgage could offer lower rates than a fixed rate mortgage, making refinancing more attractive.

While you are studying the big items like mortgage, you should also think about investments you may have in general. Growth-oriented investments (like stocks) produce small dividends (1–3 percent) but have a potential to increase in value over time. Bonds, on the other hand, can produce 5–7 percent interest and have less growth potential, but the extra interest can mean more cash in your pocket. Be sure to check where the interest and dividends are being directed. You can have them come to you as checks, which can mean additional income when you need it.

After my husband was denied tenure, we switched as much money as we could out of our stocks and into bonds. The extra income gave us a sense of security; because of our savings and our modest lifestyle, we knew we could survive even if my husband didn't find another job.

—LML

Increasing your household income should be a primary objective. If a job is in jeopardy, how about a second (even part-time) job on the side? Then, there's a fall-back position available and a "foot in the door," which might become a full-time job. There's a good chance it wouldn't pay what you used to have, but any income is better than no income at all!

If only one spouse has been working, it's time for the other to find work. If one has to "start at the bottom," the job may not initially cover the costs of child care, or produce much profit after child care and transportation are subtracted. However, job experience is crucially important, and the investment will eventually pay off as experience leads to other opportunities that offer improved compensation. Also, getting all members of the household to adjust to two working parents takes a fair bit of time. These adjustments are hard enough. It's better to get used to them now before you have the additional stress and strain of an income loss.

Similarly, going to school at night to finish a degree or to develop new vocational skills is an excellent strategy now, while you have the time and money to get it accomplished.

I became a librarian directly as a result of my husband's job loss. The moment his department denied him tenure, I began the process of shutting down my two-year-old publishing company (which was very satisfying emotionally and wasn't losing money but wasn't making money either) and investigating other career options that would bring money in. I had an expired New York State teaching certificate that wasn't valid in Wisconsin anyway, and it would have taken me two years to get fully recertified. Law school was three years. It would take two years for me to get a master's in social work, another option I considered. At the time, however, I could get a master's in library science in only one year, and since he had one year left on his contract, library school it was!

—LML

Try to get several contingency plans in place. Have short-term, long-term, and very long-term ideas in mind. The "term" will likely be in months. The important thing is that you are actively planning for this downturn all along the way.

What difference does it make if the downturn doesn't happen? Well, you might have a lower mortgage, the school degree you always wanted, and lots of money stashed away for a rainy day. That's not such a bad thing, is it? And, if it does happen, you're in the best position possible to take control of your life. That is definitely a good thing!

Divorce and Death of a Spouse

In both anticipated circumstances, it's important to have established credit in your own name. Since most married couples keep all financial records jointly, this means setting up accounts in your name only. It's wise to have a checking and savings account as well as a credit card. Buying something on the charge card and paying it off is sufficient to establish a credit rating for you in the country's complex computer systems.

For both divorce and expected death, all important financial papers, statements, wills, and trusts should be located and thoroughly understood. For a divorce situation, make yourself a copy of all these documents as well as all account statements, two to five years of tax returns, and records of every asset you want to keep or share. In the expected death scenario, you need to get cash in your own account to tide you over until probate is complete (assuming the estate will go through probate).

A divorce lawyer should be consulted if divorce is anticipated, and an accountant could be very helpful in preparing the estate when a spouse is terminally ill. There are books available too, in both areas, to provide direction and advice for the financial and emotional issues that will be involved.

When a spouse is dying, you may feel that worrying about finances is inappropriate. But that's not true! The declining spouse, if at all coherent, will most likely be quite concerned with the subject, and seeing you take proactive, determined steps to ensure your future financial security will actually comfort him or her and provide a measure of peace.

Conclusion

Remember the ants and the grasshopper? Planning ahead made the difference between surviving the winter months and perishing. If you have been given the opportunity to plan for a probable drop in income, by all means, use the time wisely.

Prepare yourself and your family mentally and financially. Teach everyone how to save and economize. Take the necessary steps to locate new jobs and career options with training or schooling. Begin to picture yourself selling the home; that mental process is very important as the first step for the separation.

People *do* survive personal economic downturns. How *well* they survive often depends on how much preparation they gave it. You have been warned. Go do what you need to do!

Chapter 15

Penny-wise, Pound-foolish

$\mathcal{D}$ecisions always have to be made in life. However, you may now feel that all the decisions you make are so difficult and important. You are constantly barraged with the need to spend money you haven't got. Weariness results from constantly evaluating and reevaluating every aspect of every expenditure. If you don't spend money now, will you end up having to pay more later? If you do spend the money, will you feel you wasted it? If you don't look at the big picture, you may end up making decisions that are "penny-wise, pound-foolish." These decisions are ones that appear to save money but end up costing you more, either now or in the future.

What kind of bad decisions do you want to avoid? You don't want to make costly decisions—things that waste money or cost more money now than they save later on. You want to avoid risky decisions—things that put your life, health, employability, or financial health at risk. You don't want to make decisions that are a waste of time and energy. Lastly, you don't want to make decisions that are simply not realistic or sustainable, that are too hard to stick to.

This chapter will give you examples of all of these kinds of bad decisions. They're meant to be representative; they certainly aren't an exhaustive list. As you face your own daily challenges, try to think about the long-range implications and try to make sure your decisions aren't "penny-wise but pound-foolish."

Costly Decisions

Costly decisions are ones that either cost a lot of money now but can't be recouped later or else save a little bit of money now but force you to spend a lot of money in the long run.

Although your intentions may be good, buying items in bulk that you can't use is a waste of money. This is particularly true of perishables. For example, you might buy a branch of bananas, because the price per pound is so low. However, they'll probably rot before your family can consume half of them, unless your family is very large or you're planning to bake and sell a lot of banana bread. All food is eventually perishable. As you try to save money by buying larger amounts, think carefully about how long it will take realistically to consume the items.

Throughout this book, you've been encouraged to do things yourself in order to save money. However, buying expensive equipment to do this is *not* a wise decision. For example, buying a rototiller to put in a lawn, a chain saw to cut your own wood, and a sewing machine to make your own clothes are likely poor decisions. Unless you can accurately calculate a savings to be realized in a short time period, you shouldn't spend money on this kind of investment. The objective right now is to save money during your transition to a downsized lifestyle. That may take months or a year or two. It's in *that* time period you want to see a payback on any money spent to save money. You could easily spend $400 on a sewing machine. Realistically, do you think you will sew over $400 worth of clothes in the upcoming months? If so, the investment is a good one; otherwise, it's best to rethink how you'll clothe your family.

One of the worst things you can do is ignore preventive maintenance on things like your car and house. Replenishing oil in the car and changing it according to the manufacturer's specifications costs very little. If you neglect it, however, you are looking at the destruction of the entire engine, a catastrophic expense.

I am not very handy with cars. Once, I destroyed the engine of my husband's car by driving it without any oil. Our marriage just barely survived the incident. Another time, I received a cursory lesson on how to change the oil in a car, so I dutifully came home and drained what I thought was the oil in my car. Unfortunately, it was the transmission fluid. The car had to be towed to a garage. I had to pay the towing charge, the cost of new transmission fluid as well as the oil, and labor for them to be replaced. What a waste of money!

—HSQ

Likewise, furnace filters have to be changed and the system checked periodically. Water leaks need to be repaired, and roofs need to be kept clear of debris and ice. Not spending money on these maintenance items can end up causing significant damage that homeowner's insurance doesn't cover. If you have ever had to replace a floor or roof with water damage, you know just how costly a mistake this can become.

A $75 gutter would have prevented the water damage that drained down the back of our house and rotted out a sliding glass door. Replacing the door cost over $600. Needless to say, there's a gutter there now!

—HSQ

Tying up money in "long shot" opportunities is another poor idea. Playing the lottery is the best example of this. However, investing everything you have in a franchise may be almost as risky. Suing your former employer may provide a great deal of satisfaction, but unless you have a strong enough case for a lawyer to take it on contingency, it should be avoided. You need to feed and house your children, not pay attorney fees, right now.

The last example of a costly decision is one that has been mentioned many times already in this book: the use of expensive forms of credit. Banks and financial institutions have too many credit cards and programs at exorbitant interest rates that take advantage of people with low incomes or those facing a monetary crisis. For regular watchers of late-night TV, these include the "no money down, no interest for twelve months" offer at the furniture store (all the interest piles up, to be paid at the end of the twelve-month period) and the auto dealership that'll pay off your credit card balance if you buy a new car from them. (Of course, they tack on the balance—and more—to the price of the new car, which you don't need in your situation anyway.) If you *really* have no choice but to charge an emergency bill or take out a cash advance on your credit card at 18 percent interest, then you have to use this avenue. However, too often, people choose it without thinking it through adequately. Withdrawing cash on a credit card at high interest instead of going through the arduous loan procedures to get money at conventional rates, if you qualify, is a terrible waste. Likewise, leaving money in a savings account or an investment that is earning money at low to moderate rates and then borrowing cash at high rates only leaves you behind in the long run.

Risky Decisions

Risky decisions, ones that threaten your ultimate health (physical, mental, and financial), are bad decisions and should be avoided.

For example, not paying your insurance premiums leave you and your family far too vulnerable. You can lose everything you own by not paying your homeowner's insurance.

Robert and Marie decided to let their homeowner's insurance lapse after he lost his job and took a new one at a reduced salary. After all, their house was paid off, so there was no mortgage company to require insurance. Furthermore, they lived across the street from the fire station, so they figured no fire would get very far.

One day, while Marie was at work, a short-circuit sparked an electrical fire, unbeknown to Robert and their three children, who were home at the time. In this 120-year old house, the fire spread quickly through false ceilings and the dry wood frame. A metal roof trapped the

heat, making the fire worse. By the time the fire depart-
ment had been notified, the house, and everything the
family owned, was totally destroyed; they were lucky to
escape with their lives. Even though they owned the
house and land outright, this uninsured loss left them
without even the money to remove the wreckage, much
less build a new house.

Not having health insurance puts you at risk of dying or ending up with astronomical medical bills that you'll pay for the rest of your life. Not having life insurance leaves the family at a financial dead end if anything happens to you.

Bill, a divorcé with children raised and gone, was laid off.
In his downsizing efforts, he canceled all the insurance
policies he could except a minimum health insurance
coverage. He felt that it was his own well-being that was
at risk, and he was willing to do it under that circum-
stance. However, he was adamant that he would never
have done any of these things if he still had responsibil-
ities to a family.

Another risky decision is deciding not to buy medications that are necessary to preserve someone's health in the household. You can't skip your blood pressure medicine when you're under stress from downsizing. The child who needs antiseizure or asthma medication must somehow get this as needed. You can certainly try to scale back on over-the-counter medicines; most Americans take too many, due to the influence of TV advertising. You can also substitute generic equivalents for most over-the-counter drugs to save money. But prescription drugs are not supposed to be used on an *ad hoc* basis. If someone in the house has a prescription, than it should be perceived as a true *need.*

Parents should also be aware that denying prescribed medication to a child for any reason, including financial need, constitutes child neglect. As a high school teacher, I once had to report a parent to the authorities for withholding antiseizure medication from her epileptic child.

—LML

If you absolutely cannot afford a child's prescription medications, you are required by law to seek assistance. You should immediately call your county Department of Social Services before the child welfare authorities come calling you.

Likewise, not seeing a doctor when you need to is a poor and risky decision. As was discussed in Chapter 11, you want to learn how to use doctors in a frugal manner—not more or less than is truly necessary. There are parents who automatically take proper care of their children or spouse but are quick to "play the martyr" and refuse to seek medical attention when they personally need it. Not only can this end up costing you more in the long run, if the problem is potentially fatal, you may be sacrificing your own life and leaving your spouse and children in an even more difficult situation.

Like most struggling musicians, Allen didn't have health insurance. When his back pains got worse and worse, he ignored them because he couldn't miss work and he didn't want to spend the money to see a doctor. He finally had no choice when he collapsed during a recording session and had to be taken by ambulance to a hospital.

Doctors quickly discovered Allen had testicular cancer that had spread throughout his body. Countless fund-raisers organized by fellow musicians paid for his treatments, but it was too late. Despite agonizing chemotherapy, Allen died two years after the initial diagnosis.

While seeing a doctor for a serious physical ailment may seem like common sense for a lot of people, many do not give their family's *mental* health the same degree of importance. But just as you risk disability or death by not seeing a doctor or taking prescription medications, you are courting a host of problems by not seeking professional help for the stress you face. In too many cases a layoff leads to divorce; perhaps the marital breakup could have been avoided by timely counseling. And a divorce following a layoff will do further harm to you, your spouse, and your children as you cope with the financial and emotional traumas. Prolonged anxiety over your financial troubles can lead to a nervous breakdown if not treated, and prolonged depression can result in suicide. You may find yourself turning your anger on your family members; studies show that domestic violence increases during periods of unemployment. Even if you are the one who lost the job, your family members may experience excessive anger, anxiety, and depression as well.

Another mental health problem you should not ignore at this time is substance abuse. Drinking alcohol, smoking marijuana, or using other mood-altering substances may help you forget your troubles for a brief time, but you are harming your body and mind (and your future employability!) if you use them. You are also spending money that can be used to feed your family and pay the mortgage, and if you drink and drive or use illegal street drugs, you are *breaking the law.* You should also be vigilant about substance abuse among members of your family during this time of stress and steer them toward getting help if it is needed. Adolescents require special attention, particularly if a divorce has precipitated your loss of income or has followed a layoff.

There *are* ways to get professional help for emotional problems, even when you have no money. Clergy are always there. Low-cost counseling is also available through Catholic Family Services, Jewish Family Services, or other community organizations. For an emergency, such as a suicide threat or attempt, your county or regional mental health center should be contacted at once; these public agencies provide crisis mental health counseling free of charge. Depending on your circumstances, you may even be able to get public assistance for substance abuse treatment or other counseling, and, of course, there are self-help groups such as Alcoholics Anonymous. For more information on these sources of help, see Chapter 16, "Getting Help."

Making risky decisions and not getting help when you need it can end up sacrificing your mental and physical health—severely impairing your chances of holding down a decent job. Having disaster strike without insurance means you'll lose your life savings, all your possessions, and still be left with unpaid bills to drag you down for years to come. It just isn't worth it!

Decisions That Are a Waste of Time

We have learned many lessons from those who lived through the Depression in the 1930s. To save money now, we can implement some of them, such as changing our way of cooking. However, those people also did things like make their own soap and sew their own clothes. In today's world, these products are mass-produced and are much cheaper to buy than to make.

A while back, my daughter asked me if she could get a denim vest to wear because they were so popular. Thinking I could save money by sewing it (I *am* a skilled seamstress), I went to the fabric store to check prices. I was shocked by the cost of the pattern and material. We went to a local department store where there were racks of denim vests at a third of what it would cost me to sew it, not even counting the time it would take to do the job. Sewing can save money on some items, but not on all!

—HSQ

Another waste of time and money is to drive all over town to catch every sale on food and household items. Although you can save a few pennies, the wear and tear on the car and the cost of gasoline may undo all your efforts. Find a couple of places to shop where you know that, over time, you have the best chance of getting good prices, and then be satisfied with that. Certainly find one good grocery store and one place to purchase your nonfood household necessities. For nonroutine purchases, "let your fingers do the walking," and comparison shop by using the telephone.

Decisions That Are Hard to "Stick To"

People can go on a crash diet and everything seems to be going along fine until one day, the person "cracks" and starts to eat everything in sight. Just like that, we sometimes try to force ourselves or our families to do something too difficult to sustain in our downsizing efforts. It's kind of like trying to push a round peg in a square hole.

Forgoing all luxuries is an easily understood example of this. The fanatic dictator orders the cessation of anything that is fun or rewarding. The stress on the family induced by this approach will be too much to handle. A far better idea is to permit small, much cheaper luxuries or rewards. One can buy a half gallon of cheap ice cream to celebrate some event, where in the past it might have warranted a restaurant dinner with champagne. Your chances of success, over the long haul, will be much greater with cheap substitutes than a "cold turkey" approach to luxuries.

Likewise, attempting to eliminate the complete use of cigarettes and alcohol in order to save money may be a noble idea, but may be a tremendous challenge during this time of stress. Absolutely, it's best to cut down the use of any health-damaging substances or overeating. Cutting back, rather than cutting out altogether, probably will be more successful. Certainly, you don't want to see an increase! Of course, it's wise to try to save money on expensive habits, and it's crucially important to preserve your health now so you can guarantee your employability. (You should also avoid gaining weight if it means you'll have to buy a new wardrobe!) If your bad habits *are* on the rise, you've lost control and need help. Now, perhaps more than ever, you need to feel in charge. Gaining control over your diet and use of cigarettes and alcohol will help you immediately in the efforts to gain control over your destiny.

Conclusion

As you make your daily decisions, try to think about the long-term consequences of your actions. If your spouse or very good friend argues with you about the wisdom of a decision you are contemplating, maybe you should listen and heed their advice.

You may make mistakes. There is no way that you can possibly anticipate all the things that might happen. If you make a decision that results in a waste of money, produces more risk than you ever wanted, or ends up costing you more in the long run, you will feel terrible. However, what is done, is done. Don't let it tear you down mentally; you don't need that on top of everything else. You just have to learn from your mistakes and try to do better next time.

Chapter 16

Getting Help

After a year of teaching in New York City's public schools, I received a layoff notice, along with about a thousand other teachers citywide who had been hired in the past two years. At a meeting to explain the layoff, the union representative told us we were not eligible to collect unemployment benefits. I knew this was not true. Some of my fellow teachers believed him, and others hesitated to collect what they saw as "welfare."

I explained to the other teachers that "welfare" and unemployment insurance are two separate programs, that working people and their employers pay into an insurance fund so that workers have money to tide them over in case of a layoff. In this sense, unemployment is an *insurance* program, much like life insurance or disability insurance.

Since my fellow teachers, like me, had to eat and pay the rent, they listened. But how do I apply for the benefits, they asked. Over the next two weeks, I personally walked half a dozen teachers through the process. (I also wrote an article for a dissident union newspaper on how to apply.) A couple of teachers got hassled, including a friend who was pregnant at the time, but nobody was denied benefits. None of us had been fired "with cause," and we had all worked the minimum period for eligibility. My application took the longest time, it turned out, because I had lost my Social Security card and had to go to the Social Security office to get a new one first.

Once on unemployment benefits (which during the

263

1982 recession lasted thirty-nine weeks), all we had to do was show up at the office every other week and certify: 1) that we had not worked during the previous two weeks (or to account for our income if we had worked part-time), and 2) that we were actively seeking work. Though the unemployment office received a few job listings, none was in the area of teaching. (You cannot be forced to look outside your area of specialty or to take a job that pays substantially less than your previous job. Today, you don't even have to appear at the unemployment office personally to certify these things either.) After six weeks, I was called back to my old school because the more experienced teacher who had "bumped" me from my position had suffered a nervous breakdown. Happily, I returned to work, but I was also glad to have had the benefits that allowed me to pay the rent and stay in town until the position opened up. Incidentally, of the six other teachers whom I helped to sign up, five were called back within the semester, and my pregnant friend chose to take a maternity leave and stopped collecting benefits altogether.

—LML

Many people who have worked all their lives don't realize they can collect unemployment and other benefits. Others consider themselves too proud to accept government help. But if you've been working, you've also been paying taxes. You've paid federal and state income taxes and payroll taxes for Medicare and Social Security. If you've ever been self-employed or employed others, you've also paid disability, workmen's compensation, and unemployment insurance.

You wouldn't even think of turning down Medicare and Social Security because it's a "government" benefit. You've paid for it, right? Well, you've also paid for unemployment, disability, and workmen's compensation, either directly or through your employer. If your employer has paid for it, it's no different from all the other things your employer pays to you as "benefits"—medical insurance, dental insurance, a pension plan. As a working person (or the stay-at-home spouse of a working person), you've also paid taxes, a small percentage of which goes toward food stamps, the school lunch program, Medicaid, the cash assistance program known as "welfare" (officially entitled Aid to Families with Dependent Children but renamed Temporary Assistance to Needy Families after the 1996 welfare reform bill), and Supplemental Security Income (SSI) for people with disabilities.

This chapter discusses the different places to which you can turn for help if you have been downsized or experienced a divorce, death, or disability. These places have been categorized according to where you go to look for help—the unemployment office, the Department of Social Services, your children's school district, religious and community organizations, and self-help groups. There is some overlap in the services offered in these different places. You are encouraged to read all sections of this chapter to see what parts are most applicable to your personal situation.

The range of services available to you is quite large. Through unemployment insurance, you can receive cash to pay the bills. You and your children can also receive food through the food stamps program, the school breakfast/lunch program, and food banks run through community organizations. Help with housing and utilities is available through government programs and through the efforts of community organizations. At this time of great stress, you may also find free or low-cost medical care and opportunities for counseling through: the government's Medicaid program; a state-run program offering subsidized health insurance for children; your local school district; community groups; and self-help organizations and support groups.

As this chapter shows, you are not entirely on your own during this crisis. Despite recent efforts to cut government programs and services to families in need, resources *do* exist. You may have to be more persistent; even if someone at the unemployment office or Department of Social Services tells you that you are not eligible or that there is a long waiting list, keep trying. Ask to see a supervisor. In an era of budget cuts, those who work in these offices feel the pressure to say no, even if you really are entitled to something. You may be made to feel guilty, unproductive, even inferior. You must resist feeling that way. You have paid for this "safety net" through your taxes. When you're back on your feet, you'll be paying for it once more.

You may still be paying taxes with one hand as you accept services with another if you are working part time or near minimum wage. Many working families receive subsidized child care, health care, housing, and food stamps simply because they do not make enough money to support a family without this assistance. It's a fact of life at a time of overall declining wages. If you work but make less than a certain amount each year, you may also be entitled to the Earned Income Tax Credit. This tax credit was enacted in 1990 to defray the burden of payroll taxes—particularly Social Security and Medicare taxes—on the small paycheck. To apply for the Earned Income Tax Credit, follow the instructions on your federal tax forms when you file in the spring.

Finally, as you experience firsthand the increasingly frayed "safety net," you should let your elected representatives know about your experiences. Many of the programs that exist today—unemployment insurance, Social Security, food stamps, to name a few—were created during the Great Depression in the 1930s, when millions of hard-working families like yours found themselves on the brink of desperation due to economic conditions beyond their control. Many people who have never undergone hard times themselves do not see the need for such programs and are seeking to get rid of them altogether. Maybe you felt that way too, before the event or events that led to your sudden loss of income. Now you know. You're a solid citizen with something to contribute to your community and your country, and you're now seeing our social system from another perspective. You've been on both sides, and your perspective is important. So speak out, and at the very least, vote!

The Unemployment Office

After you've been laid off, the local unemployment office run by your state Department of Labor (which is where you can usually find it in the phone book) is one of the first places you should visit. States differ somewhat in terms of eligibility requirements (some require you to have worked the previous six months, for instance), the amount you will receive, and for how long you can collect. However, all states provide for you to receive a percentage of your previous salary, up to a maximum amount, for a period of at least twenty-six weeks. To be eligible, however, you have to have been laid off from your position; you can't have quit or been fired. If you accepted a buyout or early retirement offer, you generally aren't eligible to collect unemployment; if you were terminated and then negotiated a severance agreement, you can collect, though states differ in their treatment of severance pay and benefits as income.

In general, you can't collect unemployment if you were fired, i.e., terminated "with cause." However, since many employers will claim that an employee was terminated with cause to get out of paying benefits, states are fairly strict in determining cause. The reasons that can deny you benefits are theft, sabotage, insubordination, or a pattern of gross incompetence that can be documented over time. A mixed performance review generally doesn't count, nor does a single negative review after a slew of positive ones.

A good guide to assessing your eligibility, benefit levels, and application procedures is *The Unemployment Survival Handbook*, by Nina Schuyler. This book describes the rules by state and offers specific information depending on where you live. Keep in mind, however, that rules change. For example, in times of recession benefits are often extended beyond the twenty-six-week period to thirty-nine or even fifty-two weeks.

When you collect unemployment, you will receive a check at regular intervals, usually every two weeks. This amount is considered taxable income, so you need to declare it when you file and budget for upcoming federal and state taxes. (This may seem like adding insult to injury, but it's the law!) In return, you have to document that you are "actively looking" for work. "Actively looking" does not mean you have to leave your field for another, nor do you have to accept a salary significantly below what you were earning before (states differ on how they define "significantly"). Occasionally, the unemployment office contains job listings and other leads. The state Department of Labor, which oversees the unemployment office, may also contain information about retraining opportunities (such as the programs described in Chapter 10) and about industries that are recruiting workers.

The Department of Social Services

In addition to issuing the Social Security cards that you will need to take to the unemployment office to collect your benefits, your county Department of Social Services (found in the phone book under county government listings) provides a wide range of benefits to you if you need them and if you qualify. These range from assistance with nutrition and medical care to aid for people, including children, with disabilities.

Perhaps the best known program run by the Department of Social Services is welfare. Until recently, the program was officially entitled Aid to Families with Dependent Children (AFDC). It provided cash grants to parents, usually mothers, who lacked any other source of income. The size of the grant, though small in any case, was based on the number of dependent children in the household. If a parent worked part time or received child support, the grant was reduced further. Many states attached other stipulations—children whose families received AFDC had to stay in school, for example.

The Personal Responsibility Act of 1996 abolished AFDC and replaced it with a program called Temporary Assistance for Needy Families. In this new program, states have wide latitude to set eligibility requirements and time limits. The maximum time any parent can collect cash benefits during his or her lifetime is five years, but some states have reduced the lifetime cap to as little as twenty-one months. This means recipients of cash grants will have to find a job—any job—as soon as possible. Noncitizens, whether they are here legally or illegally, are ineligible for benefits in any case.

When Rhonda began teaching in a public elementary school in an all-white neighborhood of Brooklyn, New

York, she was shocked to discover that two-thirds of her students lived in families receiving AFDC. The parents of these youngsters were divorced, and the fathers had skipped town or otherwise avoided paying child support. Thus, the mothers, who had raised children all their lives and possessed no job skills, had turned to welfare as a last resort.

If you have been downsized from a professional or managerial position, you probably have too many assets to qualify for Temporary Assistance to Needy Families. Most states require you to have no assets, except for a car worth less than $1,000, to qualify. However, if your income loss is the result of a divorce, or if you have "spent down" your assets caring for a disabled or dying family member, then you may very well qualify for this program. If your income loss has resulted from a divorce and you, the primary caretaker of the children, are receiving no support from your former partner, then applying for Temporary Assistance to Needy Families carries another benefit—the government will track down your deadbeat spouse and enforce the child support agreement. The government can withhold a portion of his/her wages or even threaten to send the deadbeat to jail.

If your income loss is the result of a spouse's death or disability, then you or your children are eligible for Social Security cash benefits. The cash grants paid to the children of a deceased parent are called Social Security Survivor's Benefits, and they are paid until each child turns eighteen.

My husband, his brother, and his sister received Social Security Survivor's Benefits for a number of years. Though it didn't amount to much money, it helped to pay for clothes and school books and made things a little easier for their mother.

—LML

A disabled spouse can receive cash benefits in a number of ways. If the disability is the result of an accident at work, it falls under the domain of Workmen's Compensation. If the disability occurred outside of work, it falls under the domain of either Disability Compensation (if the person who suffered the disability was employed and the employer paid into the disability insurance fund) or Supplemental Security Income, called SSI (if the person did not work or was not covered by a state disability insurance program).

Two stories illustrate the difference between Disability and SSI.

Dennis, a special-education teacher for emotionally disturbed teenagers for twenty-five years, seriously injured his neck and back in an auto accident. As a result, he failed to pass the physical exam required for his license to teach in that field. He received funds from Disability Compensation. While collecting benefits, he retrained as a computer consultant. In the end, he found a job in his new field and no longer needed his barely adequate Disability grant.

Justin was twenty-two and an aspiring rock guitarist when he suffered a near-fatal stroke that left him paralyzed on one side. Since he had never consistently worked, only occasional gigs at local clubs that were paid "off the books," he did not qualify for Disability Compensation. Instead, he received SSI. After years of collecting benefits, and in the face of tremendous obstacles due to his disability, he managed to achieve a college diploma, a master's degree in social work, and a new career as a Social Services caseworker.

If you are the parent of a disabled child, you may already be aware of the assistance available through SSI. Perhaps you have always had enough money and have been able to pay for special services yourself. Now that your income has dropped, you should take advantage of whatever free services are available through your county Department of Social Services.

If your income falls below a certain amount and you have few or no assets, you may qualify as well for food stamps. In fact, many working families receive food stamps because their earnings fall below the poverty line; if your family is large, you can make more and still qualify for food stamps. Basically, food stamps are vouchers, earmarked for food items, that you use at the grocery store instead of cash.

Many people are reluctant to apply for food stamps because they don't want those behind them in line at the supermarket to see them using the vouchers. If you are worried about what the neighbors will think, and that's keeping you from applying, you can always shop at a different supermarket—perhaps one near your workplace rather than near your house. You'd be surprised at how many people, including those who are obviously dressed for office jobs, use food stamps. Actually, it's no surprise, given the state of the economy and the declining purchasing power of most people's earnings.

If you or your wife is pregnant, or you have an infant or young child at home, you may also qualify for food subsidies through the Women, Infants, and Children (WIC) program. This program is designed to give your children a good start in life by making sure that the expectant mother and very young children have enough food, and healthy food, to eat. Not providing the food can lead to a lot of problems for your children later, such as increased susceptiblity to childhood illnesses, learning disabilities, and even mental retardation. These problems can be expensive to treat, even if you have adequate medical insurance, and some can't be treated at all. If your income is low enough to qualify for WIC, by all means take advantage of this program. Your children will thank you for it.

If you qualify for cash assistance through Temporary Assistance for Needy Families, or if someone in your family is disabled, you also qualify for Medicaid, the government-subsidized health care program administered by the Department of Social Services. Again, rules differ from state to state, and an increasing number of states are requiring

Medicaid recipients to enroll in a Health Maintenance Organization (HMO). Even if you don't get much choice for your HMO, having that access to health care is far better than the alternative. In fact, if you only have Medicaid for a short time—for instance, if you are about to take a job that does not carry health benefits—be sure to get your annual checkups and take care of any problems while the care is free. In many states, you can keep your Medicaid benefits for a set period of time even after you take a job that doesn't offer benefits of its own.

The Department of Social Services is the place you should go as well for problems with housing, utilities, and weatherization. If you cannot afford any housing, no matter how inadequate, on your current income, or if you have been burned out of your home, you may qualify for either an apartment in a public housing project or a subsidized apartment from a private landlord through a program known as Section 8. In most urban areas, there is a long waiting list for both public housing and Section 8. The picture is a little brighter in suburban areas and in smaller cities and towns.

The Department of Social Services also administers a federal program that helps with utility bills and weatherization. This is more of an issue in colder climates, where heating bills skyrocket in the winter and a utility cutoff can mean frozen and burst pipes. You should check locally to see if you qualify for this kind of aid. You may be able to receive assistance in this area even if you own a home and have other assets. You may also be able to receive aid if you are a landlord, renting out your home, a portion of your home, or other real property.

Your School District

If you have children, there are services offered through their school district that can help you save money. Specifically, you can stretch your food budget a lot further if your children eat breakfast and lunch at school free of charge or at a significantly reduced rate.

The school lunch program was implemented in the 1960s because teachers, administrators, and, finally, our lawmakers realized that children learn better when they have enough to eat. Later, breakfast was added to the menu. In comparison to Temporary Assistance to Needy Families, food stamps, and Medicaid, the income cutoff for the free breakfast/lunch program is fairly generous. Cutoffs are based on family size, but you can make more than the poverty level to qualify. Even if you make twice as much as the poverty level, your children can receive a reduced-price lunch, costing twenty-five cents per meal. There is no limit on the assets you may have (unless, of course, they provide an income). To apply, you fill out a form listing your household members and stating your income.

The application process is entirely confidential, though districts often use the raw numbers to collect statistical information. For example, a district may claim a certain percentage of its students are "at risk" based on approved applications for free and reduced-price lunches; however, individual classroom teachers do not know which of their students receive the lunches. Nor will your child's peers know. Children who do not qualify for free or reduced-price lunches buy their lunch at school and use the same tickets, only their parents have paid the full price for the tickets.

When my son was in first grade, virtually all the children bought their lunch at school. Now that he's in fourth grade, about half the kids, including him, still do. We buy our lunch tickets through the district office, where we receive a small volume discount but do not qualify for the reduced price. As a parent volunteer in the school I've often helped out in the cafeteria, and I can attest that it's impossible to tell who's receiving a free or reduced-price lunch and who's paying full fare.

—LML

Schools also offer a variety of educational and health services. If your child attends public school, you are probably aware of the special education programs. In recent years, school districts have moved away from confining children with learning disabilities, attention deficit disorders, physical disabilities, and hearing and speech problems in self-contained classrooms. Most of these children with special needs are now in regular classrooms, learning side by side with their peers. Such children may have an aide in the classroom for part or all of the day or may see a specialist or counselor on a regular basis. Unless your child has a serious disability, you should resist any effort to have him or her placed in a self-contained classroom and instead push for assistance in a mainstream classroom.

If you suspect your preschool child has some sort of disability, you should find out if your district has a program to help prepare him/her for kindergarten. Many districts do, and these types of programs can be expensive if you look in the private sector. At this time in your life, you don't need the added expense, though you want your child to get off to a good start.

Jared was diagnosed with a language disability at the age of three. The nursery school teacher suggested his parents look for another program because that school couldn't accommodate his needs. He never seemed to be able to listen to directions, and unable to communicate his own feelings, he frequently hit the other children. His parents owned a business together, and times had been hard; they could ill afford a preschool that specialized in Jared's problem. Fortunately, their school district, a large urban district, ran a free program in conjunction with a local university. Jared's parents applied, and he was accepted into the program. Since then he has made great strides and is now in kindergarten, where he is fitting in well.

If your income and lack of assets place you below the poverty line, and particularly if you are a single parent, you may qualify for Head Start. This program is designed to provide enrichment and a positive school experience to children who live in poverty and who have few other early educational opportunities. Children who have experienced Head Start do quite well in those crucial early years of school, so if you qualify, you should definitely take advantage of that excellent program. Again, you should check with your local school district and with the Department of Social Services if you think you may qualify.

Virtually all public schools have counselors, and they are an excellent resource for you as well as a source of services for your children should they need help. Many schools throughout the country feature a program called Banana Splits for children of divorced or divorcing parents. If your child has an attention deficit disorder or problems with social skills, counselors can be of great assistance, especially if you are unable to afford a private psychologist. If your child is "acting out" or withdrawn because of the crisis that led to your income loss, you should discuss the matter with the school counselor, who can then schedule an appointment with your child. Counselors exist to help students do better in school, and if any outside problem is keeping your child from doing his or her best, the school counselor is the person you should call.

All public schools also have a nurse's office, and some (particularly high schools) have full-fledged clinics. These can be useful if you have lost your health insurance, if your insurance doesn't cover checkups and immunizations, or if you have a high deductible and co-payments. At various grade levels, your children need physicals, and if you cannot afford the physical, most school districts will conduct the physical themselves through the nurse's office or clinic or will arrange for it to be done free of charge at an outside clinic. The same is true for vaccinations that are required by law. Because the school nurse sees many children whose families are uninsured or are facing financial hardship, this person is an excellent resource for finding out about free or reduced-price clinics or government programs to subsidize the cost of a child's health insurance.

Religious and Community Organizations

For many years I have volunteered with a community organization that provides a number of services to local families in need. It offers an information and referral service for callers seeking additional resources in a variety of areas (from basic needs to recreational and entertainment opportunities) and special programs for teenagers, single parents, and people with drug and alcohol problems. In addition, this organization offers a Family Assistance Program, which helps families in need to get in touch with the Department of Social Services and other sources of financial assistance within the community.

—LML

At a time when the federal government and many state governments are cutting their social spending, services provided by community organizations, churches, synagogues, and a host of other charitable organizations become increasingly important. Perhaps in the past you have donated money or even time to these organizations. As an employee, you may have given to the United Way. You may have donated canned goods to a church food drive or dropped off toys around Christmastime for the Toys for Tots program. If you have given to these charitable causes in the past, you have been a "good neighbor." You have helped others in your community. But you are a member of this community too, and now that times are tough, you should avail yourself of whatever these organizations have to offer.

Community and religious organizations can be a good source if you need food, clothing, or household goods. Even the wealthiest suburban communities have food pantries, run by churches, synagogues, and other groups, to help those in need. This is because, as you well know, massive corporate downsizing and its consequences have been a fact of life for more than a decade now, and divorce, illness, and death know no income boundaries. These same organizations often provide extras for the holiday season—turkey and trimmings for Thanksgiving, and presents for children at Christmas and Hanukkah.

In addition to providing emergency food, clothing, and other goods, community and religious organizations sometimes offer cash grants to families in need. These grants are usually for one-time expenditures—a security deposit on an apartment or the payment of a medical insurance premium until a person can become eligible for Medicaid or Medicare. These grants may also be available to take care of a small problem that can become a larger or more expensive problem later. Examples are emergency funds to help heat a home in the winter—thus preventing damage to the pipes—and a grant for someone to continue medical insurance or purchase prescription drugs.

Two months after Frank was laid off, for the third time in five years, he noticed a suspicious lump on his neck. He was eligible for COBRA, but multiple layoffs had depleted his savings, and he was having trouble keeping up with the premiums. Had he not continued his insurance payments and the lump turned out to be something serious, he would have never gotten medical insurance again, because he would have had a "pre-existing condition." The organization for which I volunteer paid his premium for a month, during which time he saw a doctor. Fortunately, the lump proved to be a harmless cyst.

How do you find out about this kind of assistance? If you have donated to local charities in the past, you are probably aware of the work they do—and that can be an excellent starting place. Another good place to start is your own church or synagogue. Talk to the priest, minister, or rabbi. If you don't have affiliations with any religious organization, ask a friend who does. If you have contacted the Department of Social Services, your caseworker is probably aware of other resources within the community, and if you have been turned down for assistance by Social Services, someone there may tell you where else you can turn. School counselors are often good sources of information as well. Finally, you might want to try the local public library. Libraries carry information about all kinds of resources within the community, and many librarians have special training in information and referral services.

When I was in library school, a significant component of the "Introduction to Public Libraries" course was on information and referral, because so many people call the library to find out about other resources within the wider community. One of the students in the class had been a library assistant in a city that is home to a large regional medical center. She had gotten a number of calls from people who needed information on serious or terminal illnesses with which they had just been diagnosed. Her library was in the process of implementing a training program on counseling the terminally ill and their families because so many people in that situation had turned to the librarians for information and assistance.

—LML

Finally, the layoff, divorce, death, illness, and subsequent loss of income has probably created a great deal of stress for you and your family. You may have had difficulties with alcohol, drugs, or gambling even before the crisis, and the stress has only compounded the problem. Or maybe you never did have a problem before—you were clearly a social drinker, for instance, but ever since you got laid off, you've been getting drunk every night. You may find yourself having anxiety attacks, trouble sleeping, or trouble getting out of bed in the morning. You may have bought a gun and are harboring fantasies of taking revenge on those who ruined your or your spouse's career, or your marriage. (For the warning signs of depression, anxiety, and excessive anger, see Chapter 1.) While the kids can see a counselor at school for their problems, where can you turn, espcially now that you don't have the money to pay a psychologist?

In most areas, Catholic Family Services and/or Jewish Family Services offer family and individual counseling and often sponsor group counseling sessions as well. Generally, these counseling services charge a sliding scale rate based on your income. You may be able to take advantage of these services even if you are not Catholic or Jewish; it doesn't hurt to check.

Many Protestant and nondenominational Christian churches offer, virtually free, individual and family counseling through the pastor or through church members who are psychologists or social workers. Ministers frequently have secondary degrees in various kinds of counseling because a divinity degree alone doesn't give them all the resources to "minister" adequately to the needs of most congregations. There may also be support groups for the newly bereaved, families facing life-threatening illnesses, couples going through a divorce (marriage counseling to prevent the divorce is also available), or people who have been laid off. If your own church does not have these services, you may be able to find a nearby congregation that does. Often people switch churches because their needs change and a different church may have the services to meet their new needs. Large churches with multiple staff members will provide the most program diversity, so you may want to target these if you are feeling uncertain and/or want to maintain some degree of anonymity.

If you haven't been religious in the past, you may feel uncomfortable with wanting to utilize the assistance available from this source. You shouldn't. Dire circumstances tend to draw people to religion. If you're experiencing any of these feelings now, why not act on them? If you can get help, it's worth it. You'll probably be surprised by how many kindred spirits you locate at a new church. Most church membership is free of charge, and any attending member should feel free to avail him/herself of whatever services and assistance the church provides, even to brand-new members.

I had joined a Protestant church only a few weeks before our first child was born. This child was born with multiple birth defects, and we were told she couldn't survive. We were advised to make funeral arrangements.

I phoned the minister of my new church (who didn't know me at all) and explained our situation. He visited us daily for the three weeks our daughter survived, arranged for visits from other church members, and performed a baptismal service at the hospital with attending Elders.

After her death he performed the memorial service. Other than a small fee for the funeral service (customary, not obligatory), we never paid anything for the hours and hours of counseling, prayer, and general support the church and its minister provided to us.

—HSQ

Other community organizations may also offer programs specially geared to substance abusers—those addicted to alcohol, drugs, or even gambling. If you still have medical insurance, you're in luck; your insurance probably covers residential or outpatient treatment for a given period of time. If you have few assets and little income, you may qualify for residential treatment through the Department of Social Services. If you fall into neither of these categories, community organizations often sponsor programs because it's such a serious and widespread problem (and one more likely to occur if you or your spouse loses a job or you face some other major crisis!). You can find out about these programs through the Department of Social Services, your local library, your church or synagogue, or a local information and referral service. If you know of a residential treatment program in your area, you can call it for more information even if you can't afford to sign up for treatment. Most residential treatment programs work hand in hand with community organizations and with self-help groups such as Alcoholics Anonymous.

Support and Self-help Groups

Often you can find support groups through community and religious organizations. These groups bring together people with similar problems to discuss their concerns and coping strategies. Usually, but not always, a social worker, psychologist, or other trained professional serves as a facilitator, and sometimes guest speakers give presentations as well. These support groups, which are usually sponsored by an organization and free of charge to participants, are an inexpensive alternative to a private psychologist. They also have the advantage of showing people in crisis that they are not alone. Participants in these groups can share information and their success stories as well as their concerns.

My son was diagnosed with attention deficit hyperactivity disorder (ADHD) at the age of five. Since then, I have attended several workshops and groups. It is reassuring to know that we are not alone, and it helps to hear about the experiences of parents of older children with ADHD so we know what to expect in later years. Although he has seen a counselor, both inside and outside school, the group offers a lot of information that we don't get from counselors, such as how to deal with teachers and with the school in general. Many of the support group members have had experience with the school our son attends, and we in turn can give information to the parents of younger children with ADHD. The school district sponsors one of the groups we've attended; it was free of charge to participants. The only fee we have had to pay for the other group is an annual $15 membership to defray the cost of mailings and renting a meeting room.

—LML

Support groups sponsored by an organization are considered formal support groups. They have regular meeting times and often send out newsletters and other mailings. You can also look for, or even start, an informal support group. These groups usually form by word of mouth and meet according to the needs of the members. Often they meet in members' homes. A common basis for an informal support group is people downsized by the same company. If that is your situation, you should try to get in contact with coworkers who lost their jobs to find out if they are getting together already. If they aren't, you should try to start something.

Self-help groups are similar to support groups, though they are

geared to confronting and resolving a specific problem, usually an addiction. One of the oldest and most established self-help groups in the
United States (and now the world) is Alcoholics Anonymous (AA).
AA, which is supported by membership donations and other charitable contributions, is free of charge to participants. Members attend
regular meetings and stay in touch with others through a system of
sponsors and mentors. AA's success has spawned a number of similar
self-help groups that address other addictions—Narcotics Anonymous, Overeaters Anonymous, Gamblers Anonymous, Debtors and
Spenders Anonymous. There are also support groups for family members of people with addictions—Al Anon for spouses or significant
others of alcoholics, Alateen for the teenage children of alcoholics.

How do you know that you have an addiction and could use the
support of a self-help group? If instead of cutting back your spending
on liquor, cigarettes, etc., you are increasing it in this period of tight
money, you have a problem. If you find yourself using illegal street
drugs, you have a problem. (In this case, you should seek help at once,
before you add trouble with the law to your list of problems.) If you
are betting the few dollars you have left on the lottery or sports events,
you have a problem. You also have a problem if you continue to go
on shopping sprees or eating binges.

To join a self-help group, you have to begin by acknowledging your
problem. Most of the self-help groups adhere to a twelve-step program in which you admit your helplessness in controlling your addiction yourself and you place your faith in a "higher power." You
recognize that you must combat your addiction "one day at a time."
In the case of alcohol, drugs, and gambling, you must pledge not to
use the substance or engage in the activity again. In the case of eating
or shopping, you have to stick to a strict plan. Meetings, which you
can attend up to twice a day in some areas (but more commonly once
or twice a week), feature members telling their stories, discussions,
and mutual support. Each member has a mentor or sponsor whom he
or she can call in an emergency.

Of all the self-help groups, AA is the largest. Most communities
have a number of AA groups, including separate groups for non-
smokers, teenagers, born-again Christians, feminists, Republicans,

and others. If you attend a meeting and you don't like that particular group, don't worry. There are bound to be other groups nearby. You can find out about the groups that are available in your area by calling the AA number listed in the phone book. The local AA office should have information about related self-help groups as well; in metropolitan areas, some of these groups have their own separate listings.

Conclusion

The government, community, and self-help resources listed here may be only the beginning. Every locality is different. The 1996 welfare reform bill turned much of the funding and administration of social services over to the states, so states also differ in terms of what public help is available, how much money is available, and who qualifies. Many of the programs and rules are still changing, and the information contained in this chapter may soon be out of date. For the specific programs that concern you, you need to check with your state Labor Department and your county Department of Social Services. For information on housing-related issues, you should also call the local branch of the U.S. Department of Housing and Urban Development.

You may not feel comfortable taking assistance from the government or from a charitable organization. But everybody needs help sometime. If people didn't need help, and people didn't offer help, we wouldn't have this thing called Community at the core of the American Dream. We would just be little family units that competed and didn't care about each other, and, in the words of the Enlightenment philosopher Thomas Hobbes, our lives would be "nasty, brutish, and short." As we come together to help each other, we grow as individuals and as a nation.

Quite by accident I found out about Hope's husband being laid off. Then, about a month later, she asked me to help her write a book about her experiences trying to cope with the downsizing and to economize. She had never written a book before; I had four published books, but none on a subject that was even remotely related.

Before we started working together, we had next to nothing in common. Our kids didn't get along. The Quinns are diehard Republicans; my husband and I are liberal Democrats. They are both scientists; I read the Science Times section of the *New York Times*, but that's about it. They vacation in the woods; we go to New York City. She teaches Sunday School at a Presbyterian church; my family is Jewish. They are avid meat-eaters; I'm a vegetarian.

You'd think all we'd be able to talk about is the book and the weather, but that's not the case. As we got to know each other, we discovered how much we really shared, even in those controversial areas of politics and religion. (We also know that life would be pretty boring if everyone we came into contact with were exactly the same.) By working together—contributing each of our strengths to the other one's weaknesses—we created this book and developed a friendship. If this book helps you, it is one more benefit of our coming together.

—LML

You, too, can contribute your strength during this time of hardship. If you accept assistance, you can offer your time in return. Volunteer at your local school to read to kindergartners or help older children with their lessons. Offer to drive senior citizens or people with disabilities to medical appointments. Help to organize a support group. Offer your services as a volunteer to a local community organization. When you're back on your feet, you can repay the help you received by donating money to the charity of your choice. You might think about keeping records of the amount you receive so you can make equivalent donations later.

Frank did not want to receive money from the community organization to pay his medical insurance—he had never taken charity from anyone before—but the lump in his neck had made him frightened for his life. As he dithered about accepting the grant, a staff member at the organization suggested an alternative. The organization's database was a mess. Frank's work experience was in designing and programming computer databases. Could he possibly come in and make the database usable?

Frank redesigned both the database and the intake forms to make them simpler and easier to use for an organization that relied on lots of volunteers. That was four years ago. Frank's database design is still in use today, working flawlessly.

Chapter 17

Conclusion—Downsized, But Not Defeated!

$\mathcal{F}$amilies downscale their lives for many reasons, but most commonly because of a drastic cut in income. Sometimes the drop in income is voluntary—such as when a parent quits working to spend more time with children—but far more often, it is the result of a grievous loss of another sort. There are eight principles to keep in mind as you downsize. Understanding (and then implementing!) these principles will help you triumph in the end.

1. Acknowledge your grief.

It's crucially important that you acknowledge your grief for the person, relationship, job, or way of life that you have lost. Remember that grief is a process; its duration and intensity are unpredictable. Every member of the home will be affected, but some will exhibit symptoms more strongly than others. Children will learn about handling grief from examples set by the parents.

One of the best ways to help the grieving process along is by participating in a support group, preferably of others who have experienced the same kind of trauma.

2. Question your assumptions.

You have to consider seriously how you've been living and question all the assumptions you've made that put you where you are. As the assumptions change, so do your future plans.

You may have assumed that your income would continue to

increase over the years and you based your mortgage and other debt burden upon that premise.

You are living in a particular place because of certain reasons—for the schools, job, commute, neighborhood, etc. Are these reasons still valid considering your present circumstances?

Your child care situation has been based on certain assumptions as well. Now that your lives have been turned upside down, you have the opportunity to examine this again. Likewise, your plans for educating your kids may be completely altered now. Before you decide what the future holds, think back to the past that led you to choose the path you took. What is still the same and what has changed?

How you spent your discretionary income was based on certain lifestyle choices. Your manner of using credit was probably based on the cash flow you used to experience. Your habits will need to change now.

3. Establish your priorities.

Some things you can easily live without to save money. Other things are too important for you to sacrifice. You have to establish these priorities. Once set, they have to be within your present income range; otherwise, you have to go through the process of prioritization all over again. This is complicated by the fact that members of the household may have different things that are sacred to them. Much discussion, negotiation, and compromise may be necessary.

Everyone in the family has to perceive clearly the difference between a necessity and a luxury. The necessities of food, housing, clothing, and insurance will come first. The money left over after meeting those obligations will need to be earmarked for debt retirement and taxes. Whatever is left after that can be fought over, but chances are, that amount won't be much.

4. Use discipline and reward yourself.

It will require massive amounts of discipline to adhere to your new, downsized budget. You will be forced to do without many items you have always considered to be part of a perfectly normal existence. However, your existence now is not normal, and while you are moving through the stage of "robbing Peter to pay Paul" (while you are trying to get out from under the burden of an excessive mortgage or debt), discipline and fortitude will be the key words for survival.

On the other hand, don't neglect rewards. There are inexpensive ways to celebrate accomplishments and reward all members of the family for the successful completion of a tough task. Take the time (and maybe even a little bit of money!) to acknowledge a job well done. It will provide a mental boost, encouragement, and an important reprieve in an otherwise difficult existence.

5. Attitude is crucial.

In the New Testament of the Bible, there is a story about two new Christians, Paul and Silas, who are beaten, shackled, and imprisoned for their beliefs. That night, in the darkness of the prison cell, they begin to sing hymns, to the astonishment of the jailer and the other prisoners. Their action demonstrates their defiance, courage, and hope regarding the path they have chosen.

You don't have to be religious to realize the value of emphasizing the positive in whatever circumstances you find yourself. Feeling guilty, continually admonishing oneself, or wallowing in self-pity produces a very unhappy person. Counting one's blessings, however, accentuates the good that can be found in almost every situation. Much has been written on the power of positive thinking.

Throughout this book, you have been encouraged to reshape your attitude on almost all subjects. Change has become a daily occurrence. You can't fight it; you simply have to accept and adapt to the new realities. Your ability to adapt is fundamentally determined by the attitude you adopt. Accept the changes. Look at them as opportunities. Focus on the positive results even though they may seem few and far between among the many discouraging signs. Encourage everyone in the family to look for the subtle "good things." Actively seeking them makes them easier to spot. Emphasizing the blessings will help ease the trauma and shape a more optimistic attitude.

6. Monitor your emotional and financial health.

It's very important to keep in touch with where you are emotionally and financially. All members of the family need nurturing through this time of adjustment. Downsizing your lifestyle may start quickly but will take months to complete and accept. Caring for the emotional well-being of the entire household needs to be encouraged. The use of family discussions has been suggested as a means of keeping the lines of communication open. This is the logical place for consistently "checking" on the family members' emotional health.

Monitoring the financial situation, of course, is mandatory. The decisions you make have to be evaluated regularly (biweekly, at least) to see if your plans are keeping you on your target budget. Emergency expenditures can destroy all your well-laid plans, and you may have to recalculate continually how you'll make ends meet.

7. Know where to get help, and take advantage of it.

You need to know where to get help and not be afraid to ask for it. This book has pointed you toward many sources of help—from books at the library, to debt counseling, to financial assistance programs provided by government agencies and schools. These services exist to help people just like you. Don't let your fear, pride, or past political feeling interfere with your use of them. You aren't going to abuse "the system." You are a decent citizen who needs help, and it's time to utilize the safety nets provided in our society for just this purpose.

8. Recognize that you can still have a piece of the American Dream.

The American Dream is a concept we all recognize—the chance to grow up, get an education, own your own home, and raise your children according to your personal beliefs. It's exactly the same dream for all of us, regardless of our income level.

For years, many people arrived at our shores, started at the bottom with nothing, and realized this dream. You may have started at the top and now, through downsizing, you are ending up moving down the economic ladder. However, the American Dream doesn't disappear in this process. It just gets resized a bit. The education is a less expensive one, or takes longer to pay off. The house is a much more affordable one. You can still provide a "good" home life for your children, raise them with love and in safety, and launch them into adulthood with more maturity and empathy for others than they might otherwise have acquired.

In the past, the American Dream was measured on the quantity and value of material goods. Perhaps now, we should redefine it to include the quality of life and the value of each other. That measure may be different, but it actually makes the American Dream even better!

It's Christmas time again—one year later. This year we get to have a holiday with gifts and trimmings. My husband has found another job! Statistics indicate that most people experiencing a layoff find a new job within six months, and he was lucky enough to help support those statistics.

But what a year this has been! We have experienced highs and lows I never dreamed were possible. We went through days of despair and sleepless nights feeling hopeless. The challenges of those dark months tested our marriage, our individual character, and our mental and physical strength. We discovered how important family is as we worked together to meet the daily problems. The family has fortitude and adaptability we hadn't anticipated. Each of us learned that you have to reach inside, reach out, and reach above to find the strength to cope.

The experience certainly took its toll. It took a significant chunk of our savings. The stress resulted in a tremendous amount of physical illness. Worst of all, it shattered the assumptions we had always held that education and experience translate into job security. It destroyed our belief that companies value their employees and are loyal to them. That simply isn't the case, and the truth really hurts. The broken trust results in much bitterness. Even locating another job cannot dispel the fear of a possible recurrence. It's just like the person who survives a heart attack and always lives in dread that it will happen again.

However, being fearful, blaming oneself for being naive, and focusing on the troubles only makes a depressed individual. It's much better to consider the good things that come out of a situation like this.

Yes, my husband was out of work for several months. But during that time, he saw more of the children than ever before. He set booby traps for them so they were hit by a sea of stuffed animals when they came home from school. Their shrieks of delight and raucous laughter as they played with Daddy were priceless. He was there to oversee their homework, and they worked together to make dinner each night. He entertained them with marvelous, inventive stories. His greatly expanded role in their life during those months may hold consequences for their personality and development that may not be seen for years to come. Now that he's back at work, he realizes how precious those moments were.

We also discovered that we can live on lots less money than we had ever realized. We would never have *voluntarily* tried such an experiment. Now we know how to save a great deal of money per month. Our plan now is to contribute significantly more to our savings and retirement accounts and waste less on frivolous material goods.

We didn't have to sell our house and move away. This was wonderful. We were lucky enough to have minimal debt and a lot of savings to rely upon.

While we are counting the "good" that has come from the downsizing experience, we have to remember the valuable financial lessons our children have learned. Affluent, suburban-raised American kids often grow up with the impression that money somehow miraculously appears whenever they want it. Our children now know that money is a valuable and limited resource that is hard to earn and has to be carefully managed. If they can retain this knowledge, it will help them the rest of their lives.

Now, the Christmas holidays have found us doing exactly what we promised ourselves all year we would do once we got reestablished. We are contributing significantly to the local food pantries and soup kitchens. The desperate circumstances that lead people to need these services are far worse than anything we ever faced. "There, but for the grace of God, go I," is a saying we can relate to all too well. This Christmas, we are counting our blessings as carefully as our pennies. At the top of the blessings list is the love and support of each member of the family. It's actually quite a long list. I hope you realize that yours probably is too.

—HOPE STANLEY QUINN

Bibliography of Literature and Resources

Note: Some of the books may be out of print and the newsletters no longer published. However, most are widely available in public libraries around the country.

Grief

James, John W. and Frank Cherry. *The Grief Recovery Handbook: A Step-by-Step Handbook for Moving Beyond Loss.* New York: HarperPerennial, 1988.

Kübler-Ross, Elisabeth. *On Death and Dying.* New York: Macmillan, 1970.

Stearns, Ann Kaiser. *Living Through Personal Crisis.* Chicago: The Thomas More Press, 1983.

Tanner, Ira J. *The Gift of Grief: Healing the Pain of Everyday Losses.* New York: Hawthorn Books, 1976.

Money Management

Breitbard, Stanley H. and Doona Sammons Carpenter. *The Price Water-house Book of Personal Financial Planning.* New York: Henry Holt and Company, 1988.

Clinton, Ellie Williams and Diane Pearl. *The Smart Woman's Guide to Spending, Saving, and Managing Money.* Hawthorne, N.J.: Career Press, 1994.

Pollan, Stephan M. and Mark Levine. *Your Recession Handbook: How to Thrive and Profit in Hard Times.* New York: William Morrow, 1991.

Turner, R. J. *A Consumer's Guide to the Mortgage Maze.* New York: St. Martin's Press, 1982.

Wall, Ginita. *Our Money Our Selves: Money Management for Each Stage of a Woman's Life.* New York: Consumers Union, 1992.

Child Care

Blum, Laurie. *Free Money for Day Care*. New York: Simon & Schuster, 1992.

Miller, JoAnn and Susan Weisman. *The Parent's Guide to Daycare*. New York: Bantam Books, 1986.

Health Care

Vickery, Donald M. and James F. Fries. *Take Care of Yourself: The Complete Guide to Medical Self-Care*. 5th ed. Reading, Mass: Addison Wesley, 1994.

Unemployment

Gleason, Barry. *Career Crash: America's New Crisis—And Who Survives*. New York: Simon & Schuster, 1994.

Kirkwood, Christopher. *Your Services Are No Longer Required: The Complete Job-Loss Recovery Book*. New York: Plume, 1993.

Poteet, G. Howard. *Starting Up Your Own Business: Expert Advice from the U.S. Small Business Administration*. Blue Ridge Summit, Pa.: Liberty Hill Press, 1991.

Schuyler, Nina. *The Unemployment Survival Handbook*. New York: Allworth Press, 1993.

"The Downsizing of America." *The New York Times*, March 3–10, 1996.

Frugal Living and Voluntary Simplicity

Brandt, Barbara. *Whole Life Economics: Revaluing Daily Life*. Philadelphia, Pa.: New Society Publishers, 1995.

Burch, Mark A. *Simplicity: Notes, Stories and Exercises for Developing Unimaginable Wealth*. Philadephia, Pa.: New Society Publishers, 1995.

Dacyczyn, Amy. *The Tightwad Gazette: Promoting Thrift as a Viable Alternative Lifestyle*. New York: Villard, 1993.

Dominguez, Joe and Vicki Robin. *Your Money or Your Life: Transforming Your Relationship with Money and Achieving Financial Independence*. New York: Penguin, 1992.

Elgin, Duane. *Voluntary Simplicity: Toward a Way of Life That Is Outwardly Simple, Inwardly Rich*. New York: William Morrow, 1993.

Kunes, Ellen. *Living Well—Or Even Better—On Less.* New York: Perigee Books, 1991.

Lewin, Elizabeth. *Say Goodbye to the Rat Race.* New York: Walker, 1993.

Long, Charles. *How to Survive Without a Salary.* Toronto: Warwick Books, 1993.

Satran, Pamela Redmond. "The Cheapest Women in America." *Good Housekeeping,* September 1996.

Simmons, Lee and Barbara Simmons. *Penny Pinching: How to Lower Your Everyday Expenses Without Lowering Your Standard of Living.* New York: Bantam Books, 1994.

Working Woman. Special Issue: "How to Create a Saner, Simpler Life." December 1995.

Newsletters and Other Sources

At-Home Dad. (North Andover, Mass.). Online at athomedad@aol.com.

Living Cheap News. 10/year, $12.00. Living Cheap Press, 7232 Belleview Ave., Kansas City, MO 64114. (816) 523–3161.

Simple Living Quarterly. Seattle, WA. ISSN 1091-5559.

The Skinflint News. $12. Box 818. Palm Harbor, FL 34682. (813) 785–7759. Editor: Melodie Moore.

The Ithaca Cooperative/ Ithaca Dollars (large co-operative arrangement located in Ithaca, N.Y. in which members trade a variety of services, from cooking to baby-sitting to home and automobile repair; the organization offers advice to individuals and community groups seeking to start other co-ops). Write for "The Home-Town Money Starter Kit" at: Ithaca Money, Box 6578, Ithaca, NY 14851. (607) 273–8025. Cost: $25.00.